MASTERMIND
QUIZ BOOK

Compiled by
Richard Morgale

Foreword by
John Humphrys

BOOKS

1 3 5 7 9 10 8 6 4 2

Published in 2012 by BBC Books, an imprint of Ebury Publishing
A Random House Group company

The Random House Group Limited Reg. 954009

Addresses for companies within the Random House Group can be found
at www.randomhouse.co.uk

A CIP catalogue record for this book is available from the British Library

ISBN 978 1 84990 396 7

The Random House Group Limited supports the Forest Stewardship Council (FSC®), the leading international forest certification organisation. Our books carrying the FSC label are printed on FSC® certified paper. FSC is the only forest certification scheme endorsed by the leading environmental organisations, including Greenpeace. Our paper procurement policy can be found at www.randomhouse.co.uk/environment

Commissioning editor: Albert DePetrillo
In-house editor: Joe Cottington
Project editor: Steve Tribe
Proofreader: Kari Speers
Production: Phil Spencer

Printed and bound by CPI Group (UK) Ltd, Croydon, CR0 4YY

To buy books by your favourite authors and register for offers,
visit www.randomhouse.co.uk

Contents

Foreword by

John Humphrys

The first email from the BBC asking me if I would like to do *Mastermind* came one sunny afternoon in 2004. I responded immediately: 'Thanks – but no thanks.' The second arrived a few days later: 'Are you sure we can't persuade you?' My reply was even briefer this time. Nothing, I said, could persuade me.

A few more days passed and this time it wasn't an email: it was a phone call to my home. And it wasn't from the humble producer who'd been emailing me, it was from God – or, at least, the nearest you get to God in this bit of the broadcasting business. It was the Head of Light Entertainment. Why, he wanted to know, was I not prepared even to consider becoming the new chairman of *Mastermind*?

What! Become chairman? I thought they'd been asking me to be a contender on the show! Nothing in the whole wide world would induce me to sit in that black chair and expose my ignorance to a national television audience. But being the man who asked the questions and had all the answers... that was something altogether different. So I said yes. Actually, I said yes please. And I haven't regretted a moment of it.

For much of my half-century as a journalist, I have laboured away asking politicians questions. I can't tell you how wonderful it is finally to be asking questions of people who really genuinely want to answer them. That's only partly a joke, by the way...

Admittedly, we occasionally get some fairly unpredictable answers on *Mastermind* – such as the contender who, when I asked him what breakfast cereal is associated with prison answered 'Cheerios' instead of porridge. Maybe he was being ironic, but I don't think so. Then there was the government minister on *Celebrity Mastermind* who proudly informed me that the king who succeeded Henry VIII was Henry VII. Ah well, they do say politicians often seem to inhabit another universe. Maybe in his particular one, time moved backwards.

But far be it from me to criticise any contender, however unlikely some of their answers may be. Without them we would have no show, and it is they who are its true stars. All of them. Even those who struggle to get their final score into double figures.

As every viewer is well aware, it is not enough to know the answers: what matters is being able to dredge them out from the back of the brain when the clock is ticking relentlessly away and the spotlight is in your eyes. It will come as no surprise to them to learn that, when the series was devised by Bill Wright in the early 1970s, he drew on his own experiences as a prisoner of war being interrogated by the Gestapo in the Second World War.

From the title of Neil Richardson's sinister theme music – 'Approaching Menace' – to that isolating spotlight on the infamous black chair, everything is designed to emphasise that the contenders are on their own. They get no encouragement, no clues, no helpful little nudges from the questioner, no opportunity to phone a friend. They are utterly alone. Either they know the answers or they don't. Indeed, for many series Magnus Magnusson was billed at the start of the programme as the 'Interrogator'. Maybe that's why they thought of me as a suitable replacement. Not that 'replacement' is quite the right word. Magnus created the role and made it his. I inherited his creation and tried not to make too big a botch of it.

In many ways, presenting *Mastermind* is a pretty straightforward job for someone with so many years of broadcasting under his belt. It's not even (unlike my day job on BBC Radio 4) as if I have to think of my own questions. That's done by specialist question-setters, and the answers are checked thoroughly by verifiers against a whole range of different sources. It's a big job. We use more than 6,000 questions every series. All I have to do is try to get the pronunciations right, occasionally tweak the grammar (once a pedant, always a pedant) and deliver the questions as fast as possible without making them unintelligible.

I am often asked why some contenders seem to get fewer questions than others. Are we giving them an unfair advantage? No, we're not. Before we go on air the questions are carefully timed by our production team and everyone gets the same number in their allotted slots. The problem is that some contenders are swifter than others at rattling through them. If they don't know an answer, they don't agonise over it: they just pass quickly. Some canny contenders try never to pass because it counts against them in dead heats, so they make a wild guess or even offer a deliberately silly answer and move onto the next question.

It's sometimes like a rather good tennis match with the contender batting the answer back to me almost as quickly as I can ask the next one. With each answer the pace increases until it seems as though the contender is almost anticipating the question before I have delivered it. That's when the programme really comes to life.

Some viewers say the real appeal of *Mastermind* is watching people struggling so desperately to find the answer. You can see their face almost contorted in anguish. I'm asked by some of our kinder viewers: 'Can't you help them a little?' And I have to say no. The truth is, I cannot even look at them. My eyes are firmly glued to the question cards and, no matter how long the pause or how great the anguish, that's the only way to make it work.

Yes, I know it can sometimes seem to take on an almost sadistic quality, but the surprising reality is that almost all those who take part end up enjoying it. People who've done really badly may well still be kicking themselves after the programme when we share a glass of (very cheap) BBC wine, but they invariably seem to have enjoyed the experience and most want to come back for more.

I like to think that's because they know they're among friends. Unlike some shows I suppose I'd better not mention, *Mastermind* is not played for high stakes. There's no prize – apart from a modest glass bowl of course – and no frantic studio audience cheering you on or howling and shrieking when you get something right. There is, instead, polite applause at the end of a good round and genuine admiration for people who are prepared to put themselves through such an ordeal for the simple pleasure of testing themselves against other clever, knowledgeable people.

Some contenders, of course, make it even more difficult for themselves by choosing specialist subjects that are anything but specialist. One of these days I'm expecting something like this:

'And your specialist subject is...?'

'The World.'

'Umm... Any particular aspect of it...?'

'Nope... All of it.'

In truth, that won't happen because, long before the final choice is made, the producer will have suggested to the would-be contender – with ever-increasing firmness – that it might be sensible to be a little more specific.

I may be the chairman, the person who appears to the audience to be in control, but of course the real work is done long before I even set foot in the *Mastermind* office when the time comes to start recording a new series. And the production team is brilliant.

I've been in broadcasting long enough to know that there has to be a special alchemy if a television programme is to stand the test of time. And not many last as long as *Mastermind*: forty years old in 2012.

Obviously the idea has to be a good one right from the beginning – and the simpler it is, the better. *Mastermind* is, for all the clever lighting and direction and tension, about as simple as it gets: a lone man or woman sitting in a chair and trying to answer two sets of difficult questions. That's it.

But I believe that for a programme to win the affection of an audience and hold it for as long as we have, there must be another factor. It must have an essential humanity. It may be easy to titillate an audience, to get newspaper headlines by humiliating contestants or making them look foolish in front of the cameras. It may well get big audiences for a while. But, sooner or later, the viewers will tire of it.

A good production team must care about the people who take part in its programme. And the *Mastermind* team does. They don't see the contenders as cannon fodder – willing victims to be fed to the mob like Christians in a Roman circus to boost the ratings. Instead, they see them for what they are: human beings entitled to be treated with dignity and respect. That is how the *Mastermind* production team behaves, and it's one of the many reasons I am so proud to be a part of it.

I said at the start of this introduction that the real stars of the show are the contenders. But obviously we would have no programme if it were not for you – our incredibly loyal viewers. Not just loyal – but extremely vigilant too. I'm delighted to say that if we ever do get something wrong you let us know – politely but very, very firmly.

So I hope you think this book is a fairly accurate representation of the standard and variety of questions that make up *Mastermind*. And if, after you've tried your hand at them, you are tempted to try it for real, why not get in touch? Who knows, one day you and I might meet in the *Mastermind* studio. And it might be you receiving that glass bowl when you become the nation's Mastermind.

Acknowledgements

I am extremely grateful to three *Mastermind* champions – Nancy Dickmann, Jesse Honey and Patrick Gibson – who kindly agreed to share their memories of the programme, and their tips for would-be contenders. Magnus Magnusson's *I've Started, So I'll Finish: The Story of Mastermind* provided a wealth of first-hand information about the programme's first quarter of a century. Thanks to those at BBC *Mastermind* for their assistance, but in particular Sue Wardrop who was an invaluable source of information and assistance. Thanks also to the many question-setters and verifiers who contributed to this book, and to Andrea Marks for her help and advice; every effort has been made to ensure that the questions and articles are correct and up-to-date, but please accept my apologies for any errors that may have crept in.

THE MASTERMIND QUIZ BOOK

Show 1

Specialist Subject 1.1
Academy Awards

1. Which legendary comedian, who died in 2003 aged 100, hosted the Oscar ceremony a record number of times?

2. For which 1997 film did Jack Nicholson win Best Actor and Helen Hunt Best Actress?

3. At the first Academy Awards ceremony, who was initially nominated as Best Actor for *The Circus*, but was eventually given a Special Award instead?

4. How old was Tatum O'Neal when she won the award for Best Supporting Actress in 1974, for her role in *Paper Moon*?

5. When Humphrey Bogart won his Oscar for *The African Queen*, the other three acting Oscars were all won by which film?

6. The Academy statuette, which came to be referred to as an 'Oscar', was designed by which M.G.M. Art Director?

7. Which Aardman Animations film, starring Wallace and Gromit, won the Award in 2006 for Best Animated Feature?

8. In 1972, who became the first Oscar winner to have parents who had also both won Oscars?

9. Which Ang Lee film won an Award in 2001 for Best Foreign Language Film and was also nominated for Best Picture?

10. In 1999, who said of her Best Supporting Actress Oscar, 'I feel for eight minutes on the screen I should only get a little bit of him'?

11. What did Robert Opal famously do at the 1974 Academy Awards ceremony?

12. Robert De Niro won Best Actor in 1981 for his portrayal of which boxer in *Raging Bull*?

13. Which film starring Elizabeth Taylor was the last to win the black-and-white Cinematography award, before the category was combined with that for colour films?

14. Whose film *Le Monde Sans Soleil* – 'The World Without Sun' – won the 1964 award for Best Documentary Feature?

15. With which song did The Beatles win the 1970 Oscar for Best Original Song Score?

16. Marcia Gay Harden won the Best Supporting Actress Oscar for playing the wife of which American artist?

17. Michael Westmore and Zoltan Elek won the 1985 award for Best Make-up, for which film starring Cher?

18. Who refused his Oscar for Best Actor in the title role of *Patton* on the grounds that he disagreed with competitive acting awards?

19. In 1999, Roberto Benigni became the first person in a foreign-language film to win a Best Actor Oscar. For which film?

20. Which film composer won Best Original Score Oscars for *Jaws*, *Star Wars* and *Schindler's List*?

21. The 1931 film *Cimarron* was the first film of which genre to win the Best Picture Oscar?

22. Which actress won a Best Supporting Actress award in 2005, for playing the real-life Oscar-winning actress Katharine Hepburn?

23. Before the success of *Chicago* at the 2002 Awards, what was the last film based on a stage musical to win the Oscar for Best Picture?

24. Who made the notorious boast 'The British are coming' at the 1981 Academy Awards ceremony, after receiving the Oscar for Best Screenplay for *Chariots of Fire*?

25. In 1991, which Disney production became the first animated feature to be nominated for Best Film?

26. Who had never won an Oscar during his lengthy career and was presented with an Honorary Award in 1980, then won Best Actor the following year?

27. For which film did Dr Haing N'Gor win the 1984 Oscar for Best Supporting Actor; it was his first film performance?

28. Who became the first person to win a Nobel Prize and an Oscar, when he shared the 1938 award for Best Screenplay with Ian Dalrymple, Cecil Lewis and W.P. Lipscomb?

29. 'When You Wish Upon A Star' was the Academy award-winning song from which Walt Disney film?

30. Which 73-year-old actor entertained the audience at the 1991 ceremony, by performing one-arm press-ups while collecting his Oscar for Best Supporting Actor?

General Knowledge 1.1

1. Which bravery award was originally made from the metal of guns captured at the siege of Sebastopol during the Crimean War?

2. Which is the first county the River Severn flows through on entering England?

3. Which work, based on thirteenth-century Latin secular poems, was set to music in 1937 by Carl Orff?

4. Who entered Parliament as MP for Doncaster North in May 2005?

5. Desirée is a red-skinned, yellow-fleshed, variety of which vegetable?

6. The actress Ellen Andree and the engraver Marcellin Desboutin were the sitters for which painting by Degas, in which they are featured sitting in a bar?

7. What is the name of the palace that Frederick the Great of Prussia had built at Potsdam between 1745 and 1747?

8. Which religious movement grew out of a Bible study group founded by Charles Taze Russell in Pittsburgh in the 1870s, and took its current name in 1931?

9. In chess, 'fianchetto' is a term for the development of which piece?

10. Who was the first presenter of the television programme *Question Time*?

11. Spider, squirrel, proboscis and rhesus are species of which animal?

12. The plot of which early Shakespeare comedy is based on the enmity between the towns of Syracuse and Ephesus?

13. Which word for a building in a sports ground in which players change their clothes and store equipment comes ultimately from the Latin for a butterfly?

14. The British astrophysicist Sir Fred Hoyle was a leading proponent of which theory of the universe that argues it has always existed in more or less the same form (with new matter being continuously created as it expands)?

15. Which film did the Coen brothers remake in 2010 with Jeff Bridges playing Reuben 'Rooster' Cogburn?

16. In horseracing, what is the name of the sharp, left-hand final bend on the Epsom Derby course?

17. What term, used to describe the virtual reality created by computers, was coined by the science fiction writer William Gibson and popularised in his 1984 novel *Neuromancer*?

18. Mahe Island is the largest of which archipelago in the Indian Ocean?

19. Which British band was formed in Birmingham in 1978 by John Taylor and Nick Rhodes?

20. Which anti-pollution component of a car usually consists of a ceramic structure coated with a blend of platinum, rhodium and palladium?

21. The furniture designer Robert Thompson used what small rodent as his signature?

22. What is the title of Shelagh Delaney's first play, written when she was nineteen and set in her native Salford?

23. Which former Portuguese colony in Africa joined the Commonwealth in 1995, the same year as Cameroon?

24. What abbreviation of the Latin for 'and others' is used especially in referring to academic texts that have more than the single named author?

25. Which spice consists of the unopened dried flower buds of a tropical evergreen tree of the myrtle family?

26. In classical mythology, who is the Greek counterpart of the Roman god Mars?

27. Which decimal coin was only in circulation from 1971 until 31 December 1984 (when it ceased to be legal tender)?

28. The American anthem 'My Country 'Tis Of Thee' is usually sung to which other well-known patriotic tune?

29. In which group of animals are the young born prematurely, completing their development attached to teats usually covered by a pouch on their mother's belly?

30. What term is widely used in the press for the police tactic of confining demonstrators for a long time, as used in the 2010 Tuition Fees protests?

Specialist Subject 1.2
The French Revolution

1. What name was commonly used for the Society of the Friends of the Constitution, an off-shoot of the Breton Club?

2. Which former Director-General of Finance was recalled to his post in 1788 and agreed that the Estates-General should be summoned for the first time in over 170 years?

3. Where was the Tennis Court in which the Third Estate took an oath in 1789 to never disband until a written constitution had been established for France?

4. Which group got its name because its members sat on the highest benches in the Assembly?

5. Whose last words to his executioner in 1794 were 'Show my head to the people. It is worth the trouble'?

6. What innovation was designed by the playwright and poet Fabre d'Eglantine and adopted by the Convention in 1793, despite being privately opposed by Robespierre?

7. Which civic religion did Robespierre create to replace Christianity and the Cult of Reason?

8. Which English radical was elected to represent Calais in 1793 as a Deputy to the National Assembly?

9. Which item of clothing, a symbol of freedom in ancient Rome, was adopted by the revolutionaries as a symbol of their cause?

10. Which political group were also known as the 'Brissotins', after their founder Jacques-Pierre Brissot?

11. What was the name of the Girondin sympathiser who murdered Jean-Paul Marat on 13 July 1793, while he was taking a bath?

12. In June 1791, the Royal Family escaped from Paris. In which town were they arrested and turned back to the capital?

13. Which body was established in April 1793 to work alongside the Committee of General Security?

14. Which painter and revolutionary, who was later banished to Brussels by the Bourbons, created pictures of the Tennis Court Oath and the Death of Marat?

15. Which agreement of 1790 effectively turned the clergy into employees of the state?

16. What was the name of the Roman Catholic priest who was confessor to Louis XVI on the night before his execution, and was with him as he mounted the steps to the guillotine?

17. Which title did the Prince known as Philippe Egalité renounce after the fall of the monarchy in 1792?

18. What name was given to the extreme radicals, led by Jacques Roux, who were concerned primarily with the critical food shortage of 1793, and attacked the Girondins in the Convention?

19. Who composed the song that became known as 'La Marseillaise'?

20. To what position was Napoleon Bonaparte appointed under the Constitution of December 1799? It was later confirmed by a public referendum.

21. By what nickname was the journalist Francois-Noel Babeuf known, because his agrarian reforms resembled those of a second-century BC Roman statesman?

22. What alternative name was given to the 'Jours Complimentaires', the spare days in the Revolutionary calendar that resulted from the year being made up of twelve 30-day months?

23. Which frequently vulgar newspaper was established by Jacques-René Hébert and became the bestselling newspaper after the death of Marat?

24. On the first anniversary of the storming of the Bastille, where in Paris did the Fête de la Federation take place?

25. Joseph Fouché crushed a revolt against the Convention in which major city in 1793? His brutality against un-armed civilians leading to a rift with Robespierre.

26. What was the name of Robespierre's brother, who was guillotined along with him during the 'Thermidorean Reaction'?

27. What name was given to the smaller of the two Chambers of the Directory?

28. Which date in 1792 was adopted as the beginning of Year One of the French Revolutionary Calendar and renamed 'primidi vendemiaire'?

29. In 1792, at which battle did the French defeat an allied army led by the Duke of Brunswick?

30. Which politician and lawyer was President of the National Convention and a member of the Committee of Public Safety? He was later executed alongside Danton.

General Knowledge 1.2

1. Seasonal allergic rhinitis, frequently caused by pollen, is commonly known by what name?

2. Which Italian fashion house uses the head of Medusa as its trademark?

3. The price of crude oil from which North Sea field is widely used as a benchmark in Europe and the OPEC countries?

4. In the television series *The West Wing*, who played President Josiah Bartlet?

5. Which relative of the giraffe is found only in the deep forests of central Africa, and was unknown to Europeans until about 1900?

6. Which cocktail is made with vodka, lime juice, triple sec, and cranberry juice?

7. The mountain K2 gets its name because it was the second peak to be surveyed in which mountain range between the Pamirs and the Himalayas?

8. Which former leader of a political party had previously served as a Royal Marines Officer from 1959 to 1972?

9. In the *Divine Comedy*, which Roman poet conducted Dante through Hell and Purgatory?

10. Which northern English city lies at the confluence of the rivers Ouse and Foss?

11. Which explorer led the Imperial Trans-Antarctic Expedition which left England on the ship *Endurance* in August 1914?

12. The Parthenon was the chief temple of which Greek goddess?

13. Which hormone, secreted by the outer layer of the adrenal glands, has been synthesised and used as an anti-inflammatory agent for rheumatoid arthritis and other ailments?

14. Which Yorkshire and England cricketer was the first bowler to take 300 Test wickets?

15. Which woodwind instrument is described in the film *The Secret Life of Walter Mitty* as 'the ill wind that no one blows good'?

16. The name of which type of ceramic comes from the Italian for 'cowrie shell', and was used by Marco Polo to describe the pottery he saw in China?

17. Which Irish poet's first full volume of poetry, published in 1966, was called 'Death of a Naturalist'?

18. What name was given to the speculative boom, centred on a company set up to trade with South America, whose collapse in 1720 ruined many British investors?

19. Which American director and screenwriter's films include *The Elephant Man* and *Dune*?

20. In 1981, which University Dramatic Club was the first winner of the Edinburgh Festival comedy award, with a revue that featured Stephen Fry and Hugh Laurie?

21. The name of which small, nocturnal lizard comes from a Malay imitation of its distinctive cry?

22. 'Noble rot' is a form of fungus that can affect which fruit, shrivelling it rather than actually rotting it?

23. Which sea is bounded on the south by Venezuela, Colombia and Panama, and on the west by Central America?

24. Which State was represented in the American Senate by John F. Kennedy and his brother Edward?

25. In 1877, Spencer Gore became the first winner of which sporting championship?

26. Which mathematician, who died in the mid-thirteenth century, was also known as Leonardo of Pisa?

27. Toxicology is the scientific study of what?

28. In *The Phantom of the Opera*, what is the first name of the young soprano, originally played on stage by Sarah Brightman?

29. Which stately home in Wiltshire stands on the site of a ruined

priory bought by Sir John Thynne in 1541 for the sum of fifty-three pounds?

30. For cars registered on or after 1 March 2001, the rate of vehicle excise duty bands are based on the type of fuel and what other criterion?

'You have two minutes on... *Mastermind*'

Mastermind made its inaugural appearance on British television on 11 September 1972, where it would remain for 25 years and 447 episodes – each presented by an Icelandic-born scholar, author and environmentalist who would later become the chairman of Scottish Natural Heritage and earn an honorary knighthood: Magnus Magnusson, known affectionately as 'the Interrogator'.

Magnus's catchphrase, 'I've started so I'll finish', soon entered the national consciousness, as did the Black Chair in which 1,231 contenders (never contestants) sat and attempted to answer more than 60,000 questions between them. The base and seat of the original chair actually came from two different chairs, and it was presented to Magnus after the final programme in 1997. Before the recording, he allowed himself to be photographed sitting in it, accompanied by dozens of former *Mastermind* contenders – or 'survivors', as Magnus described them.

Some of the 'survivors' formed a club in 1978, with annual get-togethers (and, naturally, quizzes). Entirely independent of *Mastermind*, the Club continued even after the programme ended in 1997. However, *Mastermind* refused to fade away and, following series on radio and the Discovery channel, it returned to BBC Two in 2003, with the presenter of the *Today* programme John Humphrys an apt choice of interrogator – though, unlike the politicians he questions each morning, *Mastermind* contenders are not allowed to interrupt him.

As well as the rule on interrupting, *Mastermind* also discourages contenders from choosing as specialist subjects anything related to their jobs; if you want to know why, look no further than 1990 and an unfortunate art teacher, Arfor

Wyn Hughes, who scored just five points on 'Impressionist and Post-Impressionist Art'. Following his appearance – which earned him the nickname 'Disastermind' – he had to endure pupils humming the theme tune when he walked down the corridors and answering questions with 'Pass'.

However, despite the obvious risks involved, there has never been a shortage of would-be contenders, of whom 35 have managed to claim the title. Perhaps the most famous winner of all was London taxi driver Fred Housego, whose victory in 1980 demonstrated that you didn't have to be an academic or hold a white-collar job to be a Mastermind – knowledge and recall under pressure are the only things that count. Train driver Chris Hughes reinforced the point when he took the title three years later.

Former champions like Fred and Chris are not allowed to enter *Mastermind* again, but in 1995 the restriction on *all* former contenders returning for a second attempt was lifted; among those who grasped the opportunity were Kevin Ashman (see 'High Scores') and Geoff Thomas, who surely wins the award for perseverance: having reached the semi-finals in 1994, he did so again on Discovery's *Mastermind* in 2001. When the programme returned to BBC Two in 2003, Geoff made it all the way to the final before finally getting his hands on the glass bowl in 2006; to make his victory doubly sweet, the trophy was presented to him by Magnus, who recalled Geoff telling him years earlier that he had two ambitions in life: win *Mastermind* and live to 100!

Show 2

Specialist Subject 2.1
The Apollo Space Program

1. Neil Armstrong became the first human to set foot on the Moon at 2.56 a.m. Greenwich Mean Time, on which date in 1969?

2. What name was given to the series of booster rockets that were used to launch the Apollo spacecraft to the Moon?

3. Crewed by Wally Schirra, Don Eisele and Walt Cunningham, which was the first manned Apollo flight?

4. Which astronaut honoured his wife Marilyn by naming a crater on the Moon after her during the Apollo 8 mission?

5. The Command Module was made by North American Aviation, but which company designed the Lunar Module for NASA?

6. Who was the commander of the ill-fated Apollo 1, set for launch in February 1967?

7. The Apollo 15 astronaut Dave Scott dropped a hammer and which other object before a television camera to show the effect of lunar gravity?

8. Ken Mattingly, the intended Command Module pilot of Apollo

13, had to give up his place to Jack Swigert because he had been exposed to which disease?

9. According to the Apollo 11 flight plan, what were Armstrong and Aldrin supposed to do when they landed on the Moon? However, the plan was hastily revised so that they could step out onto the lunar surface immediately.

10. What unexpected occurrence affected the electrical and navigation systems during the launch of Apollo 12?

11. What was found to be leaking from Apollo 13 after the electrical short that triggered the explosion crippling the ship?

12. What were the Apollo 10 command and lunar modules called?

13. What did the Apollo 13 crew have to construct from various objects held together with duct tape?

14. What was the name of the commander of Apollo 12's crew, who became the third man to walk on the Moon?

15. What name was given to the four-billion-year-old chunk of crystalline igneous rock that was found by Jim Irwin and brought back by Apollo 15?

16. What was always served up for the traditional astronauts' breakfast on launch day?

17. What was the name of the Apollo 13 lunar landing module used as a 'space lifeboat' to return to Earth?

18. Who was the only astronaut from the Mercury programme to subsequently walk on the Moon?

19. What was the name of the motorised vehicle first driven on the Moon by Irwin and Scott on the Apollo 15 mission?

20. What was the name of the engineer, famous for his distinctive waistcoats, who was the flight director during Apollo 13's successful return home?

21. Buzz Aldrin titled his autobiography after a phrase he used on the Moon to describe the lunar landscape. What was the phrase?

22. How did the astronauts of Apollo 8 know the precise moment that they had gone behind the Moon?

23. What was the name of the geologist on Apollo 17 who became the first scientist to walk on the Moon?

24. What was the number and type of club used by Alan Shepard to hit golf balls on the Moon?

25. What was the colour of the soil discovered at Shorty Crater during the Apollo 17 mission that provided evidence of explosive volcanic activity on the Moon?

26. In March 1969 who performed the first spacewalk of the Apollo program in order to test the spacesuit and life-support backpack?

27. What ceremony did Buzz Aldrin perform in the Lunar Module to celebrate their safe landing on the Moon?

28. Which former Gemini pilot was the Apollo 8 Mission Commander?

29. Which number Apollo mission was cancelled in January 1970 by NASA Administrator Tom Paine because of budget constraints?

30. Who, as commander of Apollo 17, was the last human (so far) to walk on the surface of the Moon?

General Knowledge 2.1

1. In pantomime, who was famously leaving London when he heard the bells telling him to 'turn again'?

2. What is the name of Milan's world-famous Opera House, which opened in August 1778 after the previous theatre had been destroyed by fire?

3. The monitor, which can range in length from twenty centimetres to three metres, is a genus of which reptile?

4. Who was born in Putney in around 1485, and rose from a humble background to become Henry VIII's chief adviser from about 1531 until his fall in 1540?

5. The name of which variety of pasta, normally served stuffed, literally means 'big tubes' or 'pipes'?

6. In which city does Robert Adam's Pulteney Bridge cross the River Avon?

7. Which film, based on a novel about a Vermeer painting, features Scarlett Johansson in the title role?

8. In which organ of the body is bile produced?

9. At which golf course does the US Masters tournament take place during the first full week in April?

10. In Greek myth, which Titan was forced to carry the sky on his shoulders as punishment for taking part in a war against the Olympian gods?

11. The chairman of which committee oversees Conservative Party leadership elections?

THE MASTERMIND QUIZ BOOK

12. Which science fiction writer's first law of robotics is: 'A robot may not injure a human being, or, through inaction, allow a human being to come to harm'?

13. In geology, what name, of Spanish origin, is given to a large crater formed by the collapse of the central part of a volcano after eruption?

14. Which classic Bruce Springsteen song begins with the line, 'In the day we sweat it out on the streets of a runaway American dream'?

15. Which soldier and statesman is credited with being the founder of the modern Turkish state? He became the first President (of the Turkish Republic) in 1923.

16. The forerunner of which cult radio comedy series, broadcast in 1951, was called *Those Crazy People*?

17. What term for a dealer in illicit alcohol, especially during Prohibition in America, is said to come from the place where illegal flasks of alcohol were concealed by early traders?

18. Which sea creature is embedded in formaldehyde in Damien Hirst's *The Physical Impossibility of Death in the Mind of Someone Living*?

19. Which landlocked West African country has a name that approximately translates as 'Land of Incorruptible People' or 'Land of Worthy Men'?

20. In Roman numerals, what letter represents the number 500?

21. Which of Shakespeare's comedies has a heroine named Hero?

22. Which anti-crime scheme was established in Britain after a group of police officers visited Chicago in 1982?

23. Which small marine creatures make up the genus hippocampus?

24. Particularly associated with New York Jewish cuisine, which meat is spiced to make the commonest version of pastrami?

25. In the film *Sylvia*, which poet was played by Daniel Craig, who starred opposite Gwyneth Paltrow?

26. With whom did Sir Isaac Newton have an increasingly bitter dispute as to which of them should take credit for the invention of calculus?

27. In which sport has Doggett's Coat and Badge been competed for annually since 1715 (in one of the world's oldest continuing races)?

28. During the Spanish Civil War, the Nationalist General (Emilo Mola) Vidal is credited with coining what term for a clandestine force of subversive agents?

29. What name is given to the sleeveless outer vestment worn by priests and bishops of the Roman Catholic and some other churches while presiding at Mass or Holy Communion?

30. Which country's flag consists of a blue cross outlined in white on a red background with the vertical part of the cross shifted to the hoist side?

Specialist Subject 2.2
Summer Olympics

1. Which country hosted the Summer Olympics in 1976, but failed to win a single gold medal?

2. At the 1908 Olympics, City of London Police defeated Liverpool Police to win gold in which event?

3. Who defeated home favourite Luz Long to win the long jump at the 1936 Berlin Olympics?

4. At which Games did the Olympic flame first burn throughout the three-month period of competition?

5. In Beijing in 2008, who added a cycling gold medal to the rowing silver she had won four years earlier?

6. Which seven-a-side indoor sport was reintroduced to the Games in Munich for the first time since 1936?

7. Which country won its first-ever Olympic Gold medal in Los Angeles in 1984, in the Men's Free Pistol shooting?

8. In 1968, cyclists Daniel Morelon and Pierre Trentin both won individual titles as well as taking gold in which other event that has since been dropped from the Games?

9. At the Melbourne Games in 1956 British gold medallist Dick McTaggart was also awarded the Val Barker Trophy, given to the competitor with the best style and technique in which sport?

10. Which famous American Second World War general finished fifth in the modern pentathlon in Stockholm in 1912, after a poor performance in the shooting?

11. On which gymnastics apparatus did Nadia Comaneci achieve a perfect score of twenty points to win the gold medal in Montreal?

12. The Hungarian fencer Aladar Gerevich won gold medals at how many successive Games?

13. Father and son Charles and Richard Burnell both won gold medals for Britain in 1908 and 1948 respectively; in which sport?

14. At which Games did Teofilo Stevenson become the first boxer to win three Gold medals in the same weight division?

15. Twelve of the thirteen Men's Swimming events in Montreal were won by Americans; which Briton won the other event, in world record time?

16. When the Games were held in South Korea in 1988, which sport was included for the first time, with the home nation winning the Men's Singles and Women's Doubles?

17. Who was the manager of the Great Britain football team at the 1948 Olympic Games?

18. Italian Klaus Dibiasi won three consecutive gold medals in which sport from 1968 onwards?

19. Who were the surprise gold medallists in the first Women's Olympic Hockey tournament, in Moscow in 1980?

20. Competitors in which athletics event at the 1932 Los Angeles games had to run an extra lap, because an official forgot to change the lap counter?

21. In 1926, Olympic gold medal winning swimmer Gertrude Ederle became the first woman to achieve which famous sporting feat?

22. In 1948, Sweden were stripped of their team gold medal in which sport after Gehnäll Persson was disqualified because he wasn't a commissioned officer?

23. In Beijing in 2008, which athlete ran the anchor leg for the Jamaican Men's Sprint Relay team that won gold in world record time?

24. In which sport did Darrell Pace win Gold in 1976 and 1984, and Team Silver in 1988?

25. Harold Sakata, who won a weightlifting silver medal in 1948, later played which character in the film *Goldfinger*?

26. Italian-born Angelo Parisi won bronze for Britain, then gold and silver medals for France; in which sport?

27. Which French player won the Women's Singles Tennis gold medal at the Antwerp Games of 1920? She also won six Wimbledon titles during her career.

28. Which team event was discontinued after the 1936 Olympics, when Argentina defeated Great Britain to take the gold medal?

29. Who won his first Olympic Sailing medal as a 19 year old in Atlanta, when he took silver in the Laser?

30. What was unusual about the re-run final of the Men's 400 Metres at the 1908 Games, won by Wyndham Halswelle?

General Knowledge 2.2

1. Which elite military unit was founded by the Scots Guards officer David Stirling in 1941?

2. In horseracing, which jockey rode all seven winners in a meeting at Ascot in September 1996?

3. The internal angles of any quadrilateral add up to how many degrees?

4. In the television series *Star Trek*, what was the name of the Communications Officer on board the original Starship *Enterprise*, played by Nichelle Nichols?

5. New York State lies on one side of the Niagara Falls; which Canadian province lies on the other?

6. Which former lawyer, now a bestselling writer of legal thrillers, served in the Mississippi House of Representatives from 1983 until 1990?

7. In English business law, what name is given to the insolvency process whereby a company's debts are frozen while a rescue package is attempted by a person appointed by the Court to take over the company?

8. Who said, on becoming Prime Minister in 1868, 'I have climbed to the top of the greasy pole'?

9. Which small fruit, that resembles an orange and originated in China, can be eaten whole as the rind is edible?

10. Which form of musical composition has a name derived from the past participle of the Italian verb meaning 'to sound'?

11. The name of which member of the cat family native to Central and South America comes from a Tupi-Guarani word for any large carnivore?

12. Which influential Post-Impressionist artist once said that, 'For an impressionist to paint from nature is not to paint the subject, but to realise sensations'?

13. What word for a large lorry comes from a statue of the god Krishna which is dragged through the streets on a heavy wagon during an annual festival at Puri in India?

14. Which 1998 film stars Jim Carrey as an insurance agent whose life has been recorded on television without his knowledge?

15. What expression for noble descent comes from the Spanish 'sangre azul' and is thought to derive from the visible veins of their fair-skinned aristocracy?

16. Which number puzzle first appeared in its modern form in a New York magazine in 1979 under the title 'Number Place', before reappearing in Japan in 1984?

17. Which City of London institution is based at 10 Paternoster Square?

18. In which musical does the character Grizabella (originally played by Elaine Paige) sing 'Memory'?

19. Ludwig II, who was known as Mad King Ludwig, ruled which German state from 1864 to 1886?

20. What is the title of the allegorical fourteenth-century poem usually attributed to William Langland?

21. What acid is secreted into the stomach by the parietal cells, also known as the oxyntic cells?

22. Which country co-hosted the 2011 ICC Cricket World Cup, along with India and Sri Lanka?

23. Which bitter extract from the leaves of the plant 'Artemisia absinthium' is an important flavouring ingredient in absinthe?

24. Which name of Old French or Middle Dutch origin is given to an anchored float that serves as a navigation mark?

25. The radio series *The Archers* is set in which fictional county?

26. The name of which Norwegian army officer, who collaborated with the Nazis during the Second World War, has become a synonym for a traitor?

27. What answer did the French social thinker Pierre-Joseph Proudhon give to the question he posed in Chapter One of his work *What Is Property*?

28. Which small South Atlantic island group, a dependency of St Helena, is named after the Portuguese sailor who discovered it in 1506?

29. In 1987, which soul singer became the first woman to be admitted to the Rock and Roll Hall of Fame?

30. In 1994, the Globe Theatre on Shaftesbury Avenue in London was renamed in honour of which actor (as well as to avoid confusion with the reconstructed Shakespearean theatre)?

Bill Wright

More often than not, *Mastermind* resembles an interrogation rather than a mere quiz show – contenders sit alone in a chair, with a spotlight in their faces, desperately trying not to say the wrong thing; most hope merely to survive the experience. A young BBC staffer called Bill Wright, who joined the RAF during the Second World War and had the misfortune to be shot down, knew the feeling only too well.

The Gestapo were convinced that Bill was a spy and questioned him for three weeks; all he could do was endlessly repeat his name, rank and number – the standard information that POWs were obliged to give their captors – with the realisation that at any moment his time could be up... Fortunately, his identity was eventually confirmed and after the War he returned to the BBC and rose to the level of producer.

In 1971, Bill devised a show based on a concept he remembered only too well, with each contender giving their name, occupation and specialised subject, then facing an interrogation against the clock. He produced the programme himself, before his death from motor neurone disease at the age of 58; *Mastermind* stands as his legacy... He started it, and it's still not finished.

Show 3

Specialist Subject 3.1
The Plays of Shakespeare

1. In which play does Jaques deliver the speech that begins 'All the world's a stage, and all the men and women merely players'?

2. In *Julius Caesar*, who is described as 'the last of the Romans'?

3. While disguised as a doctor of law in *The Merchant of Venice*, Portia makes a celebrated speech in which she says that the quality of what 'is not strained'?

4. Printed in 1594, what is Shakespeare's first Roman tragedy?

5. In *Richard III*, which eight words complete the opening sentence that begins 'Now is the Winter of our discontent...'?

6. According to the report of Mistress Quickly, who 'babbled of green fields' on his deathbed?

7. The proverbial expression 'The course of true love never did run smooth' is a line from which of the plays?

8. In which of the history plays does the title character look into a mirror and say 'Is this the face which fac'd so many follies, that was at last out-fac'd by Bolingbroke?'

THE MASTERMIND QUIZ BOOK   39

9. In *Romeo and Juliet*, the Friar urges Romeo to flee to which town after killing Tybalt?

10. Which play was also known in Jacobean times as 'All Is True'?

11. What is the name of the tragic heroine whose final line is 'Shall we not see these daughters and these sisters'?

12. Which Shakespearean king is described as 'More sinned against than sinning'?

13. How are Valentine and Proteus known in the title of a Shakespeare comedy?

14. According to Thersites in Act Five of *Troilus and Cressida*, two things 'hold fashion'. One is 'wars'; what is the other?

15. What is the name of the 'simple constable' in *Measure for Measure*?

16. According to Tennyson, the tenderest lines in Shakespeare – 'Hang there like fruit, my soul, Till the tree die!' – are from which play?

17. In *Love's Labour's Lost*, what does Ferdinand, the King of Navarre, make his courtiers agree to forswear for three years along with food and sleep, and instead devote themselves to study?

18. Which of Shakespeare's comedies has a heroine called Hero?

19. In *Antony and Cleopatra*, an asp is brought to Cleopatra in a basket said to contain which fruit?

20. In *Henry IV Part One*, whom does the king describe as a 'Mars in swaddling clothes'?

21. Counting the lines printed in the 1623 folio, which is the shortest of Shakespeare's plays?

22. Before which besieged town does Henry V make his speech beginning 'Once more unto the breach, dear friends, once more'?

23. What is the profession of Nick Bottom in *A Midsummer Night's Dream*?

24. Which play that opens at Antioch and ends in Ephesus did not appear in the 1623 Folio?

25. In *Romeo and Juliet*, what is the name of Capulet's niece, with whom Romeo was enamoured before he met Juliet?

26. Which fruit is embroidered on Desdemona's handkerchief, which Iago makes Othello believe she has given to Cassio?

27. In *Macbeth*, Malcolm was one of Duncan's sons; what is the name of the other?

28. In *King John*, what disguise has Arthur adopted when he is killed leaping from the castle walls while attempting to escape?

29. Who was the pedlar, the self-styled 'snapper-up of unconsidered trifles', in *The Winter's Tale*?

30. In Act One of *Richard III*, Lady Anne insults Richard by calling him a toad, and which other animal?

General Knowledge 3.1

1. The modern name of which planet comes from the Roman Goddess of Love and Beauty?

2. Which bank was brought down in 1995 by the dealings of the 'rogue trader' Nick Leeson?

3. Who presented the programme *Time Team* and the series *The Worst Jobs in History*?

4. Which animal was unknown in the West until 1869, when the French missionary Armand David obtained some furs?

5. The name of which orphan, created by the American novelist Eleanor H. Porter, is now used for anyone of a particularly sunny and optimistic disposition?

6. Which American state is known as the 'Green Mountain State'?

7. Which jazz trumpeter recorded the classic albums *Kind of Blue* and *Sketches of Spain*?

8. According to the Bible, what is the name of the hill in Jerusalem on which the existing Jebusite fortress became David's royal capital?

9. In Indian cuisine, what is the characteristic feature of the meat in a dish described as 'keema'?

10. What description of the English was used by Adam Smith in *The Wealth of Nations*, and has also been attributed to Napoleon?

11. In which part of the body is the brachial artery found?

12. The Clore Gallery, an extension to what is now Tate Britain, was built to hold the works of which British artist?

13. In heraldry, what name is given to an X-shaped cross usually occupying the entire field in which it is placed?

14. As part of the Treaty of Versailles in 1919, the German company Bayer was made to surrender the brand name of which common painkilling drug to the Allies?

15. Which English football team, founded in 1862, claims to be the world's oldest surviving professional Football League club?

16. Which South American Republic derives its name from an Italian city after European explorers observed Indian villages on stilts over water?

17. What name is given to the plant disease caused by fungi which produce a dusty white surface, particularly on leaves?

18. What is the name of the top film award at the Cannes Film Festival?

19. What nickname was Margaret Thatcher given when she ended free school milk for (the) over-sevens, as Secretary of State for Education and Science in 1971?

20. In which ballet, with music by Tchaikovsky, has Odette been turned into a bird by the magician Rothbart?

21. What name is given to the two instances each year when the Sun is exactly above the Equator, making the night and day equal in length?

22. Which French author wrote *The Second Sex*, which became a classic of feminist literature when it was published in 1953?

23. Which cocktail of Mexican origin is made from tequila, an orange liqueur and lime or lemon juice? It is typically drunk from a glass whose rim has been coated with salt.

24. In Greek mythology, the minotaur had the body of a man and the head of which creature?

25. Which album by the Rolling Stones, released in 1968, includes the tracks 'Sympathy For The Devil' and 'Street Fighting Man'?

26. Which painting by Velazquez, completed in 1635, shows

the symbolic handing over of the keys of a Dutch city to the victorious Spanish army after a siege?

27. Anosmia is a loss of which of the senses?

28. In April 1998, which Northern Line underground station was reopened by the team of the BBC Radio Four game show *I'm Sorry, I Haven't a Clue*, after modernisation?

29. Jack Slipper, known as 'Slipper of the Yard', was particularly famous for his pursuit of which escaped criminal?

30. Who scored 766 runs during the 2010–2011 Ashes series in Australia, the second-highest total by any English batsman in a Test series?

Specialist Subject 3.2
World Geography

1. Which mountain with strong Biblical connections is, at 16,853 feet, the highest point in Turkey?

2. Tokyo is situated on which of the Japanese islands?

3. What name for the vast plains of Central Argentina comes from a Quechua word meaning 'flat place'?

4. In which country is Lake Disappointment?

5. Which island, with an area of 195,000 square miles, is the largest in the Canadian Arctic and the fifth largest in the world?

6. Derived from the Arabic for 'coastal region', what name is given to the semi-arid region of Africa, which forms a transitional zone between the Sahara to the north and the wetter tropical areas to the south?

7. What is the name of the square in Prague which saw the start of the Velvet Revolution in 1989?

8. In the early seventeenth century, Potosi in Bolivia was one of South America's richest and largest cities. What was discovered there in 1545 that resulted in this wealth?

9. Which landlocked salt lake, at up to 1,312 feet below sea level, is the lowest body of water on Earth?

10. Which strait, up to 70 miles wide, contains the island of Krakatoa and links the Java Sea with the Indian Ocean?

11. What is the most northerly of the five Great Lakes of North America?

12. In December 1991, Nigeria changed its capital from Lagos to which purpose-built new federal city, the first planned city to be built in the country?

13. Lake Titicaca, which at an altitude of 12,500 feet is the world's highest lake navigable to large vessels, is astride the border of Bolivia and which other country?

14. Four capital cities lie on the River Danube. Vienna, Belgrade and Budapest are three; what is the fourth?

15. In which US state is Mount McKinley, the highest peak in North America?

16. Which lake in eastern Siberia contains one-fifth of the fresh water on the Earth's surface, and is the largest freshwater lake on Earth?

17. In which country is the Vredefort Dome, which is the second-largest known meteorite impact crater on Earth?

18. Extending some 3,200 miles from east to west and consisting

of 13,670 islands, which country makes up the world's largest archipelago?

19. In which European capital city is the Uspenski Orthodox Cathedral, one of the few remaining reminders of a period of Russian rule?

20. In which country is Fiordland National Park, established in 1952 and one of the largest in the world?

21. Which city in western Uruguay became important in the early 1860s when the 'Liebig Extract of Meat Company' was established there?

22. What is the name of the Canadian territory that was created as a homeland for the Inuit?

23. Which country, whose capital is Asmara, became a separate state in May 1993 when it gained independence from Ethiopia?

24. Opened in 1958 as part of the World Fair, what is the name of the visitor attraction in Brussels which takes the form of a giant model of an iron crystal?

25. What is the name of Ecuador's principal port and largest city?

26. The Great Barrier Reef extends for some 1,250 miles off the North Eastern coast of which Australian State?

27. Vientiane, or Viangchan, is the capital of which Asian country?

28. Which river flows into the Mediterranean through two principal branches, the Rosetta and the Damietta?

29. The Polish Glacier provides one of the more challenging routes up which South American mountain?

30. What name was given to the main crossing point between East and West Berlin, situated in Friedrichstrasse?

General Knowledge 3.2

1. Squire Trelawney and Ben Gunn are characters in which novel by Robert Louis Stevenson?

2. In 1846, which Prime Minister was responsible for the repeal of the Corn Laws that had restricted imports of grain?

3. In which hit song for The Kinks does Terry meet Julie 'every Friday night'?

4. Dutch is the official language of which South American republic?

5. Which fish hatch in the Sargasso Sea, the larvae turning into immature adults as they are carried by currents across the Atlantic before entering British rivers?

6. In 1903, Frenchman Maurice Garin became the first winner of which annual event?

7. What word that means 'the act of throwing someone out of a window', is associated with an event that occurred in Prague in 1618?

8. Who played secret agent Harry Palmer in a trilogy of films in the 1960s?

9. In computing, what does the acronym RAM stand for?

10. Which Impressionist, noted for his admiration of the female form, said, 'I never think I have finished a nude until I think I could pinch it'?

11. In Greek mythology, which monster terrorised the Thebans by asking them a riddle and devouring them when they couldn't answer it?

12. Which television hospital drama series was created by the novelist Michael Crichton?

13. Which spicy soup originated in India and takes its name from the Tamil for 'pepper water'?

14. Which organ of the body is affected by hepatitis?

15. In which novel had the language 'Newspeak' been invented to meet the ideological needs of 'Ingsoc' or 'English Socialism'?

16. Which town, now a city, was by-passed by the first stretch of motorway to be opened in Britain in 1958?

17. On which musical instrument was Yehudi Menuhin a virtuoso performer?

18. Who was Chairman of the British Railways Board from 1961 to 1965, and gave his name to the plan under which Britain's railway mileage was substantially reduced?

19. Which word for a plan of action designed to achieve an overall aim comes from a Greek word meaning 'generalship'?

20. The mouflon, native to Corsica and Sardinia, is a small, wild form of which farm animal?

21. *In Sickness and in Health* was the sequel to which television comedy series?

22. What adjective meaning 'disdainfully superior in manner' comes from the Latin for 'eyebrow'?

23. Sabres and epees are types of which weapon?

24. What is the lightest chemical element?

25. In 1931, Sir Edward Elgar conducted 'Land Of Hope And

Glory' at the opening ceremony of which recording studio in St John's Wood in London?

26. In Islam, what name is given to the prophet Muhammad's journey from Mecca to Medina in July 622?

27. Which shipping forecast area off the east coast of Scotland gets its name from the approximate depth in fathoms of its seabed?

28. In which part of the body are the cuboid and cuneiform bones?

29. Which novel by James Jones, about the experiences of a serviceman in Hawaii just before the attack on Pearl Harbor, was made into an award-winning film starring Burt Lancaster, Deborah Kerr and Frank Sinatra?

30. In which country did the Second World War battle of El-Alamein take place?

'Approaching Menace'

Conductor and arranger Neil Richardson wrote a number of memorable tunes, including 'The Riviera Affair'; he also orchestrated the music for *Four Weddings and a Funeral*.

However, his most famous composition is surely 'Approaching Menace', which was chosen as the *Mastermind* theme for the very first series in 1972 and has introduced the programme ever since – the current version was recorded by the BBC Philharmonic in 2010 for that year's Grand Final.

Show 4

Specialist Subject 4.1
British Political History since 1900

1. Who joined the Cabinet at the age of just 31, when he was appointed President of the Board of Trade in 1947?

2. What name was given to the historic series of Constitutional proposals about Northern Ireland, signed on 10 April 1998?

3. Who wrote in her diary 'She is so clearly the best man among them' on Margaret Thatcher's election as Conservative Party leader?

4. Who was Britain's Prime Minister at the outbreak of the Great War in 1914?

5. What name, taken from a left-wing journal, was used for the group of Labour MPs who were at the heart of Bevanite support in the early 1950s?

6. Who resigned as Foreign Secretary in 1935, after details of his pact with Pierre Laval were leaked to the press?

7. Whose comment on Macmillan's drastic Cabinet reshuffle of July 1962 was 'Greater love hath no man than this, that he lay down his friends for his life'?

8. What was the slogan on the famous poster, used by the Conservatives at the 1979 General Election, showing a queue of people at an Unemployment Office?

9. Who is the only Prime Minister to have also held all three great offices of state: Home Secretary, Foreign Secretary and Chancellor of the Exchequer?

10. In the expenses scandal of 2009, what term was adopted by the media for the MPs' practice of switching the designation of main and second homes in order to qualify for maximum allowances?

11. Which British Prime Minister wrote the novel *Savrola*, which was first published in 1900?

12. In November 1974, which former Government minister was supposedly drowned while swimming in the sea off Miami, only to turn up several weeks later in Australia?

13. Which party took part in a general election for the first time in 1992, fielding 310 candidates all of whom lost their deposits?

14. Which Conservative MP lost Enfield Southgate at the 1997 General Election, despite defending a majority of 15,545?

15. In October 1960, who told a largely hostile Labour Party conference, 'There are some of us who will fight and fight again to save the party we love'?

16. The statement issued on 25 January 1981 by the so-called 'Gang of Four', announcing their intention to leave the Labour Party, is known by what name?

17. Which Liberal Democrat resigned from his position as Chief Secretary to the Treasury in May 2010, just weeks after the Coalition government had taken office?

18. Who was the first person to disclaim a title under the 1963 Peerage Act?

19. In a parliamentary debate in 1907, what did David Lloyd George describe as 'Mr Balfour's poodle. It fetches and carries for him. It barks for him. It bites anybody that he sets it on to'?

20. Which future leader of the Conservative Party was first elected to Parliament in 1989, in a by-election at Richmond in Yorkshire?

21. Who became Scotland's First Minister in 1999, following the first elections to the Scottish Parliament?

22. In a speech at the Guildhall in November 1914, what did Winston Churchill say was the maxim of the British people?

23. Who was forced to resign as an MP in 1974, while facing bankruptcy after investing in the Canadian company Aquablast?

24. Who was appointed as Home Secretary in Tony Blair's first Cabinet, in May 1997?

25. What was the two-word election slogan used by Stanley Baldwin and the Conservatives during the 1929 General Election campaign?

26. Who was Margaret Thatcher's chief press secretary from shortly after the 1979 General Election until her resignation in 1990?

27. Whom did Michael Foot beat by ten votes to become leader of the Labour Party in 1980?

28. Which party's first MP was J.T. Walton Newbold, who won Motherwell in 1922?

29. In 1995, who announced that he had brought a libel action in

order to fight 'bent and twisted journalism... with the simple sword of truth and the trusty shield of British fair play?'

30. With which name, taken from a Surrey hotel, did Harold Wilson brand the Conservatives as uncaring in the run-up to the 1970 General Election?

General Knowledge 4.1

1. 'DE' is the internet code abbreviation for which country?

2. Who assassinated Archduke Franz Ferdinand and his consort Sophie in June 1914, triggering the Great War?

3. Which musical direction, denoting a moderately slow tempo, literally means 'going' in Italian?

4. Which desert has a name meaning 'waterless place' in Mongolian?

5. Which Shakespearean character has been played on film by Sir Laurence Olivier in 1948 and Mel Gibson in 1990?

6. The battles of Blenheim, Ramillies, Oudenaarde and Malplaquet were the principal engagements of which war?

7. Who played Mr Spock in the original *Star Trek* TV series?

8. In which city, the place of his birth, are most of the surviving works of the architect Charles Rennie Mackintosh?

9. Who won the Whitbread Award for a first novel with *Oranges Are Not the Only Fruit*?

10. What name is given to the salted belly of pork that is an important ingredient in Italian cooking and very similar to streaky bacon?

11. In Ancient Greece, which city-state in the southern Peloponnese was characterised by its rigorous military discipline?

12. Which series of eight engravings by William Hogarth details the decline of a spendthrift young man?

13. Which religious philosopher was born in Copenhagen in May 1813, and became a major influence on existentialism and Protestant theology?

14. Which ligaments that are found in the knee and other parts of the body are so named because they form an X-shaped cross?

15. Which play by Terence Rattigan was based on the true case of George Archer-Shee, who was expelled from Osborne Naval College for petty theft?

16. Quezon City was the capital of which Asian country from 1948 until 1976?

17. The popular 'Humming Chorus' is from which opera by Puccini?

18. Which drug, that for three centuries was the only treatment for malaria known in the West, is obtained from the bark of the cinchona tree?

19. Which director's films include *The Terminator*, *Titanic* and *Avatar*?

20. Which town in Cornwall is the centre of the china clay industry, the white spoil mounds that surround it being known locally as the 'Cornish Alps'?

21. Who took Bonnie Prince Charlie from Benbecula to Skye, disguised as her Irish maid Betty Burke?

22. The footballers Tommy Hutchison and Des Walker both scored

own goals, ten years apart, against which team in FA Cup finals?

23. What name for an animal's den, especially that of an otter, is a variant of an Old English word for a stronghold?

24. Whose work 'Ode To Joy' did Beethoven set to music in the last movement of his Ninth Symphony?

25. Boxing Day is also the feast day of which Saint, the first Christian martyr?

26. What is the meaning of 'Scottorum malleus', part of the inscription on Edward I's tomb in Westminster Abbey?

27. Mikhail Gorbachev became the effective ruler of the Soviet Union in March 1985 after whose death?

28. What name for the periods into which a game of polo is divided comes from the Sanskrit for 'circle' or 'wheel'?

29. Which major Paris museum and art gallery, opened in 1986, is situated in a former railway station?

30. Cochise and Geronimo were leaders of which Native American tribe that inhabited the south-western states?

Specialist Subject 4.2
Pop Music of the 1970s

1. Which group topped the UK charts with the album *Physical Graffiti*, which they released on their own label Swansong?

2. Which 1976 record by The Damned is generally regarded as the UK's first punk single?

3. Which singer topped the charts as part of a famous duo in 1970, and later had number ones with his first two hits as a solo artist, in 1975 and 1979?

4. Which Scottish 1970s group got their name from a town in Michigan when their manager stuck a pin in a map?

5. Which David Bowie song contains the line 'I've never done good things, I've never done bad things'?

6. Under what name did comedian Graham Fellows, also known as John Shuttleworth, have a top ten hit in 1978?

7. Which former member of The Animals produced Slade's hits in the 1970s, after seeing them perform at a London club?

8. Chicory Tip's 'Son Of My Father', a number one hit in 1972, was the first chart-topping single to feature which instrument, invented by Robert Moog?

9. Deep Purple were inspired to write which track, when the Montreux Casino caught fire while they were doing a gig with Frank Zappa?

10. Midge Ure replaced John Foxx as lead vocalist of which band, formed in the mid 1970s as Tiger Lily?

11. Who co-wrote Smoky Robinson's chart-topper 'Tears Of A Clown' with Henry Cosby and Smoky himself?

12. Queen's 'Bohemian Rhapsody', was originally released as a track on which of the band's albums?

13. After the break-up of Deep Purple in 1976, David Coverdale formed which group?

14. Who wrote and produced all of The Wombles' top twenty hits?

15. Between December 1975 and February 1978, Abba had a run of seven consecutive top three hits; which of these was the only one not to top the UK charts?

16. Which guitarist replaced Brian Jones in the Rolling Stones, before leaving the group in 1974?

17. Feargal Sharkey was lead singer with which group, formed in Londonderry in the mid Seventies, before he began his solo career?

18. Who wrote the song 'I Shot The Sheriff', which was taken to number nine in the British charts in 1974 by Eric Clapton?

19. Which Beatles song reached number one in the American singles charts in 1965, but wasn't a top ten hit in the UK until 1976?

20. Which rock guitarist was born John Graham Mellor in Ankara, Turkey, in 1952?

21. 'I could be a writer with a growing reputation, I could be the ticket man at Fulham Broadway Station' were lines from which 1978 hit song by Ian Dury and the Blockheads?

22. Which chart-topping disco artist had her final top ten hit with 'Dr Love' in 1976?

23. Which group, formed in Sheffield in 1977, took its name from a computer game called *Star Force*?

24. Whose biggest hit single as a solo artist was 'Let's Stick Together (Let's Work Together)' which reached number 4 in the UK charts in 1976?

25. Session player Raphael Ravenscroft played the memorable saxophone riff on which 1978 hit single?

26. Which 1970s chart-topping singer had his first success as Shane Fenton in the early 1960s?

27. Which song gave Cliff Richard a number one hit in 1979, his first since 'Congratulations' in 1968?

28. Whose first chart entry was '2-4-6-8 Motorway', a top ten hit in 1977?

29. Which single by The Police failed to chart when it was first released in 1978, but reached number 12 on re-release in 1979?

30. Which singer and songwriter's debut album, released in 1977, was called 'My Aim Is True'?

General Knowledge 4.2

1. Which classic novel features the lawyer Atticus Finch and his daughter Scout?

2. Who performed the first human heart transplant operation at the Groote Schuur Hospital in Cape Town in December 1967?

3. Which family of musical instruments includes the oboe and the bassoon?

4. Which shipping forecast area lies between the Irish Sea to the north, Fastnet to the west, and Plymouth to the south?

5. In English folklore, who was Robin Hood's chaplain?

6. Which Mexican artist, noted for her brilliantly coloured self-portraits, was twice married to her fellow artist Diego Rivera?

7. In the western Christian church, what name is given to the day that follows Shrove Tuesday and marks the first day of Lent?

8. In March 1957, Kwame Nkrumah became the first Prime Minister of which newly independent country?

9. What name is given to a sweet pancake served in a flaming tangerine or orange sauce?

10. Whose 1630 treatise 'Dialogue Concerning the Two Chief World Systems' led to him being tried for heresy by the Inquisition in Rome?

11. Which film actor, who starred in *Captain Corelli's Mandolin*, is the nephew of the director Francis Ford Coppola?

12. In architecture, what name is used for the decorative end or ridge of a gable, often in the form of a spike or bunch of leaves?

13. Which symphonic fairy tale for narrator and orchestra by Prokofiev was first performed in 1936?

14. King Henry I of England reportedly died from eating 'a surfeit' of which eel-like creatures?

15. Which actor played the photographer Lawrence in the film *Calendar Girls* and DCI Gene Hunt in the television series *Life on Mars* and *Ashes to Ashes*?

16. The north-eastern corner of the island of Corfu lies just off the coast of which country?

17. Whose novel *Germinal*, first published in 1885 and widely considered his masterpiece, is a study of working-class life in a French mining community?

18. Which of its former allies declared war on Nazi Germany on 13 October 1943?

19. Which small town near Borehamwood in Hertfordshire gave its name to a group of film and television studios in the area?

20. Three, six and nine-banded are species of which mammal found mainly in Central and South America?

21. In his work *Man and Superman*, George Bernard Shaw claims every man over forty is a what?

22. Which metal is present in the ores malachite and azurite?

23. Which American boxer known as the 'Boston Strongboy' was the last holder of the World Heavyweight Championship under the London Prize Ring bare-knuckle rules?

24. What name is given to the position on the Earth's surface directly above the point of origin of an earthquake?

25. On a roulette wheel, what colour is the compartment containing the number zero?

26. Which Gilbert and Sullivan operetta has the alternate title 'The Lass That Loved A Sailor'?

27. Which London park that gets its name from its landscape of grass and trees was once used as a duelling ground?

28. Which Impressionist painter's reclining nude *Olympia* was based on Titian's *Venus of Urbino*?

29. In which American state is the Petrified Forest National Park?

30. In the film *The Lavender Hill Mob*, the gang plan to melt down their gold bullion booty and ship it to France as models of what?

The first Master-mind

The first three *Mastermind* champions were female – Nancy Wilkinson, Patricia Owen and Elizabeth Horrocks – leading to the light-hearted suggestion that the programme's title should be changed to 'Mistressmind'! In 1975, however, a 'master' finally triumphed; doubly so in fact as John Hart, as well as being male, was a schoolmaster at Malvern College.

Many years later, John took on another formidable opponent – the Inland Revenue – in the landmark legal case now known as 'Pepper v Hart', which went all the way to the House of Lords where the Law Lords decided in favour of John and his colleagues.

Show 5

Specialist Subject 5.1
British TV Comedy and Sitcoms

1. What is the name of the tower block where the Trotters live in *Only Fools and Horses*?

2. Which scriptwriter's successful sitcoms include *Bread*?

3. In *Blackadder III*, which nineteenth-century writer does Edmund Blackadder describe as 'a huge Yorkshireman with a beard like a Rhododendron bush'?

4. Which character in *Dad's Army* was known for his catchphrase 'We're doomed, we're doomed!'

5. In an episode of *Fawlty Towers*, an American guest demands what type of salad that Basil has never heard of?

6. What was the name of the obnoxious cockney plasterer created by Harry Enfield in the late 1980s?

7. Which show, written by John Sullivan, featured the characters Vince Pinner and Penny Warrender?

8. Which fictional character's autobiography, entitled *Bouncing Back*, describes his battles with weight and depression?

9. In which sitcom does the lead female character (played by one of the show's co-writers) have a son named David Keanu Ronan?

10. Which harassed executive's loyal secretary, Joan Greengross, was played by Sue Nicholls, who also appeared in *Coronation Street*?

11. In *Citizen Smith*, Wolfie Smith (played by Robert Lindsay) was the self-elected leader of the Popular Front in which district of London?

12. In *Birds of a Feather*, what was the name of Sharon and Tracey's toy-boy-loving next-door neighbour?

13. The original title characters of which sitcom were called Beryl and Dawn, though the latter was replaced by Sandra (played by Nerys Hughes)?

14. Who plays Edina Monsoon's PA, Bubble, in *Absolutely Fabulous*?

15. In which series were Simon Peel and Oliver Smallbridge rival antique dealers?

16. In the classic Monty Python sketch, who plays the man from the Ministry of Silly Walks?

17. What was the name of the Crimpton-on-Sea holiday camp in *Hi-de-Hi!*?

18. In *The Good Life*, what was the surname of Tom and Barbara's next-door neighbours, Margo and Jerry?

19. In *The Office*, paper merchants Wernham Hogg were based in which town?

20. What was the full name of the character played by Ronnie Barker in *Porridge*?

21. Which spoof soap opera that appeared in *Victoria Wood – As Seen on TV* starred Julie Walters as Mrs Overall?

22. In *The Young Ones*, who played the students' landlord Jerzy Balowski (and all of his family)?

23. Which sketch show featured an invented language that had phrases including 'scorchio', 'Chris Waddle' and 'Boutros Boutros Ghali'?

24. Lenny Henry played the title character, Gareth Blackstock, in which sitcom?

25. What was the name of the fictional Tory MP for Haltemprice, who used to shout 'Go back to Russia!' whenever Labour MPs spoke in the House of Commons?

26. In the *Yes, Minister* episode 'Party Games', Jim Hacker helps to prevent what being re-named as an 'Emulsified High-Fat Offal Tube'?

27. What is the name of Audrey fforbes-Hamilton's butler, who moves into one of the lodges of Grantleigh Manor with her after her husband dies?

28. Better known for his portrayal of policemen, who played Henry Willows in the sitcom *Home to Roost*?

29. Which duo played George and Anne in the Enid Blyton spoof *Five Go Mad in Dorset*?

30. What was the name of the voluptuous movie star, created by Kenny Everett, who did everything 'in the best possible taste'?

General Knowledge 5.1

1. Which reference work, first published in 1768, was the idea of two Edinburgh printers, Andrew Bell and Colin Macfarquhar?

2. Which town on the Island of Lewis and Harris is the largest town in the Outer Hebrides?

3. Which of Lord Byron's mistresses wrote in her diary after their first meeting, that he was 'mad, bad, and dangerous to know'?

4. The Polish refusal to hand over which port to the Germans was used by Hitler as a pretext for invading the country to start the Second World War?

5. Elgar's Opus 36, 'Variations on an Original Theme', is more usually known by what title?

6. The insect-repellent citronella is derived from a close relative of which perennial grass, often used in Thai cooking?

7. The name of which religion means 'disciple' in Hindi?

8. What is the surname of Leon and Michael who became the first brothers to be World Heavyweight Boxing Champions?

9. What name for the only bear native to South America comes from the light-coloured marks that partly or wholly encircle their eyes?

10. Which French artist, whose works include *Sunday Afternoon on the Island of la Grande Jatte*, founded the School of Neo-Impressionism?

11. In biology, what name is given to the threadlike structures normally occurring in pairs in the cell nucleus that carry hereditary information in the form of genes?

12. Which dramatist wrote the plays *Entertaining Mr Sloane*, *Loot* and *What the Butler Saw*?

13. What name, from the Greek for 'weapon', was given to the heavily armed foot soldiers of Ancient Greece?

14. In classical architecture, what name is given to a roof structure supported by columns that forms the entrance to a building, or is extended into a colonnade?

15. Which self-governing island is known as Kalaallit Nunaat in the language of its indigenous people?

16. Which American band have had hit albums with *Hot Fuss* and *Sam's Town*?

17. In a standard three-pin electrical plug, two of the pins should be connected to the live and earth wires, respectively; what should the third pin be connected to?

18. Which Anglo-Saxon king, whose name means 'noble counsel', was given a nickname that meant 'bad' or 'no counsel'?

19. A cartoon by Richard Doyle was used continuously from 1849 to 1956 on the front cover of which magazine?

20. What London landmark was originally designed by John Nash as the main entrance to Buckingham Palace?

21. The annual music writing awards presented by the British Academy of Songwriters, Composers and Authors are named after which songwriter and actor?

22. Which genus of plants, also known as the sensitive plants, gets its name from the Greek for 'to mimic'?

23. Which hit television series starred James Gandolfini as a New Jersey mafia boss?

24. What unit commonly used for measuring land area is equal to 10,000 square metres?

25. The French designer Rene Lalique was especially noted for his Art Nouveau and Art Deco objects made from what material?

26. Which Latin term is used to describe the period of time between two reigns when the throne is unoccupied?

27. Which cycle of sixty-three nostalgic poems by A.E. Housman was first published in 1896 at the author's own expense?

28. The popular name of which religious group is said to have been coined in 1650 by Justice Bennet of Derby, in mockery of the exhortation 'to tremble at the word of God'?

29. The motto of Sir Thomas Bond, after whom Bond Street is named, was used as the title for which James Bond film?

30. The North Star, the brightest star in the constellation Ursa Minor, is commonly known by what other name?

Specialist Subject 5.2
The Human Body

1. What is the largest internal organ in humans? It plays a major role in detoxifying the body.

2. Which long bones in the mid-foot are often broken by football players? This is sometimes attributed to the modern lightweight design of football boots.

3. Which major extensor muscle in the thigh is so-called because it comprises four distinct parts?

4. The stapes, incus and malleus, meaning stirrup, anvil and

hammer, are the three small bones located in which part of the body?

5. The bile and pancreatic ducts enter which one of the three sections of the small intestine?

6. In humans, which is the principal pigment determining the colour of skin, hair and eyes?

7. Which segmented valve of the heart that lies between the right atrium and the right ventricle, prevents the backflow of blood?

8. Which is the largest of the three paired muscles in the buttocks?

9. Which are the smallest blood vessels? They have very thin walls that enable blood and cells to exchange materials.

10. Which group of illnesses are specifically characterised by a reduction of haemoglobin below the normal range?

11. A combined total of how many phalanges, metacarpals and carpals make up the skeletal structure of a human hand and wrist?

12. The maxilla forms the upper part of the jaw; which bone forms the lower?

13. The body's immune system is based on which specialised white cells, with two types called 'T' and 'B', which respond to infection or cell abnormalities by producing antibodies?

14. Which bone of the upper arm extends from the shoulder to the elbow?

15. What name is given to the small clusters of endocrine cells in the pancreas, which secrete insulin and lucagon?

16. What is the common name of parotitis, the infection

characterised by swelling of the largest pair of salivary glands located in front of the ear?

17. The sac surrounding the heart, comprising an outer fibrous layer and an inner thinner membrane, is known by what name?

18. Which pads of lymphatic tissue at the back of the nasal passages, above the tonsils, form part of the body's defences against infection but have mainly disappeared by puberty?

19. What is the inner region of the adrenal gland called, from which the hormone adrenalin is produced as part of the body's response to fear or stress?

20. Which is the principal acid in gastric juice, the human digestive fluid?

21. In the eye, what clear jelly-like substance fills the chamber between the lens and the retina?

22. What name from the Greek is given to the white blood cells that defend the body against both infectious disease and foreign materials?

23. Which lymph gland, in the upper part of the chest above the heart, is involved in the body's immune system and is large at birth but gradually shrinks in adulthood?

24. What name is given to the normal openings in the skull of an infant, resulting from the incomplete closure of the sutures?

25. The Sabin vaccine, named after the Polish-American doctor who developed it in Cincinnati in the 1950s, is an oral preparation that is used against which disease?

26. What name is given to the wavelike process whereby food is moved through the digestive track by muscular contractions?

27. Which units in the kidney, numbering around one million, filter waste products from the blood and reabsorb salts and water as required?

28. Commonly referred to as the tailbone, what is the anatomical name of the triangular bone that forms the final segment of the spine?

29. Which pair of ligaments inside the knee joint, attached to the tibia and condyle of the femur, help prevent excessive antero-posterior glide of the joint?

30. Which gland at the base of the brain, often referred to as 'the master gland', controls the activities of many other endocrine glands?

General Knowledge 5.2

1. What colour does litmus paper turn in acid solutions?

2. Who played Indiana Jones's father, Dr Henry Jones, in the 1989 film *Indiana Jones and the Last Crusade*?

3. Which fifth-century BC writer, whose nine-volume history includes an account of the wars between the Greeks and the Persians, is known as the 'father of history'?

4. In musical notation, which note, also called the whole note, has double the value of the minim?

5. Who resigned as President of Argentina in the wake of his country's defeat in the Falklands War?

6. Whose first successful play was *The Glass Menagerie*, about a southern family living in a tenement?

7. The Gulf of Finland and the Gulf of Riga are inlets of which sea?

8. Which sixteenth-century Venetian artist, who is thought to have trained briefly under Titian, was responsible for the vast series of paintings for the Scuola di San Rocco produced between 1565 and 1587?

9. In Greek mythology, who was chained to a rock as a sacrifice to a sea-monster, until she was rescued by her future husband Perseus?

10. Which group's first chart-topping UK single was 'Good Vibrations' in November 1966?

11. Leek and which other vegetable is used to make the soup Vichyssoise, which is usually served chilled?

12. Which Romantic novel begins with the lines '1801 – I have just returned from a visit to my landlord – the solitary neighbour that I shall be troubled with'?

13. What general term is used for a small, woody, often bushy plant that has several stems, none of which are dominant?

14. What Latin term was given to a darkened room or box into which light is admitted through a small hole producing an inverted image of an outside scene?

15. The Stirling Prize, named after Sir James Stirling, was first awarded in 1996 in which field of the arts?

16. What is the second largest of the English Lakes? It is drained at its northern end by the River Eamont.

17. The trademark of which film studios, formed in 1928, was a radio tower on top of the Earth, transmitting rhythmic signals?

18. Which Italian-born astronomer discovered four moons of Saturn and also the gap in its ring system that has been named after him?

19. What is the name of Rugby League's premier knockout tournament, which was first won by Batley in 1897?

20. Lilongwe is the capital of which African country?

21. Which London club was founded in 1831 as a place where 'actors and men of refinement and education might meet on equal terms'?

22. Which Jewish festival commemorates the Hebrews' liberation from slavery in Egypt?

23. Which children's novel, written by Roald Dahl, features Aunt Sponge and Aunt Spiker and a group of friendly insects?

24. Which powerful analgesic drug was isolated from opium at the beginning of the nineteenth century by the German chemist Friedrich Wilhelm Sertürner?

25. Which of Rossini's operas is known in Italian as 'La Gazza Ladra'?

26. What is the alternative name for the caudal fin of a fish?

27. What is the name of the small Russian pancakes traditionally served with sour cream and caviar?

28. Which island is divided into two French départements with Bastia and Ajaccio as their respective capitals?

29. Which historical drama series, shown on BBC Two in 1976, featured a supporting cast including John Hurt, Brian Blessed, George Baker and Sian Phillips?

30. What is featured on the badge of John of Gaunt and the arms of Scotland and is said to be the commonest pub name in Britain?

The Trophy

Every *Mastermind* champion receives a glass bowl, each of which is unique. Designed and engraved by Denis Mann, the theme is always the Muses – the Greek goddesses of the arts, sciences and intellectual pursuits generally.

The Muses were the offspring of Zeus – the greatest of the Greek gods – and Mnemosyne – the goddess of memory. An apt choice then, for the supreme test of knowledge and recall.

Show 6

Specialist Subject 6.1
English and Scottish History, 1066–1707

1. Three days before William the Conqueror landed in England in September 1066, King Harold defeated a Viking army that included his own brother, Tostig, at which battle?

2. Which places of popular entertainment were closed by the Puritan Parliament in 1642?

3. Who was excommunicated for killing his rival John Comyn during a meeting in Dumfries in February 1306?

4. After reading Henry VIII's anti-Lutheran tract 'The Defence of the Seven Sacraments', what title did Pope Leo X confer on him in October 1521?

5. What name was given to the series of trials, conducted in 1685 by Judge Jeffreys, in which over two hundred people were executed after the failed Monmouth Rebellion?

6. One of the terms of the Treaty of Medina Del Campo in March 1489 was the marriage of the two-year-old Arthur Tudor, son of Henry VII, to which three-year-old princess?

7. Born at Selby in Yorkshire, who was the first English-born King of England after the Norman Conquest?

8. The Company of Scotland made a disastrous attempt to colonise which area on the Isthmus of Panama that they renamed 'New Caledonia'?

9. Which lawyer led the Pilgrimage of Grace, which began in Yorkshire in October 1536?

10. Generally regarded as being the centre of London, where was a memorial to the last resting place of the coffin of Edward I's queen, Eleanor of Castile, erected in 1291?

11. In which year did the Scottish army, led by Robert the Bruce, rout the English at Bannockburn?

12. What was the name of the pretender to the throne who claimed to be Richard III's nephew, Edward Earl of Warwick, and was 'crowned' in Dublin Cathedral (as 'Edward VI') on 24 May 1487?

13. In which city did Charles I raise the royal standard on 22 August 1642, and proclaim the Commons and their soldiers traitors?

14. What name is popularly given to the meeting of Henry VIII and Francis I of France, which took place south of Calais in 1520?

15. Which district of the West End of London takes its name from the type of collar popular in the early seventeenth century that was a speciality of Robert Baker, a local tailor?

16. In the spring of 1297, who killed the English Sheriff of Lanark, sparking a movement of national resistance across Scotland?

17. What nickname was given to the cavalry troops commanded by Oliver Cromwell, which were a key factor in the Parliamentary victory at Marston Moor?

18. James I and VI eased his financial concerns in 1611 by establishing and selling which hereditary title?

19. What informal name was given to the group of Whigs in the reigns of William III and Queen Anne that included Lord John Somers, the Earl of Wharton, and the Earl of Orford?

20. As well as the Isle of Man, King Magnus of Norway ceded which island group to Scotland, by the Treaty of Perth in 1266?

21. In 1619, which architect designed the new Banqueting Hall in Whitehall, where King Charles I was executed on 30 January 1649?

22. Sir Isaac Newton abandoned his scientific enquiries at Cambridge after being made the Warden of which institution?

23. The 'Popish Plot', a fictitious conspiracy alleging that Jesuits planned to kill Charles II, was based solely on false statements made by Israel Tonge and who else?

24. Which battle, fought on 9 September 1513, saw James IV of Scotland killed and the Scottish army annihilated by the English?

25. The Great Fire of London began on 1 September 1666 in Thomas Farynor's bakehouse in which lane?

26. Under which Act of 1701 were Roman Catholics and anyone married to a Catholic explicitly excluded from the line of succession to the English throne?

27. Which royal favourite was assassinated by John Felton in August 1628?

28. What name was given to the Plot of 1683 to assassinate Charles II and his brother on their way home from Newmarket racecourse?

29. In December 1648, which Colonel 'purged' the House of Commons of those MPs who wanted to negotiate with King Charles I?

30. By which act of parliament of 1534 was Henry VIII declared to be the 'Supreme Head on Earth of the Church of England'?

General Knowledge 6.1

1. In the UK, what name is given to a strip of countryside around a town or city protected under Planning Regulations and intended to limit urban sprawl?

2. Who was excommunicated by the Catholic Church in 1521 and appeared before an assembly of the Holy Roman Empire known as the Diet of Worms?

3. What name is given to the clear, savoury jelly used to coat food such as cold meat or fish?

4. Which sculptor, born in Wakefield, has a gallery dedicated to her work in the city, which opened in May 2011?

5. What season does Keats describe as 'Season of mists and mellow fruitfulness'?

6. What term for the theory or philosophy of law comes from the Latin for 'knowledge of the law'?

7. What name is shared by an island off the coast of Northumberland and an island off the west coast of Anglesey?

8. Which composer, who died at the age of 31 in 1828, had been a torch-bearer at Beethoven's funeral and was buried near to him?

9. Which marsupial, native to the south-eastern part of Australia and Tasmania, is the largest burrowing herbivorous mammal?

10. In Parliament, what name is given to either of the corridors, entered from each side of the Speaker's Chair, through which MPs pass to register votes?

11. Which town in Australia's Northern Territory is referred to in the title of Neville Shute's novel about an Englishwoman who settles in nearby Willstown?

12. What name is given to the process discovered in 1839 by the American inventor Charles Goodyear, whereby rubber is heated with sulphur to toughen it?

13. Which filmmaker first teamed up with Robert de Niro for the 1973 film *Mean Streets*?

14. When the Soviet Union broke up in 1991, which Central Asian republic became the world's largest landlocked country?

15. In the *Iliad*, which Trojan hero, killed by Achilles, was the son of King Priam and the husband of Andromache?

16. Which public school has former pupils including Lord Byron, Sir Robert Peel and Sir Winston Churchill?

17. Which ornamental, highly poisonous, evergreen shrub, that has thick lance-shaped leaves and striking red or white flowers, is also known as rose-bay or rose-laurel?

18. John Howard and Elizabeth Fry are both noted for their contributions to the reform of which institutions?

19. Which 1979 UK number one hit for the Boomtown Rats begins with the line 'The silicon chip inside her head gets switched to overload'?

20. What name is given to the side opposite the 90-degree angle of a right-angled triangle?

21. In cricket, who was appointed as the England team Director in 2009? He coached them to their Ashes victory in the winter of 2010–2011.

22. Which writer and member of the Bloomsbury Group was the sister of Vanessa Bell?

23. The region around Palo Alto on San Francisco Bay is known by what name because of the concentration of electronics and computer companies situated there?

24. Which modern-day musical instrument normally has eighty-eight keys and covers over seven full octaves?

25. Which of the seven hills of Rome was the home of the wealthy during the Republican era, and under the Empire became the site of the imperial palaces?

26. What is the usual term, originating in America, that describes a spirit, especially whisky, served undiluted over ice cubes?

27. Which sea monster of Norwegian folklore, mentioned by Tennyson among others, is thought to have been inspired by sightings of a giant squid or octopus?

28. Who won the first of her four Best Actress Oscars for the 1933 film *Morning Glory* and the last for the 1981's *On Golden Pond*?

29. The femur is the medical term for which bone?

30. Which small fountain sculpture in Brussels, depicting a young boy, is known affectionately by local people as the 'oldest citizen'?

Specialist Subject 6.2
James Bond Novels and Films

1. What is the title of the first of the James Bond novels by Ian Fleming? It was published on 13 April 1953.

2. Which of James Bond's adversaries was played by Richard Kiel?

3. Which 1967 Bond film had a screenplay written by Roald Dahl?

4. Which character has been played in Bond films by actors including Jeffrey Wright, David Hedison and Jack Lord?

5. In which 1973 film did Roger Moore make the first of his seven appearances as James Bond?

6. In *Dr No*, M instructs Bond to change his gun from which weapon, described by the armourer as a 'Ladies' gun', to the Walther PPK?

7. In which city did the Bond film *A View to a Kill* have its world premiere, as a gesture of gratitude to the mayor for allowing the filming of the climactic sequences of the film on the city's bridge?

8. Which actor played Valentin Zukovsky in the Bond films *Goldeneye* and *The World Is Not Enough*?

9. In which novel and film does Bond get married, only for his bride to be killed as they set off for their honeymoon?

10. What is Goldfinger's first name, which is derived from the Latin for 'gold'?

11. Whose first appearance as Bond was in *The Living Daylights*?

12. In the 2006 film version of *Casino Royale*, starring Daniel Craig, Bond plays a high-stakes card game against which villain, who provides a 'banking service to the world's terrorists'?

13. Sean Connery returned to the role of James Bond in the 1983 film *Never Say Never Again*, which was a virtual remake of which earlier Bond film?

14. In *On Her Majesty's Secret Service*, Sable Basilisk of the College of Arms tells Bond that which villain was born in the Polish town of Gdynia on 28 May 1908?

15. What is the name of Karl Stromberg's undersea base from which he aims to control the world in the film version of *The Spy Who Loved Me*?

16. In which Bond novel and film do the hired killers Mister Wint and Mister Kidd appear?

17. The full name of Bond's controller, 'M', is revealed in the novel of *The Man with the Golden Gun*. What is it?

18. Which group had a hit single in Britain with the theme from the Bond film *A View to a Kill*?

19. What is Goldfinger's reply when Bond, who is about to be cut in half by a laser beam, asks him 'Do you expect me to talk?'

20. The villain Rosa Klebb attempts to kill Bond with her poison-tipped shoe in which of the novels, as well as in the subsequent film version?

21. What is the name of Elliot Carver's newspaper, which is also part of the title of the film he appears in?

22. Desmond Llewelyn played which character in numerous Bond films?

23. In which film does Bond uncover a plot by a renegade Russian general and an ex-Afghan prince to detonate an atomic bomb on an American airbase?

24. What was unusual about Charles Gray's performances in *You Only Live Twice* and *Diamonds Are Forever*? Joe Don Baker did the same in reverse in *The Living Daylights* and *GoldenEye*?

25. In which of the films does Bond take on the Colombian drugs baron Franz Sanchez?

26. Simone Latrelle, a telepath and fortune teller, is the real name of which character in *Live and Let Die*?

27. In which city is Emile Leopold Locque an 'underworld enforcer', in *For Your Eyes Only*?

28. Who has a cameo as Verity, a fencing instructor, in *Die Another Day*?

29. What circus act do the murderous twins Mischka and Grischka perform in *Octopussy*?

30. One of Scaramanga's distinguishing features is that he has three... what?

General Knowledge 6.2

1. What term, meaning 'beautiful writing', is used to describe the art of fine penmanship?

2. Which city was founded in Roman times as Aquae Sulis, and dedicated to the Celtic goddess Sul?

3. Who wrote *The Life and Strange Surprising Adventures of Robinson Crusoe*, first published in 1719 and based on the real-life adventures of Alexander Selkirk?

4. In mathematics, what name is given to a system of equations that are to be solved together? The simplest example is a pair of linear equations in two unknowns.

5. Which Verdi opera features the characters Zaccaria, the high priest of the Hebrews, and the King of Babylon?

6. In classical mythology, who is the Muse of epic poetry?

7. What name was given to the question originally posed by the MP Tam Dalyell, which asked whether Scottish MPs at Westminster could justifiably vote on purely English matters after devolution?

8. Which British-born director achieved his first commercial success with the film *Alien*, followed by *Blade Runner*?

9. Which peninsula forms the mainland portion of Denmark and also includes part of the German state of Schleswig-Holstein?

10. In the mid-nineteenth century, who invented jeans as durable work clothes, reinforced with small copper rivets?

11. The order Acarina comprises ticks and which other small arthropods, whose name means anything very tiny?

12. What two-word Hindi name, translating roughly as 'hot mixture', is given to a combination of roasted spices, sometimes blended with water or vinegar, that are often used in Indian cookery?

13. In around 182 BC, which military leader poisoned himself in Bithynia in Asia Minor, where he was taking refuge from the Romans?

14. Which band, formed in Leeds, have had hit singles including 'I Predict A Riot' and 'Never Miss A Beat'?

15. Which channel linking the Atlantic and Pacific Oceans lies between the tip of mainland South America and the island of Tierra del Fuego?

16. Which author's work *A Rose for Winter*, published in 1955, tells of his return to Spain with his wife, fifteen years after the Civil War in which he fought on the Republican side?

17. Which country joined Rugby Union's Five Nations Championship in 2000 to make it into the Six Nations?

18. According to the Gospels of Mark and John, who was the first person to see Christ after his resurrection?

19. Which word for a pithy statement of the truth comes from the Greek for 'a distinction' or 'a definition'?

20. Which composer's orchestral works include the ballet *Appalachian Spring*, written for the dancer Martha Graham?

21. Which shrub, that is similar to gorse but without the spines, grows on heathland and sandy soil over most of Britain?

22. Which English painter and engraver's works include six scenes entitled *Marriage à la Mode*, criticising the marriage customs of the upper classes?

23. French reinforcements were transported to the front in a fleet of Paris taxis during which battle of September 1914 that halted the German advance on the city?

24. The Chief Electrician responsible for the lighting of the set in a film or television studio is known by what title?

25. What is the world's highest uninterrupted waterfall, which is

situated on the Churun river in Venezuela and named after the first outsider to see it?

26. Which aromatic plant has a stalk that turns bright green when candied, and is used to decorate cakes and trifles?

27. Which disease of children, characterised by improper hardening and development of bones, is caused by a deficiency of vitamin D?

28. The hero of which 1749 novel by Henry Fielding is described as 'a foundling' in its full title?

29. Which city is the second largest in California and lies just across the border from the Mexican city of Tijuana?

30. In February 2011, a blue plaque was unveiled on Bournemouth seafront, celebrating Britain's oldest example of what type of building?

Morecambe-mind

Mastermind had truly entered the national consciousness by 1974 – proof came when Magnus Magnusson was invited to appear in a sketch with Morecambe and Wise, with the former 'winning' on the final question: 'It is the most important route from Afghanistan into Pakistan, it is the Khyber... what?' Eric Morecambe, with a resigned shrug: 'Pass.' Magnus: 'Correct.'

Show 7

Specialist Subject 7.1
Impressionist Art and Artists

1. Which artist's *Impression: Sunrise*, painted at Le Havre in 1872, is generally regarded as the picture that gave the Impressionist movement its name?

2. What name was given to the art exhibition of 1863, held by command of Napoleon III, for those artists whose work had been rejected by the jury of the official salon?

3. Which of the Impressionists, although born in France, had English parents and was known as the 'English Impressionist'?

4. Which French term is used for a painting done in the open air instead of in the studio, a central feature of Impressionism?

5. Which journalist, writing in the satirical magazine *Charivari* in 1874, gave the painters the name 'Impressionists'?

6. With which country's ethnic art did Monet have a life-long fascination? It was the inspiration for his 1876 portrait of his wife Camille surrounded by fans.

7. Whose last great painting, *The Bar at the Folies-Bérgère*, is part of the collection of the Courtauld Institute and has been displayed at Somerset House?

8. What was the nationality by birth of Mary Cassatt, who settled in Paris and exhibited in four of the Impressionists' group shows between 1879 and 1886?

9. Which artist, who was born in the West Indies, had his work shown in all eight of the Impressionist group exhibitions between 1874 and 1886?

10. Which of Manet's paintings appears in the background of his 1868 portrait of Emile Zola?

11. Writing in *Le Temps* in 1877, critic Paul Mantz described which female artist as 'the one real Impressionist'?

12. In which resort area on the River Seine, now a suburb of north-west Paris, did Monet live in the 1870s, often working from a studio boat he had there?

13. Which of the Impressionists joined the Tenth Cavalry Regiment at the start of the Franco-Prussian War in 1870 and was posted to Libourne in the Bordeaux region, where he contracted dysentery?

14. Whose works include *Mont Sainte-Victoire* and *The Cardplayers*?

15. In 1897, Pissarro produced a series of paintings, in the classic Impressionist style, showing which famous street 'on a Winter Morning'?

16. Which popular open-air dance hall and café-bar in Montmartre is the subject of Renoir's well-known painting of 1876 showing people seated, talking and dancing in dappled sunlight?

17. Who painted *Sunday Afternoon on the Island of La Grande Jatte* as a companion piece to his *Bathers at Asnières*?

18. Which colour, subject of much opprobrium by his fellow Impressionists, did Renoir come to appreciate after a trip to Italy, where he discovered Raphael?

19. Whose works include *Dancers at the Bar*, *Woman in a Tub* and a sculpture entitled *The Little 14-Year-Old Dancer*?

20. What profession did Cezanne give up to move to Paris in 1861?

21. *Jane Avril Dancing* is a famous work by which artist?

22. Along with Seurat, who was the other major exponent of the Pointillist style of Impressionism? They both exhibited at the last Impressionist show in 1886, on the encouragement of Pissarro.

23. In the third Impressionist Exhibition of 1877, Monet exhibited views of which Paris railway station and its immediate surroundings?

24. Which French painter, who posed for Renoir, was encouraged to draw and paint by Degas, and was the mother of the artist Maurice Utrillo?

25. What title is shared by Manet's painting of 1863, a parody of a Renaissance painting in a modern setting, and Monet's uncompleted work showing picnickers in the forest of Fontainebleau?

26. In which medium did Degas produce *At the Milliner's* and *Two Dancers Resting*?

27. What was the name of the art dealer who organised the one-man show of Monet's Antibes paintings, at the Boussod and Valadon gallery in Paris in 1888?

28. Which London landmark did Monet begin painting from a window or balcony of St Thomas' Hospital in 1903?

29. Which artist spent part of his childhood near Lima in Peru, exhibited with the Impressionists in the early 1880s and also lived briefly in Denmark and other places before dying in the Marquesas?

30. Which group of artists, whose name means 'wild beasts' in French, took inspiration from the late- or post-Impressionists?

General Knowledge 7.1

1. In 1975, who founded the Microsoft Corporation with his friend Paul Allen?

2. Which small European Principality is traditionally divided into two regions known as the Upper Country or Oberland, and the Lower Country or Unterland?

3. Which Shakespeare play features the line 'That which we call a rose by any other name would smell as sweet'?

4. What alternative name for the European wolf spider comes from the city in southern Italy where it is commonly found?

5. Joaquin Rodrigo composed his 'Concierto De Aranjuez' for which solo stringed instrument, with orchestra?

6. Which tenth-century Bohemian martyr prince, noted for his piety, was murdered by his brother Boleslav on his way to Mass?

7. Which sauce, originally from Genoa, is made by adding olive oil to pounded basil, pine nut kernels, garlic and Parmesan cheese?

8. In the human body, the clavicle is more commonly known by what name?

9. The works of which poet and designer, associated with the Pre-Raphaelite Brotherhood, include *News From Nowhere* that describes a Socialist rural utopia?

10. The political upheaval that was launched by Mao Zedong in 1966, and attacked traditional values, is generally known by what name?

11. In snooker and billiards, what term is used to describe a series of successive scoring shots made by any one player?

12. What is the most abundant element in the Earth's crust, consisting of nearly half of its mass?

13. Which 1972 film, starring Liza Minnelli and Michael York, was based on Christopher Isherwood's 'Berlin' stories?

14. In law, what does the acronym ASBO stand for?

15. Which novel by Nicholas Monsarrat tells of the trials and tribulations of the crew of the corvette HMS *Compass Rose* during the Battle of the Atlantic?

16. Which range of hills, situated mainly in Northumberland, form the border between England and Scotland for around thirty-five miles?

17. Which rock festival was the subject of a song written by Joni Mitchell that became a number one hit for Matthews' Southern Comfort in 1970?

18. What is the fourth letter of the Greek alphabet, the equivalent to the Roman letter 'D'?

19. Which hand-held percussion instruments take their name from the Spanish for 'chestnut'?

20. Entomology is the scientific study of which creatures?

21. Graham McPherson, who is better known as Suggs, was the vocalist with which group, who started out as The Invaders?

22. In the 1840s, British troops in India were first issued with uniform in which colour? The name derives from the Persian for dust.

23. In Greek mythology, which youth, who pined away after falling in love with his own reflection, was turned into the flower that bears his name?

24. Which river, the longest in Ireland, enters the Atlantic Ocean through an estuary about seventy miles in length below the city of Limerick?

25. In which television series did teams representing their home towns compete over a series of obstacle courses for the right to represent Britain in the European finals of *Jeux Sans Frontières*?

26. Which word for a substance that acts as a biological catalyst, regulating the rate at which biochemical reactions proceed, comes from the Greek for 'in leaven'?

27. Which work by William Makepeace Thackeray is sub-titled 'A novel without a hero'?

28. What name is given to the group of six Dorset farm labourers who were sentenced to seven years' transportation to Australia? They had been involved in early trade union activities.

29. In 1969, who became the first person to sail solo, non-stop, around the world in his boat *Suhaili*?

30. Which farm animal appears, along with the Union Jack, on the Falkland Islands' flag?

Specialist Subject 7.2
The Bible

1. Which is the only one of the four New Testament Gospels that is not synoptic?

2. In Leviticus Chapter 16, what is the cover on the Ark of the Covenant called, where God will appear in a cloud?

3. In the genealogy of Jesus recounted in Luke, Joseph was descended from which of Adam's sons?

4. In John's Gospel, who expressed annoyance at Mary for anointing the feet of Jesus with perfume, claiming it should have been sold and the money given to the poor?

5. How old was Moses when he died, according to the Book of Deuteronomy?

6. 'And, lo, I am with you always, even unto the end of the world. Amen' is the closing line of which Gospel?

7. Which queen, the wife of King Ahab, was thrown to her death from a window and trampled underfoot?

8. Chapter 1 of Acts describes the ascension of Christ from which point that was 'from Jerusalem a Sabbath Day's journey'?

9. Which Jewish festival commemorates the foiling by Esther of a plot by Haman to kill all the Jews on a date chosen by lot?

10. What did Jesus compare to a mustard seed in a parable that appears in three of the Gospels?

11. To which of the tribes of Israel did Samson belong?

12. According to Chapter 13 of the Revelation of St John the Divine, what is the number of the Beast?

13. John relates that when Jesus first met Simon Bar Jona, later to be called Peter, he gave him the name Cephas, meaning 'stone' in which language?

14. Which of the major prophets was the son of Amoz?

15. According to Matthew and Mark, which single word of praise did the people shout as Jesus made his triumphal entry into Jerusalem?

16. In the Book of Joshua, what mark was put in the window of the harlot's house in Jericho, to protect Rahab and her family after she gave help to the Israelite spies?

17. The Apostles voted to replace Judas Iscariot among the Twelve with whom, in preference to Joseph Barsabbas?

18. Which miracle prompted a meeting of the Sanhedrin, where the high priest, Caiaphas, prophesied that Jesus would die for the Jewish nation?

19. In the Book of Daniel, who interprets the vision of the ram and the he-goat to Daniel?

20. What is the opening line of Psalm 22, according to Mark, the words that Jesus called out at the ninth hour of his crucifixion?

21. In which trade were Simon Peter and his brother Andrew working when Jesus called them to follow him?

22. Which prophetess, one of the Judges who ruled Israel, urged Barak to fight Sisera, the song of triumph celebrating his victory often being called after her?

23. According to Matthew, who did Jesus say, in his Sermon on the Mount, 'shall be called the Children of God'?

24. Which book contains the prophetic verse 'For from the rising of

the sun even unto the going down of the same, my name shall be great among the Gentiles?'

25. According to Luke, the Ascension of Jesus took place in the vicinity of which village?

26. Who had friends called Eliphaz the Temanite, Bildad the Shuhite and Zophar the Naamathite?

27. Verse 35 of Chapter 11 in John's Gospel is the shortest verse in the Bible, describing the grief felt by Jesus at the death of Lazarus. Which two words make up this verse?

28. In Kings, what is the name of the priest who anoints Solomon with oil?

29. In Chapter 3 of his First Epistle to Timothy, Paul speaks of the qualities, such as having just one wife, that are required of a bishop and which other official of the Church?

30. What is the opening line of Psalm 137?

General Knowledge 7.2

1. Sugar Loaf Mountain overlooks which South American city?

2. What name is given to a painting or carving on three panels hinged together to form a single work of art?

3. Which novel was Mervyn Griffith-Jones QC referring to when he asked the jury at the Old Bailey in October 1960, 'Is it a book that you would even wish your wife or your servants to read'?

4. Which branch of mathematics, that uses letters as symbols when calculating, takes its name from the Arabic for 'resetting'?

5. What symbol of authority is carried in procession in and out of the Chamber of House of Commons by the Serjeant at Arms at the beginning and end of each working day?

6. What name for the toxic substance used by South American Indians to tip arrows for hunting comes from an Indian word for 'poison'?

7. An *ushanka* or *shapka* is a Russian type of what item of clothing?

8. Which Greek islands became a British protectorate after the fall of Napoleon, but were ceded back to Greece in 1864?

9. Who composed 'The Hebrides' Overture, also known as 'Fingal's Cave'?

10. On Ordnance Survey Explorer and Landranger maps, what symbol is used, along with a date, to indicate a battlefield?

11. Which Oscar-winning director had early successes with the films *Shallow Grave* and *Trainspotting*?

12. What term for the order of aquatic mammals, primarily comprising whales, dolphins and porpoises, comes from the Latin for 'whale'?

13. Which duo's first UK chart entry 'Tainted Love' in 1981 was their only UK number one hit?

14. In about 1190, Henry Fitzailwyn became the first holder of which civic office?

15. Who created the radio programme *Desert Island Discs* in 1942, and was its host until his death in 1985?

16. In which European country did women only win the right to vote in national elections in 1971, and at all local elections in 1990?

17. The liqueur Cassis, a speciality of Dijon, is made from which soft fruit?

18. In Greek mythology, the name of which ill-fated king of Thebes means 'swollen-footed'?

19. Pyrophobia is an extreme fear of what?

20. What is Britain's smallest breed of duck? It gives its name to a shade of greenish-blue resembling the coloured patches over its eyes.

21. In Oscar Wilde's *The Importance of Being Earnest*, what is the name of Algy Moncrieff's formidable aunt?

22. What is the common name of the herb Armoracia rusticana, grown for its roots, which are crushed to make a pungent sauce, sometimes served with roast beef?

23. Which Italian word, meaning 'little book', is used for the text of an opera?

24. What name is given to the process whereby heat is transferred by the mass movement of a fluid such as air or water?

25. According to Shakespeare's *Richard III*, at which battle did the King shout 'A horse! A horse! My kingdom for a horse!'?

26. What name is given to the ninety-mile-long system of gorges and rapids on the River Danube that forms part of the border between Romania and Serbia?

27. In skiing, what name is given to the braking technique that involves moving the skis into the shape of an inverted 'V', while digging the inner edges into the snow?

28. Which English city holds an annual Goose Fair dating back to 1284?

29. Who was nominated for an Oscar for Best Supporting Actress for her portrayal of Queen Elizabeth in the film *The King's Speech*?

30. What name is commonly given to the war of 1739 between England and Spain? It refers to an incident of 1731, where a British sea captain had part of his anatomy removed by Spanish coastguards who had boarded his ship?

Stories of *Mastermind* champions
Nancy Dickmann: Mastermind 2009

Nancy grew up in the USA and appeared on the popular TV quiz *Jeopardy* while still in school. She applied for *Mastermind* not long after moving to the UK, and thinks her foreign upbringing may have helped her as, unlike most contenders, the black chair didn't have the same depth of cultural resonance (and fear) for her!

When she applied for *Mastermind*, however, Nancy wasn't sure she would be able to take part if selected as she was seven months pregnant with her first child. Fortunately the filming schedule fell kindly and night-time feeds proved to be a chance to revise her specialist subjects.

As *Mastermind* is pre-recorded, Nancy was able to go to the pub to watch herself in the final, accompanied by some work colleagues. She had managed to keep the result secret from them though they didn't act too surprised when she won. She says she takes that as a compliment.

Fittingly, when Nancy was asked to appear on the 'Champion of Champions' series in 2010, her heat fell just two weeks after the due date of her second child.

Show 8

Specialist Subject 8.1
The Solar System

1. Which planet orbits the Sun at an average distance of approximately 150 million kilometres?

2. Whose heliocentric model of the solar system was finally published in 1543 in *Six Books Concerning the Revolutions of the Heavenly Orbs*?

3. What name is given to the continuous flow of charged particles that are ejected outward from the Sun's corona and released into interplanetary space?

4. Which planet is a near twin of the Earth in terms of size and mass?

5. What is the name of the tenuous layer of gas that lies below the Sun's corona? It gets its name from its reddish-pink colour.

6. Which extinct volcano on Mars rises to a height of around 25 kilometres and has a base measuring around 600 kilometres? It is the largest volcano in the solar system.

7. The temperatures on the surface of which planet can range from around 430 degrees Celsius during the day to minus 170 degrees Celsius at night?

8. In 1639, who made the first recorded observation of a Transit of Venus, from his Lancashire home?

9. What name is given to the time taken by a planet to make one complete orbit of the Sun, measured by reference to the background of stars?

10. With a specific gravity of 0.71, which is the least dense of the planets?

11. Suisei, meaning 'water star', is one of the plains or planitiae on Mercury and is also the name of the planet in which language?

12. Now known not to exist, what name was given to the major planet thought, during the nineteenth century, to orbit the Sun within the orbit of Mercury?

13. On which body in the solar system are there craters named Anaxagoras, Crookes, and H.G. Wells?

14. The axis of which planet lies almost parallel to its orbital plane, meaning that the planet spins nearly on its side?

15. Carbon dioxide comprises about 96.5 per cent of the atmosphere of Venus; which gas makes up virtually all of the remainder?

16. Pandora and Prometheus are known by what collective name, because they keep Saturn's F Ring narrow by orbiting just inside and outside it?

17. The surface gravity on which planet is around two and a half times that of Earth?

18. The planet Uranus appears blue-green in colour, because of the absorption of red light by which gas in its upper atmosphere?

19. The ring systems of the gas giants all lie within a gravitational

boundary inside which any large satellite would be torn apart by tidal forces. What is the name of the boundary?

20. Proteus and Nereid are among the moons of which planet?

21. Which of the Galilean satellites of Jupiter is the densest and was shown to have volcanic activity when the two Voyager spacecraft flew by in 1979?

22. What is the name of the huge rift system on Mars that straddles the planet just south of its equator?

23. Which of Saturn's moons is the most highly reflective satellite in the solar system?

24. Which space probe, launched on 3 March 1959 and designed to photograph the Moon and measure radiation, became the first American space craft in solar orbit?

25. Discovered in 1948 by the Dutch-American astronomer Gerard P. Kuiper, which is the smallest and innermost of the moons of Uranus?

26. What feature of Jupiter, millions of kilometres across with a tail up to 650 million kilometres long, is thought to be the largest structure in the solar system?

27. Which annual meteor shower is caused by the debris left by the comet Tempel-Tuttle?

28. What name is given to the roughly spherical halo of comet nuclei surrounding the solar system beyond the Kuiper Belt? It is named after one of the astronomers who proposed its existence in 1950.

29. Which word of German origin is used for a fissure or narrow channel on the Moon's surface?

30. To the nearest mile or kilometre per second, what velocity would a rocket launched from the surface of Earth have to achieve to escape from the planet's gravity?

General Knowledge 8.1

1. What is the popular name for the overture composed by Tchaikovsky to commemorate Napoleon's retreat from Moscow?

2. What was the name of the tax, representing one-tenth of the annual produce of land and labour, that was traditionally taken for the support of church and clergy?

3. Fino is a very dry and Oloroso a sweeter type of which fortified wine?

4. What alternative name for the rowan tree reflects the fact that it can grow at a higher altitude than most other trees in Britain?

5. Who wrote the song 'Mr Tambourine Man', a number one UK hit for The Byrds in 1965?

6. Which of the United States is sometimes nicknamed the 'First State' because it was the first to ratify the Constitution in 1787?

7. Benjamin Braddock, played by Dustin Hoffman, is the title character of which 1967 film?

8. The River Dart flows for its entire length through which English county?

9. In Shakespeare's *Twelfth Night*, what is the name of Olivia's steward, who is fooled into thinking that his mistress is in love with him?

10. What name is given to the measure a backbench MP may introduce before public business on Tuesdays and Wednesdays? It takes its name from the time its sponsor may speak for.

11. In mathematics, how many faces does a dodecahedron have?

12. What agricultural device was developed and used by the inventor Jethro Tull in around 1701?

13. In June 1994, who made an innings of 501 runs, setting a new record for the highest ever score in first-class cricket?

14. In the Church of England, what name is given to the Sunday before Easter, commemorating Christ's triumphal entry into Jerusalem?

15. What part of the brain coordinates voluntary movements, maintains balance, and has a Latin name meaning 'little brain'?

16. For which event of 1951 did the sculptor Henry Moore construct a large 'Reclining Figure' that stood on the South Bank of the Thames?

17. *The Hitchhiker's Guide to the Galaxy* was whose first science fiction novel? It was based on his radio series.

18. In the English peerage, what title ranks immediately below that of Duke?

19. Ned Maddrell, who died in 1974, is generally known to be the last person to speak which form of Gaelic as his first language?

20. What common name of the New World bird Mimus polyglottos comes from its ability to imitate the calls of other birds?

21. Which Italian painter and architect is best known for his work *Lives of the Artists*, the fundamental source of information on Italian Renaissance art?

22. Which island is separated from the mainland of North Wales by the Menai Strait?

23. 'The Bridal Chorus', more familiarly known as 'Here Comes The Bride', is from which Wagner opera?

24. Hussein ibn Talal was the king of which Middle Eastern country from 1953 to 1999?

25. Which French chef created the Peach Melba in honour of the Australian soprano Dame Nellie Melba, while he was working at the Savoy Hotel in London?

26. The Maenads were the followers of which Greek god?

27. In Robert Louis Stevenson's *Treasure Island*, in what capacity was Long John Silver employed on board the *Hispaniola*?

28. Which word, now especially applied to a retired professor, originally meant 'honourably discharged from public duty'?

29. In the Channel 4 comedy series, which Bolton night-club was run by Brian Potter, played by Peter Kay?

30. Which English navigator commanded the ships *Endeavour* and *Resolution* on successive voyages of exploration?

Specialist Subject 8.2
The Football World Cup

1. Who was the captain of the 1970 Brazilian team that won the World Cup for the third time?

2. Which team were undefeated during the 1974 World Cup finals, but were still eliminated from the tournament on goal difference?

3. In which year did England, Scotland, Wales and Northern Ireland all play in the World Cup finals?

4. Who scored the winning penalty in a shoot-out against Romania, to take Ireland through to the quarter-finals in 1990?

5. Who scored thirteen goals, a record for a single tournament, in the 1958 World Cup in Sweden?

6. Which Brazilian scored in every game in every round in the 1970 World Cup finals?

7. Who were the beaten finalists in both the 1974 and the 1978 World Cups?

8. For which country did Jose Luis Brown score in a World Cup final?

9. With six goals, who won the Golden Boot award at the 1998 World Cup finals?

10. Who was the coach of West Germany when they won the World Cup on home soil in 1974?

11. In which stadium did Uruguay beat Brazil in the 1950 final, in front of a world record crowd of around 200,000 people?

12. At which World Cup was there, for the first time, a quarter-final stage involving teams from Europe, North and South America, Africa and Asia?

13. Who did West Germany beat 2-1 in the semi-finals of the 1966 World Cup?

14. Who scored the only goal when Brazil beat Wales 1-0 in quarter-finals of the 1958 tournament?

15. Which fullback scored a goal in the 1974 World Cup final and

repeated the feat in 1982?

16. Which country beat the holders Argentina 1-0, in the opening game of the 1990 World Cup?

17. Who scored the first Golden Goal in World Cup history when France beat Paraguay in the Second Round of the 1998 finals?

18. In 1934, which country became the first from Africa to take part in the World Cup finals?

19. Who was the top scorer at the 1954 finals, with eleven goals?

20. What was unusual about Luis Monti's appearances in the 1930 and 1934 finals, losing the first but winning the second?

21. What was the surname of the twin brothers who played for the Netherlands in the 1978 tournament?

22. Which Mexican goalkeeper played in five World Cup final tournaments between 1950 and 1966, a record equalled in 1998 by Lothar Matthaus?

23. Which country did Hungary beat by ten goals to one margin in the group stages of the 1982 finals?

24. Who selected the Romanian squad that took part in the first World Cup, in 1930?

25. Which Brazilian won the World Cup twice as a player and then managed them to success in 1970?

26. What was the nationality of Gottfried Dienst, the referee of the 1966 World Cup final between England and West Germany?

27. What was the name of the Yorkshireman who managed Sweden in the 1950 and 1958 tournaments?

28. How old, officially, was Cameroon's Roger Milla when he scored at the 1994 World Cup finals?

29. The 1954 quarter-final between Hungary and Brazil, a game marred by numerous fouls and three sendings-off, is generally referred to by what nickname?

30. Why did the Argentine captain 'Nolo' Ferreira have to return home midway through the 1930 tournament and miss his team's match against Mexico?

General Knowledge 8.2

1. Which famous picture, by John Constable, shows a wagon in the water on the River Stour near Flatford?

2. The name of which chemical element comes from the Latin for 'charcoal' or 'coal'?

3. Which 1965 hit song for The Beatles contains the line 'When I was younger, so much younger than today'?

4. Napoleon's favourite horse was named after which battle in northern Italy where he defeated the Austrians in 1800?

5. Lucy Honeychurch is the heroine of which novel by E.M. Forster, later made into an award-winning film?

6. There are three National Parks in Wales. Snowdonia and the Pembrokeshire Coast are two; which is the third?

7. Which fruit juice cordial is mixed with an equal quantity of gin to make a gimlet cocktail?

8. A person with the letters LLB after their name, which is short for *Legum baccalaureus*, has a degree in which subject?

9. In which present-day country was the composer Jean Sibelius born in 1865?

10. The name of which friend of Odysseus is used for someone who is a wise and faithful adviser?

11. Which playwright was killed in a tavern brawl in Deptford in 1593, allegedly after a quarrel over the bill?

12. The Anglo-French agreement of April 1904, aimed ultimately at curbing growing German power, is known by what name?

13. Who won the first of his seven Wimbledon Men's Singles titles when he beat Jim Courier in the final in 1993?

14. Which bird has the longest annual migration; it breeds in northern polar regions and winters in southern polar regions?

15. An oxide of which heavy metal is used to make crystal glass?

16. Members of which religious order, named after the Spanish priest who founded it, are known as Black Friars because of the colour of the cloak they wear?

17. Which legendary soul singer appeared as the Rev Cleophus James in the film *The Blues Brothers*?

18. What word of Arabic origin is used for a dry valley or watercourse found in arid regions and subject to flash flooding?

19. On television, Terry Collier (played by James Bolam) and Bob Ferris (played by Rodney Bewes) are better known by what collective name?

20. Who produced a White Paper called 'In Place of Strife' aimed at curbing the power of the unions, while she was Secretary of State for Employment and Productivity in Harold Wilson's government?

21. Which actress co-starred with Geena Davis in the 1991 film *Thelma and Louise*, and with Goldie Hawn in the 2002 film *The Banger Sisters*?

22. Which Greek philosopher poisoned himself by drinking hemlock, after being sentenced to death on charges of corrupting the young?

23. In the third part of *Gulliver's Travels*, what is the name of the flying island run by mad scientists?

24. In sailing, what name is used for steering a zigzag course with the boat either left or right of the wind direction, in order to make progress upwind?

25. Which nineteenth-century composer was a Professor of Chemistry at St Petersburg Academy of Medicine?

26. On which major river does the city of Worcester stand?

27. Which vegetable, also known as zucchini, is a variety of marrow usually eaten when it is young and immature?

28. In a suit of armour, what part of the body is protected by the greave?

29. *Ranunculus repens* is the creeping form of which common wild flower, dreaded by gardeners and farmers because it spreads so quickly?

30. In 1924, which Sunday broadsheet, owned by Lord Beaverbrook, became the first British newspaper to publish a crossword puzzle?

Stories of *Mastermind* champions
Jesse Honey: Mastermind 2010

Jesse admits that before he applied for *Mastermind* he spent several years building up his general knowledge to the point where he thought he had a realistic chance of winning. He even scheduled his application for the year before he planned to start a family so he wouldn't have to combine revision with being a new parent, unlike Nancy who managed to do both simultaneously. I've resisted the obvious joke about multi-tasking…

Jesse quizzes regularly as a member of the Quiz League of London and is clearly not a man to leave anything to chance: as his potential subject for the *Mastermind* final he chose a single building – in his case, Liverpool Anglican Cathedral – as he knew that this tactic had proved successful for a number of previous champions, most famously Fred Housego who had answered questions on the Tower of London.

More prosaically, Jesse was also aware that he would have less time to revise the Cathedral than his semi-final subject 'the Life and Work of Gaudi'. In the first round he took 'the London Borough of Wandsworth', which had considerable revision advantages as that was where he was living at the time.

Show 9

Specialist Subject 9.1
Gilbert and Sullivan

1. In *The Pirates of Penzance*, what claim do potential victims of the pirates generally make to ensure they are released unharmed?

2. What is the secret sign of those involved in the plot to depose *The Grand Duke* and put the Theatre Manager Ernest Dummkopf in his place?

3. In *The Yeomen of the Guard*, Wilfred Shadbolt holds which post, along with Head Jailor?

4. In *Princess Ida*, what does Lady Psyche say is 'nature's sole mistake'?

5. In *Trial by Jury*, when Edwin offers to marry both Angelina and his new sweetheart, the Counsel says that 'to marry two at once is...' what?

6. At the end of *Iolanthe*, whom does the Fairy Queen marry?

7. In *Ruddigore*, what is the word that, when uttered by Despard, immediately calms Mad Margaret?

8. According to his song in *The Gondoliers*, why did the Duke of Plaza-Toro lead his regiment from behind?

9. In *Utopia, Limited*, what is the name of the journal that details the King's alleged 'abominable immoralities'?

10. In *The Mikado*, among Pooh-Bah's many job titles, he is Master of the Buckhounds and Groom of... what?

11. In *The Sorcerer*, Sir Marmaduke tells Alexis that Aline Sangazure is the 7,037th direct descendant of whom?

12. In *HMS Pinafore*, what is the real name of the bumboat woman known as 'Little Buttercup'?

13. Despite the operetta's subtitle, who is the only character left at the end of *Patience* without a bride?

14. In *The Pirates of Penzance*, Frederic's old nursemaid Ruth confesses that through a misunderstanding she had apprenticed him as a pirate instead of what?

15. At the beginning of *The Grand Duke*, a theatrical troupe has arrived in the town square to perform which play?

16. According to Gama's song in Act III of *Princess Ida*, 'isn't your life extremely flat / With nothing whatever to...' what?

17. In *Trial by Jury*, how does the Learned Judge announce he will settle the Breach of Promise of Marriage case between Edwin and Angelina?

18. In the Lord Chancellor's 'Nightmare Song' from *Iolanthe*, at which stations was he joined by a 'ravenous horde of friends and relations'?

19. In *Ruddigore*, what reason does Sir Ruthven, also known as Robin Oakapple, give for not having committed a crime on the previous Monday?

20. In *The Gondoliers*, what is the name of the Grand Inquisitor?

21. What is the occupation of Tarara in *Utopia, Limited*, according to the dramatis personae?

22. In *The Mikado*, what part of Katisha does she claim is 'A miracle of loveliness'?

23. What is the full name of 'the dealer in magic and spells', as disclosed in his patter song in *The Sorcerer*?

24. The original set of *HMS Pinafore* was a facsimile of the quarterdeck of which ship?

25. When Bunthorne is rejected by Patience, his solicitor suggests he should choose one of the twenty maidens to marry, by what means?

26. In the 'Nightmare Song' from *Iolanthe*, which stretch of land does the Lord Chancellor cross on a bicycle, wearing a shirt and black silk socks?

27. In *The Gondoliers*, Luiz tells the Duke that he cannot 'tootle' like a cornet but he can imitate what?

28. In *The Mikado*, Pooh-Bah claims he can trace his ancestry back to 'a protoplasmal primordial' what?

29. In *The Sorcerer*, what is the title of the drinking song which begins 'Eat, drink and be gay'?

30. In *HMS Pinafore*, Sir Joseph Porter was based on which First Lord of the Admiralty, best remembered for the chain of book shops he founded?

General Knowledge 9.1

1. Who painted the ceiling of the Sistine Chapel in the Vatican between 1508 and 1512?

2. The city of Sunderland lies at the mouth of which river?

3. What is the name of the opera in which the character Canio, dressed as a clown, sings 'Vesti la giubba'?

4. Where, on the human body, are the so-called Mount of Apollo, Mount of the Moon and the Girdle of Venus?

5. Who played Idi Amin in *The Last King of Scotland*?

6. In Norse mythology, what is the name of the dwelling place of the gods?

7. What word, indicating that a reference will be found in several places throughout a text, is derived from the Latin for 'scattered'?

8. Common and Darwin's are the two species of which ostrich-like birds native to South America?

9. Who wrote the novels *Men at Arms*, *Officers and Gentlemen* and *Unconditional Surrender*, which were republished as the *Sword of Honour* trilogy in 1965?

10. The period of industrial unrest at the end of the 1970s that led to the fall of the Callaghan government is known by what name, borrowed from a Shakespeare play?

11. Closely related to the nasturtium, what peppery plant grows submerged in water in fast-flowing streams? Its sharply flavoured leaves are often used in green salads or as a garnish.

12. Which element, a vital component of the common match, was originally discovered in, and distilled from urine?

13. Which famous 1818 novel contains the words 'I beheld the wretch – the miserable monster whom I had created'?

14. In which country is Cape Nordkinn, the northernmost point of mainland Europe?

15. According to the Noel Coward song, who 'go out in the midday sun'?

16. The Popes Callistus III and Alexander VI were members of which notorious family?

17. In which sport is the rank of 'yokozuna' the highest attainable title?

18. The Saguaro, which gives its name to a National Park in Arizona, can reach a height of about fifteen metres and live for around 200 years, and is a giant species of which plant?

19. In Arthur Miller's play *Death of a Salesman*, what is the full name of the salesman?

20. Which famous street in New York is named after an embankment built by Dutch settlers in about 1653 to repel attacking forces?

21. Which fashion designer launched the prêt-à-porter Rive Gauche range in 1966?

22. The name of which Scottish festival comes from the old Norman French for 'a gift at the New Year'?

23. Who was the manager of The Beatles from 1961 until his death in 1967?

24. What name is given to the incident in Manchester in 1819 when local magistrates ordered troops to clear a peaceful meeting about Parliamentary reform, resulting in eleven deaths and hundreds of injuries?

25. Which classic Ealing comedy features Katie Johnson as the elderly landlady, Mrs Wilberforce?

26. The ruins of which Cistercian abbey, founded in 1131, lie on the banks of the River Wye between Monmouth and Chepstow?

27. Who wrote his only novel, *Rasselas*, during the evenings of a single week in 1759, to pay for his mother's funeral expenses?

28. What name is given to the traditional British system of weights, based on the grain and the pennyweight, and used to weigh precious metals?

29. What is the premier French Order of Distinction, founded by Napoleon Bonaparte in 1802?

30. Which American chat show host was born in a London underground station in 1944?

Specialist Subject 9.2
British Birds

1. How are ducks such as the teal and wigeon commonly known because they tend to feed by sieving the surface water as opposed to diving?

2. Which British bird spends more time in flight than any other species and on the ground is often helpless and easily caught?

3. With the scientific name 'Lagopus scoticus', which is the only bird indigenous solely to the British Isles?

4. Derived from the Greek for 'Pan Pipes', what is the name for the vocal organ of a bird?

5. Attaining speeds of up to 217 miles per hour when stooping at 45 degrees from great heights, what is the fastest bird found in Britain?

6. 'Saxicola torquata' has what common name because its call resembles two pebbles being knocked together?

7. Which British falcon is well known for its ability to hang in the air for a long time, giving it the nickname 'windhover'?

8. The fruit of which tree is eaten all year round by the jay, which has a habit of hiding and recovering food?

9. Pairs of which of the British owl emit the characteristic 'too-wit, too-woo' call?

10. Which bird, officially recorded as extinct in 1916, returned to breed in Scotland in the 1950s, at Loch Garten?

11. In which remote island group, around forty miles west of North Uist, is the largest gannetry in the world to be found?

12. What is the common name for the bird also known as a green plover or peewit?

13. Which is Britain's smallest bird of prey? The male of the species helps to incubate the eggs?

14. Which bird is also known as the 'Storm Cock' because of its habit of singing even in the worst of weather?

15. Special structures in the peregrine's nostrils enable the bird to breathe at great speed when stooping. What are they generally called?

16. The male of which large bird, related to the heron, has a call known as a 'boom' that resembles a distant foghorn?

17. What is the common name of 'Buteo buteo' whose numbers dropped greatly in the 1950s when a favourite food – rabbits – were decimated by myxomatosis?

18. The most distinctive feature of which duck is its large, flat, spade-like bill that it uses to filter out food particles from its watery feeding grounds?

19. Why was the peregrine falcon shot dead in large numbers during the Second World War?

20. Which oceanic bird has the scientific name 'Puffinus puffinus', but isn't a puffin and hasn't bred on the island after which it is named since the early nineteenth century?

21. What is the common name of the small passerine birds of the genus 'anthus' that has species called 'rock', 'tree' and 'water'?

22. The garefowl was an alternative name for which now-extinct bird, which was probably last seen in Britain on St Kilda in 1840?

23. Unlike other gulls, what colour legs does a kittiwake have?

24. A white heart-shaped face and an eerie shriek are distinguishing features of which owl?

25. Which resident shore bird, with the scientific name 'Hematopus ostralagus', is sometimes called the 'Sea-Pie'?

26. What is the name of the Wildfowl and Wetland Trust nature reserve in Lancashire that attracts huge flocks of pink-footed geese each winter?

27. The wetland bird the little grebe, the smallest of the British

grebes, has what alternative common name?

28. What type of woodland is the stronghold of Britain's smallest birds, the goldcrest and the firecrest?

29. The 'whip-whip-whip' call of which migratory game bird is said to sound like 'wet my lips'?

30. What do members of the Falcon family use their so-called 'tomial tooth' for, if they take their prey alive?

General Knowledge 9.2

1. The notorious naval mutiny against Captain Bligh took place on which ship in 1789?

2. The adjective 'vulpine' refers to which animal?

3. Whose works include *The Life and Opinions of Tristram Shandy, Gentleman*?

4. Antananarivo is the largest city and capital of which island republic off the coast of Africa?

5. Which conductor founded both the London Philharmonic and Royal Philharmonic Orchestras?

6. Which term for the band of colour formed when a beam of visible light is split into its constituent wavelengths was coined by Isaac Newton in 1672?

7. Angus Deayton was the original host of which topical satirical quiz show, first broadcast in 1990?

8. Most English translations of the Bible (including the Authorised Version) begin with which three words?

9.   Which architect's work includes the rebuilding of Brighton Pavilion in oriental style?

10. In which battle of 480 BC did Leonidas, King of Sparta, and a small force unsuccessfully defend a pass against a much larger Persian army?

11. Founded in 1858, Blackheath, who play at the Rectory Field, claim to be the oldest continuously existing English club in which sport?

12. What is the name of the chalk headland, situated near Eastbourne, which is one of the highest cliffs on the South Coast of England?

13. The 1966 film *Walk, Don't Run* was the last screen appearance of which debonair, British-born film actor?

14. In anatomy, what name for the soft lower part of the outer ear can also be applied to divisions of the lungs and brain?

15. Who wrote the plays *Dirty Linen* and *Rosencrantz and Guildenstern Are Dead*?

16. What name is given to the male reproductive part of a plant where pollen is produced, consisting of the anther and the filament?

17. What seventeenth-century invention is called a tire-bouchon in France, a kurketrekker in the Netherlands and a cavatappi in Italy?

18. Who was leader of the Liberal Party from 1976 until 1988, when it merged with the SDP to become the Liberal Democrats?

19. Graham Nash left which group in 1968 to join David Crosby and Stephen Stills?

20. An 'unkindness' or a 'conspiracy' is the collective noun for which members of the crow family?

21. Who is the Commanding Officer of the *Nautilus* in Jules Verne's *Twenty Thousand Leagues Under the Sea*?

22. Taken from the Old Norse for 'third part', what is the name of the administrative divisions into which the old county of Yorkshire was divided?

23. Dr Evil is the arch enemy of which spoof film hero?

24. What first name and surname were shared by the father and son who both served as British Prime Minister during the eighteenth century?

25. What alternative name is commonly used for Leonardo da Vinci's famous pen and ink drawing of a naked man with arms outstretched, also known as 'The Proportions of the Human Figure'?

26. The Taj Mahal is in which Indian city?

27. The works of which Nobel Prize-winning author include *One Hundred Years of Solitude* and a fictional account of the last days of Simon Bolivar called *The General in his Labyrinth*?

28. What is the name of the train service that links London with Paris and Brussels via the Channel Tunnel?

29. Who wrote the music and lyrics for the musical *Oliver!*?

30. The word for which financial arrangement comes from the Old French words for 'death' and 'pledge'?

Stories of *Mastermind* champions
Patrick Gibson: Mastermind 2005

How do you top winning the highest prize on British TV? Well for Pat Gibson – who walked away with £1 million on *Who Wants To Be A Millionaire?* – the answer was obvious ... win *Mastermind* as well.

Pat chose subjects that he thought he would enjoy revising: 'Quentin Tarantino films', 'The Novels of Iain M. Banks', and for the final '*Father Ted*', the last of which he hoped would defuse the tension of the occasion due to the humour of the subject. As for his strategy, well that was simple: ensure that his pace of answering didn't slacken, and 'on *Mastermind*, pausing is not an option.'

So how do you top winning *Mastermind*? By becoming the second *Mastermind* 'Champion of Champions' of course – despite encountering that most dreaded of scenarios in his heat: getting a question he knew ('Who discovered blood groups?') but being unable to recall the answer (the Nobel Laureate Karl Landsteiner). Given Pat's refusal to consider passing, he ended up giving the answer Erdinger ... a Bavarian Weissbier! However, in the end that proved to be an inspired 'wrong' answer as he finished tied for first on points, but won the contest thanks to having fewer passes.

Show 10

Specialist Subject 10.1
US Presidents

1. Which President was born in a backwoods cabin three miles south of Hodgenville, Kentucky in 1809?

2. Which term for the wife of an American President is said to have been coined by Zachary Taylor in 1849, at the funeral of Dolley Madison, wife of James Madison?

3. Barack Obama was born in which state, in 1961?

4. Which American President said that the proper way to conduct foreign affairs was to 'speak softly and carry a big stick'?

5. What did John Adams describe as 'The most insignificant office that ever the invention of man contrived or his imagination conceived'?

6. Who is the only American President to have never been married?

7. For which book did John F. Kennedy win the Pulitzer Prize for biography in 1957?

8. Which President captured the prevailing sentiment of the 1920s when he said 'The chief business of the American people is business'?

9. Millard Fillmore was the last President to represent which political party, formed in 1834 to oppose Andrew Jackson and the Democratic Party?

10. What was the surname of the grandfather and grandson who became the 9th and 23rd Presidents of the USA respectively?

11. What government post was occupied by future President George Bush Senior between 1976 and 1977?

12. Which President's campaign pledge was to restore 'the great, confident roar of American progress and growth and optimism'?

13. What was the headline in the first edition of the *Chicago Daily Tribune* on 3 November 1948, the day after voting in the Presidential election that saw Harry Truman re-elected?

14. Two assassinated American Presidents have been succeeded by men with which surname?

15. Which group's song 'Don't Stop' was used by President Clinton as his campaign song? They later performed it at his Inauguration Concert.

16. What nickname was given to the wife of President Rutherford B. Hayes because she banned alcohol in the Executive Mansion?

17. In 1957, Dwight Eisenhower sent troops into which state capital to enforce the desegregation of schools, in compliance with the orders of a federal court?

18. Who was the first President to be an American citizen from birth, rather than British, having been born after the Declaration of Independence?

19. Which law did Benjamin Harrison have passed in 1890 to limit anti-competitive business practices?

20. What name was popularly given to the Progressive Party founded by Theodore Roosevelt when he ran for President in 1912?

21. Nixon's first Vice-President, Spiro Agnew, resigned in 1973 and subsequently pleaded no contest to which criminal offence?

22. Which President gave his name to the doctrine outlined in 1823 to prevent further colonisation of the Americas by European nations?

23. In 1785, future President John Adams became the first American to serve in which diplomatic post?

24. Theodore Roosevelt was awarded the 1906 Nobel Peace Prize for his mediation that helped to end which conflict?

25. Who was the first woman to be nominated as Vice-Presidential candidate by one of the two main parties?

26. What name did Lyndon Johnson give to his sweeping programme of reforms, specifically in the areas of Civil Rights and the 'war on poverty'?

27. Who is the only US President to have served two non-consecutive terms of office?

28. Which organisation was created by John F. Kennedy in March 1961 to send volunteers to developing countries for two years to aid in public service projects?

29. Former President Taft was appointed to which post by Warren Harding, in 1921?

30. On becoming President, who said in his acceptance speech 'My Fellow Americans our long national nightmare is over'?

General Knowledge 10.1

1. The name of which online reference work comes from the Hawaiian for 'fast' and the classical Greek for 'education'?

2. In geometry, what name is given to a triangle with two equal sides and angles?

3. Which novel by James Joyce features the characters of Leopold Bloom and his estranged wife Molly?

4. Montgomery is the capital of which American state?

5. What name is shared by Beethoven's Sixth Symphony and Vaughan Williams' Third?

6. Which Roman Emperor is widely assumed to have been poisoned by his fourth wife Julia Agripinna, to ensure the succession of her son Nero?

7. Which American cartoonist created a fictional sinister family who were named after him, and were first televised in the 1960s?

8. The Siberian or Amur is a sub-species of which endangered animal?

9. What vegetable is the essential ingredient in a dish described as Lyonnaise?

10. Italians use the word 'tedesco' for which European nationality and language?

11. In classical Greek architecture, there are three orders of column: Doric, Ionic and which other, the newest and most elaborate?

12. What is the name of the Duke of Bedford's family home, situated near Whipsnade Zoo?

THE MASTERMIND QUIZ BOOK

13. In the film *The Great Dictator*, who appeared in a dual role as a Jewish barber and as Adenoid Hynkel, dictator of Tomania?

14. In Norse mythology the bridge Bifrost connected Earth with Asgard, the home of the Gods. What form did the bridge take?

15. On board ship, what is housed in a binnacle?

16. What word for the testing of a metal to determine its ingredients or purity comes from an Old French word meaning 'trial' or 'attempt'?

17. According to the sonnet by Shelley, which ancient tyrant's ruined statue carries the words, 'Look on my works, ye mighty and despair'?

18. What is the name of the early flowering deciduous shrub with yellow bell-like flowers, which is a member of the olive family and is widespread in the UK?

19. 'Lara's Theme' was part of the Oscar-winning musical score for which 1965 film?

20. Which Falls on the Argentine-Brazilian border are four times wider than Niagara and consist of a series of around 275 cataracts?

21. The works of which Surrealist artist, who died in August 1967, feature recurring symbols such as the 'female torso', 'the bowler hat', and 'the castle and the rock'?

22. Which is the larger of the two bones in the lower leg, also known as the shinbone?

23. In 1992, the Summer Olympic Games were held in which Spanish city?

24. Which Caribbean island, along with Puerto Rico, gained

independence from Spain as a result of the 1898 Spanish-American War?

25. Who wrote *Love on the Dole*, a 1933 novel about working-class poverty?

26. In 1981, who became the first socialist President of France since the founding of the Fifth Republic in 1958?

27. With which protest song did Bob Dylan first enter the UK Singles Chart in March 1965?

28. What determines the number of men and women who receive Maundy money from the monarch, and also the amount they are given?

29. What was the name of the puppet made by Geppeto who was eventually granted his wish to be 'a real boy'?

30. The Kama Sutra was originally written in which ancient language?

Specialist Subject 10.2
The *Star Wars* films

1. Who plays Princess Leia in the original three *Star Wars* films?

2. At the beginning of the first film, R2D2 and C3PO escaped in a lifepod and landed on which remote planet?

3. Which character is played by Jake Lloyd in *The Phantom Menace*, Hayden Christensen in *Attack of the Clones* and *Revenge of the Sith*, and Sebastian Shaw in *Return of the Jedi*?

4. In *The Empire Strikes Back*, Han Solo reveals that he won the Millennium Falcon in a card game with which of his friends?

5. Obi-Wan Kenobi tells Luke that he 'will never find a more wretched hive of scum and villainy' than which spaceport?

6. The 7 feet 3 inch tall actor Peter Mayhew played which character?

7. In how many means of communication does C3PO claim to be fluent?

8. Who provides the voice for Yoda in the *Star Wars* films?

9. In *The Empire Strikes Back*, what does Darth Vader say to the late Captain Needa after choking him to death?

10. In the original *Star Wars* film, which actor, who is best known for his horror roles, plays Grand Moff Tarkin?

11. According to the on-screen text at the beginning of *Revenge of the Sith*, which droid leader had kidnapped Chancellor Palpatine?

12. Which creatures, who live on the forest Moon of Endor, capture Luke, Han and Chewbacca and mistakenly think C3PO is a god?

13. At the beginning of *Attack of the Clones*, who is said to be the leader of the separatist movement?

14. What is the name of the all-powerful and omnivorous beast who lives in the Pit of Carkoon in the Dune Sea?

15. Which British actor plays Supreme Chancellor Valorum in *The Phantom Menace*?

16. The young Luke Skywalker, unaware that his father was a Jedi knight, believed that he had been a navigator aboard which type of freighter?

17. In *The Empire Strikes Back*, C3PO says that the possibility of successfully navigating what, is 3,720 to 1 against?

18. Obi-Wan Kenobi and which other Jedi are sent as ambassadors to settle a trade dispute in *The Phantom Menace*?

19. What is the call sign of Luke's X-Wing Starfighter on his mission to attack the original Death Star?

20. What is the common surname of Boba and Jango, who both appear in *Attack of the Clones*?

21. In *The Empire Strikes Back*, Luke travels to which planet to seek training from Yoda?

22. As what is Princess Leia disguised, when she enters Jabba the Hutt's Palace in *Return of the Jedi*?

23. Who first appears as the Jedi Mace Windu in *The Phantom Menace*?

24. With what type of torpedo does Luke destroy the original Death Star?

25. What is Han Solo encased in before being sent to Jabba the Hutt?

26. From which planet had Obi-Wan Kenobi returned at the beginning of *Attack of the Clones*?

27. According to C3PO, who was his previous master before he became the property of Luke Skywalker?

28. Who completed the script for *The Empire Strikes Back* after the death of Leigh Brackett?

29. What was the name of the monster in the pit below Jabba the Hutt's throne room, which Luke kills by causing a heavy door to fall on it?

THE MASTERMIND QUIZ BOOK

30. What links Peter Serafinowicz's performance as Darth Maul in *The Phantom Menace* with that of James Earl Jones as Darth Vader?

General Knowledge 10.2

1. What name is traditionally given to the black pirate flag showing a skull and crossbones?

2. Jethou, Lihou and Brecqhou are smaller members of which island group?

3. What is the title of the play by Arthur Miller, set around the Salem witch trials of 1692?

4. Which rare, bearlike mammal has an enlarged wrist bone that functions rather like a thumb, enabling it to handle food?

5. Which cult film of 1969 stars Peter Fonda and Dennis Hopper as a pair of motorcycling dropouts?

6. In Ancient Greece, what general name was given to the Chief Magistrate in many city-states?

7. Which Dutch artist painted *The Garden of Earthly Delights* in the early sixteenth century?

8. What name is given to any of the group of twenty organic molecules that are the basic building blocks of proteins?

9. Which disgraced politician was Secretary of State for War from 1960 to 1963?

10. In English verse, what name is given to a pause in the middle of a metrical line?

11. Which British fighter unified the WBA, WBC and IBF World Heavyweight titles when he beat Evander Holyfield in Las Vegas, in November 1999?

12. What is the name of the large marshy island in the delta of the River Rhône, famed for its bulls and wild birds?

13. Emerson, Lake and Palmer's only British hit single was composed by Aaron Copland. What is its title?

14. In the mythology of Ancient Egypt, Thoth was the Patron of Scribes and a god of which celestial body?

15. What Italian dessert is made by whisking egg yolks, wine and sugar together over a gentle heat?

16. In anatomy, what name is given to the fibrous sac surrounding the heart?

17. Which opera by Puccini is set in the days of the Californian Gold Rush?

18. Which book of the Bible gets its English name because it starts with a census of the 'children of Israel'?

19. Frederick William Lanchester, who built one of the first motor cars in Britain, patented what type of brake now standard on motor cars?

20. Who founded the American Institute of Public Opinion in 1935 and developed the polls for testing opinion that still bear his name?

21. What word for a nickname comes from an early French word for a 'playful tap under the chin'?

22. What well-known revolutionary socialist hymn was the National Anthem of the Soviet Union from 1917 until 1944?

23. Whom did Henry VIII appoint as Archbishop of Canterbury in 1533 following the death of William Warham?

24. Who was nominated for a Best Actress Oscar for her role as Mrs Robinson in the 1967 film *The Graduate*?

25. What name was adopted by the former British colony of the Gold Coast when it gained independence in 1957?

26. Who wrote the poem, one of his 'Sonnets dedicated to Liberty', that opens, 'Milton! Thou shouldst be living at this hour'?

27. What general name is given to any tree that produces its seeds in cones?

28. The architect Sir Frederick Gibberd, best known for the 'Crown of Thorns' design of Liverpool's Catholic cathedral, was responsible for planning which New Town in Essex?

29. In 1925, the teacher John T. Scopes was put on trial in Tennessee for teaching what?

30. In *The Magic Roundabout*, what type of creature was Brian?

High scores

Over the years, the length of the rounds and the questions has varied, so direct comparisons are difficult; however, the following are believed to be the best performances ever achieved on *Mastermind* in the traditional format of two minutes on specialist subjects and two minutes on general knowledge:

In the 2010 'Champion of Champion' series, Jesse Honey scored 23 points on his specialist subject 'National Flags of the World' – breaking the record set by Joe West in 1979, who scored 22 points on Lord Nelson.

Jennifer Keaveney scored 22 on General Knowledge in the 1986 final; Chantal Thompson matched this in the final four years later. Jennifer also established a record points total for a single show during that series – scoring 40 in her semi-final and then equalling that to win the final. Another champion, Mary-Elizabeth Raw, equalled that in her heat in 1989.

Their record was eventually beaten by Kevin Ashman in a first-round heat in 1995. After scoring 20 points on 'Martin Luther King and the Civil Rights Movement', he added another 21 points on General Knowledge for a total of 41 – a feat even more impressive given that he was only offered a place on the show at short notice when another contender had to drop out.

Kevin went on to score 38 in his semi-final, and then 39 to win the final – he subsequently became the first person to hold the titles of 'Mastermind' and 'Brain of Britain' simultaneously, along with many other achievements in the world of quizzing.

Show 11

Specialist Subject 11.1
Agatha Christie's Hercule Poirot Novels

1. In which country house did Hercule Poirot solve both his first and his last murder cases?

2. In *The Big Four*, Poirot unexpectedly produces his 'twin brother'; what is his first name?

3. In which novel does a member of the Cloade family attempt to hire Poirot for the purpose of finding grounds to disinherit Gordon Cloade's unsuitable young widow?

4. What was the name of Poirot's dentist, who was shot after Poirot had paid him a visit in *One, Two, Buckle My Shoe*?

5. In *Peril at End House*, how much does Jim Lazarus offer Nick Buckley for the portrait of her grandfather, so as to deliberately raise her suspicions?

6. In *Hickory Dickory Dock*, Patricia Lane tells Nigel Chapman that she found the bottle of morphine sulphate hidden in which specific place, before she replaced it with bicarbonate of soda?

7. What was the name of the girls' school where Miss Springer, the gym mistress, was murdered in *Cat among the Pigeons*?

8. In which of Poirot's cases did he first work with the lady mystery writer Ariadne Oliver?

9. In *Three Act Tragedy*, what is the title of the play by Muriel Wills that Angela Sutcliffe is putting on?

10. In *The Mysterious Affair at Styles*, which poison actually killed Emily Inglethorpe?

11. In the first of *The Labours of Hercules*, who asked Poirot to investigate the kidnapping of his wife's pet Pekinese dog?

12. In *Third Girl*, who does Norma's flatmate, the so-called art student 'Frances Cary', turn out to be?

13. In *Hallowe'en Party*, what is the ancient symbol from Mycenae or Crete that is carved on the stone at Kilterbury Ring, where Miranda is to be sacrificed?

14. Elinor Carlisle's trial for murder after being caught in a love triangle is the centrepiece of which novel?

15. In *Lord Edgware Dies*, who partnered Poirot in a game of bridge that ended in a 'heavy financial gain' for the two of them?

16. For some time, Poirot was the owner of a large expensive car that broke down at the beginning of 'The Arcadian Deer'; what make was it?

17. Which of the *Five Little Pigs* says in his narrative that he stood as godfather to Amyas and Caroline Crale's daughter, Carla?

18. What was the occupation of Mrs Boynton, before her marriage to Elmer in *Appointment with Death*?

19. In the 1920s, Poirot and Captain Hastings were the tenants of which landlady at No. 14 Farraway Street?

20. Hercule Poirot first encountered Countess Vera Rossakoff, the love of his life, while working on which jewel robbery case?

21. In *Murder in Mesopotamia*, what was the name of the archaeologist who called in Poirot to investigate the death of his wife, Louise?

22. In *The A.B.C. Murders*, what is the name of the product that Poirot used on his hair to get rid of the grey?

23. What name is written across the corner of the small travelling clock found in the room where R.H. Curry's body is found in *The Clocks*?

24. When Poirot moves to King's Abbot, what dominates his time before he begins to investigate the murder of Roger Ackroyd?

25. In *Dumb Witness*, Emily Arundell fell down the stairs after tripping over her wire-haired fox terrier's tennis ball. What was the dog' name?

26. In which novel did Superintendent Battle's youngest daughter, Sylvia, play a small but important part?

27. In *Elephants Can Remember*, who had replaced Miss Sedgewick as Ariadne Oliver's secretary?

28. In *Cat among the Pigeons*, Julia Upjohn finds the hidden jewels in what item of sports equipment?

29. In *One, Two, Buckle My Shoe*, what is the name of the hotel in which Miss Sainsbury Seale was staying, immediately before she was murdered?

30. According to Captain Hastings in *Curtain*, what were the last words he ever heard Poirot say?

General Knowledge 11.1

1. According to legend, which eleventh-century king of England ordered the waves to recede, while on Bosham beach in West Sussex, to demonstrate the limit of his powers?

2. Second Viscount Townshend, who directed Britain's foreign policy from 1721 to 1730, was given what nickname, because of the root vegetable he favoured in his crop rotation system?

3. Who won the Booker Prize in 1981 for *Midnight's Children*?

4. What is the general name for an arachnid with a pair of grasping pincers and a segmented curved tail terminating in a venomous sting?

5. Who created the television series *Grange Hill*, *Brookside* and *Hollyoaks*?

6. The statement 'L'état, c'est moi', which literally means 'I am the state', is usually attributed to which French king?

7. Under what surname did the Brontë sisters publish a volume of poems in 1846?

8. Which Caribbean island, a British Overseas Territory, was sighted in 1493 by Christopher Columbus, who named it after a monastery in Catalonia and the jagged mountain it stands on?

9. Which group's song 'Flowers In The Rain' was the first to be played on BBC Radio One, when it began broadcasting in 1967?

10. In Buddhism, what name, of Sanskrit origin, is given to the universal truth or law as expounded by the Buddha?

11. Which film, based on a novel by Michael Ondaatje, won nine

Oscars at the 1997 ceremony, including Best Supporting Actress for Juliet Binoche?

12. The BCG vaccine is given to protect against which disease?

13. Which Pop artist featured in Ken Russell's *Pop Goes the Easel* and produced the collage *Toyshop* in 1961, using glass and cut-outs?

14. By what slang name were FBI agents commonly referred to in the 1930s? It was also the title of a James Cagney film.

15. The French city of Dijon is particularly associated with which condiment?

16. What numbers, when used in table form to simplify calculations, consist of an integral part called the 'characteristic' and a decimal part called the 'mantissa'?

17. In which winter sport is a match or tournament known as a bonspiel?

18. What river forms most of the boundary between Devon and Cornwall?

19. The heroine of which novel by Tolstoy commits suicide by throwing herself under a train?

20. Which flightless bird has nostrils at the tip of its bill rather than the base? It also lays a larger egg relative to its body size than any other bird.

21. In the Aztec empire, a bitter version of which familiar beverage was used as a drink for warriors and the social elite?

22. Which Scottish public school did Prince Charles and his brothers attend?

23. Cape Comorin is the southernmost point of which Commonwealth country?

24. The climax of which Alfred Hitchcock film takes place on Mount Rushmore?

25. In German mythology, who brings about the death of Siegfried after she finds out that he has won her for someone else?

26. In 1925, the wearing of what type of hat was prohibited in Turkey?

27. What term for a large urban area is derived from the Greek for 'mother' and 'city'?

28. Which opera by Puccini opens on a freezing Christmas Eve in Paris, where the poet Rodolfo burns some of his manuscripts to keep warm?

29. What name is given to the method of sending messages using two flags, held in different positions by a signalman, to represent individual letters or numbers?

30. Douglas Hogg made newspaper headlines in 2009 when he was alleged to have claimed the cleaning bill for what part of his country estate on Parliamentary expenses?

Specialist Subject 11.2
Ancient Rome

1. In 64 BC, who defeated Catiline for the following year's consulship and subsequently played a leading role in the capture and execution of his followers?

2. The year AD 69, which was marked by civil war, is known as 'The Year of Four ...' what?

3. Rome fought a succession of wars against which Italian people whom they eventually subdued, despite a famous defeat at the Caudine Forks?

4. Of which Emperor's unwilling accession did Gibbon write, 'While the Senate deliberated, the Praetorian Guard had resolved'?

5. The Emperor Septimius Severus died in which British city?

6. What was the name of the leader of the Gauls who surrendered to Julius Caesar after the siege of Alesia?

7. Which imperial province could not be visited by a senator without the Emperor's permission?

8. Who seized power by force and was declared dictator in around 82 BC, but later relinquished his office voluntarily after completing his programme of legislation?

9. Where did Constantine the Great hold the church council of AD 325, which was originally scheduled to be held in Ancyra?

10. Which title did Augustus assume on the death of Lepidus, the former triumvir, in 12 BC?

11. Two great cities of the ancient world were captured and sacked by Roman armies in 146 BC; one was Carthage, what was the other?

12. What was the name of Caligula's favourite horse, which he allegedly planned to appoint as a consul?

13. Which 37-mile-long turf wall was built from the Firth of Forth to the Firth of Clyde in around AD 142, but was eventually abandoned as the Romans withdrew to Hadrian's Wall?

14. In 67 BC, who was given authority, by the Lex Gabinia, to solve the problem of piracy in the Mediterranean?

15. Which 'rose-red' city of the Nabataeans became a metropolis of Roman Arabia under Trajan?

16. Who was recalled from exile on Corsica to become Nero's tutor?

17. Rome suffered its bloodiest defeat to Hannibal in which battle of 216 BC, when their forces were encircled in a pincer movement?

18. Which dynasty was initiated by Vespasian and ended with the assassination of Domitian, although it was later adhered to by Constantine the Great and his family?

19. The series of speeches in which Cicero attacked Mark Antony are generally known by what name?

20. Which reformer, who was killed in 121 BC, brought in a law that guaranteed corn to all the citizens of Rome, often at a subsidised price?

21. Which city did Hadrian rename Aelia Capitolina in honour of the tribe to which he belonged, after it was destroyed and rebuilt in the second century?

22. Who was the governor of Britain when Boudicca and the Iceni rose up against Roman rule in AD 60?

23. During the Republic, which office was held by the ten elected representatives of the plebeians, who had the power to summon the Senate or to veto legislation?

24. Cassius Dio described the assassination of Caligula as a practical demonstration for the Emperor 'that he was not ...' what?

25. In the early fifth century, the Western Imperial government was

moved to which city, protected by marshes and lagoons, in order to avoid the attacks of the Visigoths?

26. During Julius Caesar's triumph for defeating Pharnaces II at Zela, how did he summarise the battle concisely?

27. Which Emperor of the second century wrote a fragmentary book of 'Meditations' based on Stoic philosophy?

28. Which Christian heresy, that proclaimed that the Son was 'of a different substance' from the Father, was supported by the Emperors Constantius II and Valens?

29. Who commanded the Roman army that captured Tigranocerta in Armenia before being recalled to Rome, where his lavish lifestyle in retirement made him a by-word for extravagance?

30. As reported by Suetonius and Dio Cassius, what were Nero's last words?

General Knowledge 11.2

1. What French word is used for an additional song or piece at the end of an artist's performance?

2. In the early 1970s, which American surgeon pioneered an eponymous emergency procedure to restore breathing to a person who is choking, by means of a sequence of abdominal thrusts?

3. The Norfolk town of Cromer is particularly famed for which seafood?

4. Shami Chakrabarti was appointed Director of which human rights organisation in 2003?

5. Which twentieth-century artist had a ten-year relationship with Dora Maar, who inspired his painting *Weeping Woman*, as well as other major works?

6. Europe's longest river, the Volga, empties into which sea?

7. On which instrument did Anton Karas play the theme music to the film *The Third Man*?

8. In Greek mythology, who abducted Helen of Troy?

9. In Cockney rhyming slang, what is a 'butchers'?

10. What is the name of the Safari Park near Liverpool, situated at the ancestral home of the Earls of Derby?

11. Created by John Le Carré, which fictional British intelligence officer's long-term adversary was the Soviet spymaster Karla?

12. What name, from the Latin for 'seaweed', is given to the simple plant-like organisms, that typically lack true stems, roots and leaves?

13. Which hit American TV comedy series starred David Hyde Pierce as Niles Crane, and John Mahoney as his father Martin, who has a Jack Russell terrier named Eddie?

14. Which city and its surrounding area was the last English possession in France? It was taken back by the French in January 1558.

15. What is the popular name for the floating capsule that is intended to make canned beer taste like draught?

16. The 'pascal', which is named after the French philosopher and scientist, is the international standard unit of which physical quantity?

17. In Coleridge's poem, which bird does the Ancient Mariner kill?

18. What was the self-appointed office of Matthew Hopkins, who came to prominence in 1645?

19. Which comedy duo starred in the 1932 film *The Music Box* about two delivery men attempting to take a piano up a flight of steps to a house?

20. What is the capital and chief port of the Northern Territory of Australia?

21. Which baseball star became Marilyn Monroe's second husband when they married in 1954?

22. Heath, Marsh, and Dark Green are species of which butterflies, whose name comes from the Latin for 'dice box' because of their spotted markings?

23. In the novel by Robert Louis Stevenson, which fictional doctor discovers a drug that absorbs all his evil instincts?

24. The Galton-Henry system that was officially introduced at Scotland Yard in 1901, is a method of classifying what?

25. In *Star Trek*, which character was the son of Ambassador Sarek and a human teacher named Amanda Grayson?

26. Which Hindu deity is worshipped as 'the Preserver', one of the three gods who oversee and maintain justice and the world order?

27. Which cartoon character's falsetto voice was provided by Walt Disney until 1946, when Jimmy MacDonald took over the role?

28. What is the proper name of the flag that is sometimes known as the 'Red Duster', and which is flown by the British Merchant Navy?

29. Which Swiss ski resort was the first venue to host the Winter Olympics twice?

30. What term for a younger man, who is paid by an older woman to act as her escort, was used as the title of a book by Edna Ferber published in 1922?

Celebrities and their specialist subjects

Mastermind returned to the BBC in 2002 with a special series of Celebrity programmes and, each year since then, famous faces have braved the Black Chair to raise money for charity.

Understandably, many celebrities prefer to answer questions on subjects that are close to home: the comedian Dave Spikey, who worked in a hospital before finding fame on *Phoenix Nights*, chose 'Human Blood', Sir Clive Sinclair went for 'British Inventions', and Sir Ranulph Fiennes selected 'Captain Scott's expeditions to Antarctica'.

In 2005, the novelist Iain (M.) Banks made an unusual piece of *Mastermind* history by appearing on the show as a celebrity contestant *and* as a subject in the same year. Iain answered questions on 'Malt Whisky and the distilleries of Scotland', while Pat Gibson took Iain's 'Culture' novels as his semi-final subject.

The challenge of facing questions rather than asking them has enticed the hosts of several other quizzes onto Celebrity Mastermind: *QI* presenter Stephen Fry answered some (presumably 'Quite Interesting') questions on 'Sherlock Holmes'; *15 to 1*'s William G. Stewart tackled 'Lord Elgin and the Marbles' and *Just a Minute*'s Nicholas Parsons attempted to answer questions on Edward Lear without 'hesitation, repetition or deviation'.

In January 2012, the presenter of (dare we say it) the most prestigious quiz show of them all was chosen by comedian Andi Osho as her subject on *Celebrity Mastermind* ... so John Humphrys had the surreal experience of asking questions about himself for two minutes!

Her fellow comedian Tony Hawks chose the life and career of the American skateboarder Tony Hawk, after receiving numerous emails from skateboard fans who had confused the two of them ... when he reappeared on a later series, Tony went all sensible and chose to answer questions on Fridges.

The award for the most original choice of subjects goes jointly to journalist and broadcaster Janet Street-Porter, who selected 'British ceramic teapots 1735–1970', and comedian Gina Yashere, who went for 'The History and Mechanics of the Lift'!

Show 12

Specialist Subject 12.1
World History since 1800

1. Which sea-battle took place off the Spanish coast on 21 October 1805?

2. The first Soviet Politburo, elected in March 1919, consisted of five members: Lenin, Stalin, Krestinsky, Kamenev and who else?

3. In April 1939, after King Zog and his queen had escaped from the invading Italian army, which country's Constituent Assembly was forced to vote for union with Italy?

4. In a radio broadcast from Madrid in July 1936, Dolores Ibárruri proclaimed 'They shall not pass', which became a republican slogan in the Spanish Civil War; by what nom-de-guerre is she better known?

5. In April 1867, Emperor Louis Napoleon of France attempted to buy which territory from the King of the Netherlands but was prevented from doing so by Bismarck?

6. In 1929, Mussolini restored the temporal power of the Pope with which treaty, giving him 108 acres to rule as the Vatican City?

7. In November 1917, a declaration was made to Lord Rothschild, favouring 'the establishment in Palestine of a national home for the Jewish people', by which former Prime Minister who was then the Foreign Secretary?

8. What was the name of the trade union that the Polish General Jaruzelski tried to suppress by declaring martial law in December 1981?

9. Which American general's plan for the post-war recovery of Europe was unveiled in a speech at Harvard University in June 1947?

10. Which country exploded its first nuclear weapon in October 1964?

11. Who was the Prefect of the Seine for most of the French Second Empire, and was responsible for the reconstruction of Paris?

12. Which conclusive battle in 1954 saw the defeat of the French forces in Indo-China by the Viet Minh?

13. What was the occupation of Alexei Stakhanov, whose efforts in the 1930s to improve his own productive power inspired a movement amongst fellow Soviet workers to follow his lead?

14. What name is generally given to the period in Japanese history that was instigated by the fall of the Tokugawa Shogunate, and the return of power to the Emperor in 1868?

15. Who was appointed First Secretary of the Moscow Communist Party Committee by Mikhail Gorbachev in December 1985 but was forced to resign in disgrace after criticising Gorbachev two years later?

16. What name is commonly given to Bismarck's edited version of the final interview between the Prussian King Wilhelm and the French ambassador, which precipitated the Franco-Prussian

War in 1870?

17. Which American army general commanded the forces that liberated Kuwait in the 1991 Gulf War?

18. In which country did the revolutionaries of the '26th of July Movement' seize power in January 1959?

19. What name was given to Willy Brandt's policy that was intended to create closer ties between West and East Germany, and to improve relations with Poland and the Soviet Union?

20. Whom did Éamon de Valera appoint as the Minister of Finance in the first Dáil Éireann, which formed after the 1918 General Election?

21. Which decisive battle of December 1805 is also known as the Battle of the Three Emperors?

22. What three-word term was coined for the doctrine which claimed that the possession of huge stockpiles of nuclear weapons by the superpowers actually enhanced global security?

23. Opened in New York in May 1930, what was the first building in the world to exceed 1,000 feet in height. It is still the world's highest brick-clad building.

24. The term 'Velvet Revolution' refers to the peaceful overthrow of the Communist regime in which country?

25. What was the name of the Chinese leader who was forced to retreat to the island of Taiwan with the remnants of his Nationalist forces, after the victory of the Communists in 1949?

26. Which former lawyer was President of France throughout the First World War and headed a Government of National Unity from 1926 to 1929?

27. What name, the Russian for 'fist', was given to the wealthy peasants whom the Soviet government sought to 'liquidate as a class' in a campaign launched in 1929?

28. Between 1865 and 1870, the Triple Alliance of Brazil, Argentina and Uruguay fought a war against which country?

29. The Soviet Union ceased to exist on which date in 1991? Mikhail Gorbachev resigned as President on the same day.

30. In 2011, Osama bin Laden was located and killed by US Special Forces in which town, named after a nineteenth-century British army officer?

General Knowledge 12.1

1. Which embroidered artefact begins with Edward the Confessor meeting the future King Harold II and ends with the Battle of Hastings?

2. The name of which sea comes from the Latin for 'middle of the land'?

3. The common or blue species of which mollusc, found growing in tight clusters on rocks, is widely harvested for food in Europe where it is often served with french fries?

4. What was Margaret Thatcher's first Cabinet post when the Conservatives were returned to power under Ted Heath in 1970?

5. Bonnano Pisano was the engineer in charge of which famous building, begun around 1174?

6. In the New Testament, what was the name of the prisoner

released by Pontius Pilate instead of Jesus at the behest of the crowd?

7. The name of which sea monster from the Book of Job was used by Thomas Hobbes for the title of his best-known work, first published in 1651?

8. What was the last Royal House to rule an independent Scotland?

9. On what subject did Albert Einstein publish his Special Theory in 1905 and his General Theory in 1916, concerning bodies in motion with respect to each other?

10. The gemsbok, the scimitar-horned and the Arabian are three species of which large antelope? The latter two are listed as endangered species.

11. Which playwright is the subject of John Lahr's biography *Prick up Your Ears*? It was made into a 1987 film starring Gary Oldman and Alfred Molina.

12. What fabulous fire-breathing monster, slain by Bellepheron, had a lion's head, a goat's body and a snake or dragon's tail?

13. Which 1968 film starring Jane Fonda is set in the forty-first century and features Milo O'Shea as the villain Durand Durand?

14. What name is shared by a river that flows through the Derbyshire Peak District and one that forms part of the English-Welsh border?

15. What sport combines cross-country skiing and rifle shooting?

16. The name of which natural pigment comes from the Greek for 'green leaf'?

17. The theme tunes to which long-running television programme included a version of Led Zeppelin's 'Whole Lotta Love', Phil Lynott's 'Yellow Pearl' and 'The Wizard' by Paul Hardcastle?

18. What term, the first part of which is derived from the German for 'rag' or 'rabble', did Karl Marx coin for the lowest stratum of the industrial working class, including tramps and criminals?

19. What is the destination of the annual rally for veteran cars starting in London and inaugurated to commemorate the lifting of the 'Red Flag' Act in 1896?

20. In mathematics, what general term is used for any two-dimensional polygon with four sides?

21. Which novel by Daphne du Maurier begins 'Last Night I dreamt I went to Manderley again'?

22. The salient around which Belgian city was the scene of three important battles in the First World War, in 1914, 1915 and 1917 respectively?

23. Judy Garland is the mother of which Oscar-winning actress?

24. On the River Thames, which birds are owned either by the Crown or by one of two City of London companies: the Dyers and the Vintners?

25. What title did J.S. Bach give to his set of twenty-four Preludes and Fugues for keyboard in each of the major and minor keys, and also to a second set composed later in Leipzig sometimes called the '48'?

26. What dish on a Greek menu, similar to shish kebabs, consists of marinated lamb chunks, generally skewered and grilled with vegetables such as onions and green peppers?

27. An ampersand is a symbol used in printing to replace which three-letter word?

28. What road in Chelsea, running south-west from Sloane Square, has been particularly associated with fashion since the 1960s?

29. What word is used for a hole emitting gases or steam in a volcano or volcanic region, and is derived from the Latin for 'smoke'?

30. In 1935, which theoretical physicist devised a thought experiment about the fate of a cat in a box to highlight some of the conceptual problems posed by quantum physics?

Specialist Subject 12.2
English Test Cricket

1. During the 1981 Ashes series, who scored 149 not out in the Third Test, took 5 wickets for 1 run to win the following match and then scored a century off 86 balls in the game after that?

2. Who scored an unbeaten double century at Lord's in 1984 to help the West Indies beat England by 9 wickets, after they had been set 342 to win?

3. How many runs did Alastair Cook score in seven Test innings during the 2010–2011 Ashes series?

4. When Duncan Fletcher was appointed England coach in June 1999, who was selected as the new captain?

5. Which Australian player attempted to use an aluminium bat during the Perth Test in the 1979–1980 Ashes series?

6. Which English ground staged its only Test match in 1902?

7. Who captained the England side that regained the Ashes in 1953?

8. England were officially ranked the number one Test-playing nation in 2011, after a 4-0 series victory over which country?

9. Who captained England in 19 home Test matches between 1977 and 1981, and was never on the losing side in any of them?

10. At which ground did Jim Laker take 19 Australian wickets in a single Test match, in 1956?

11. Which batsman made his England Test debut in the first Test of the 2005 Ashes series?

12. Which country hosted the famous 'timeless Test' of 1939, which was abandoned as a draw on the tenth day so England could catch their ship home?

13. Kapil Dev hit which spinner for four consecutive sixes at Lord's in 1990, to ensure India avoided the follow-on?

14. The 1977 Centenary Test in Melbourne finished with an identical result to the inaugural Test match played 100 years previously; by how many runs did Australia win both games?

15. Which South African batsman made double centuries in the first two Tests against England in 2003?

16. What notable feat did Geoffrey Boycott achieve during the third Ashes Test in 1977, equalling the Indian batsman Jaisimhha, before making his 100th first-class century in the following match?

17. Who took 189 Test wickets for England at an average of just 16.43 runs, between 1901 and 1914?

18. In 1978, which country finally beat England in a Test match at the 48th attempt?

THE MASTERMIND QUIZ BOOK

19. Who did Shane Warne dismiss with his first ball in an Ashes series, at Old Trafford in 1993?

20. What unusual method of dismissal accounted for Graham Gooch in the first Ashes Test of 1993, and for Michael Vaughan against India in 2001?

21. Who played in three Test matches for England in the 1930s, before playing for India against England in 1946?

22. Who scored a century against England from just 56 deliveries, at St John's in Antigua in 1986?

23. In December 2000, England beat which country by 6 wickets in near darkness to claim a famous series victory?

24. Who took 8 for 43 at Headingley in 1981, as Australia were bowled out for 111 in their 2nd innings and lost by 18 runs, despite having made England follow on?

25. What was unusual about the Test series staged in England in 1912? The experiment wasn't repeated until a series staged in Asia in 1999.

26. In the second innings of the 1952 Headingley Test, Alec Bedser and which other bowler took four wickets between them before India had scored a run?

27. What was England's margin of victory in the 2005 Edgbaston Test against Australia?

28. In Pakistan, during the 1972–1973 tour, who was chosen to captain England on his Test debut?

29. In Don Bradman's final Test innings, which English bowler dismissed him for a duck to deny him a career Test average of 100?

30. When (the former England spinner) Rockley Wilson heard that Douglas Jardine had been appointed England captain, he commented that 'We may well win the Ashes, but we may very well lose a ...' what?

General Knowledge 12.2

1. Which sign of the Zodiac takes its name from the Latin for 'fish'?

2. What name is given to the fertile low-lying area of reclaimed marshland to the west and south of the Wash?

3. Who said, in his work *An Essay on Criticism*, 'A little learning is a dangerous thing'?

4. In which ancient Greek city-state were the state-owned slaves known as helots?

5. What martial art was introduced as an Olympic sport at the Tokyo Games of 1964?

6. The nineteenth-century Russian explorer Nikolai Przewalski gives his name to the only living wild species of which animal?

7. Which famous American bandleader and composer disappeared while on a flight from England to Paris in December 1944?

8. In astronomy, what name is given to either of the days of the year when the Sun's apparent path is furthest north or furthest south of the Earth's Equator?

9. Who starred as the gang boss Charlie Croker in the original 1969 version of *The Italian Job*?

10. Which legendary giant bird that is said to carry off animals as large as elephants for food, is mentioned in *The Thousand and One Nights* and also in *The Travels of Marco Polo*?

11. Pinot noir, pinot meunier and which other grape variety are the only three permitted in the production of champagne?

12. The Catskill, Blue Ridge and Allegheny are all part of which range of mountains in eastern North America?

13. In which classic science fiction novel by Ray Bradbury do firemen burn books instead of putting out fires?

14. The name of which garden shrub comes from the Greek for 'water vessel', an allusion to the cup-like shape of its seed-capsules?

15. The opening of which of London's bridges in 1817 is the subject of one of the few paintings by Constable not to feature a pastoral scene?

16. In 1535, who completed the first translation of the Bible to be printed in English, and edited it for what became known as the 'Great Bible' of 1539?

17. In *Monty Python's Flying Circus*, what institution did Cardinal Ximinez and his sidekicks Fang and Biggles represent?

18. How often does a Hebdomadal Council normally meet?

19. In 1944, the alleged medium Helen Duncan was the last person in Britain to receive a prison sentence under which Act of 1735?

20. What name is given to an alloy of mercury with one or more other metals, especially one used for dental fillings?

21. According to Shakespeare's play, who struck the first blow when Julius Caesar was assassinated?

22. What French term is used in ballet for dancing on the tip of the toe in specially designed stiffened shoes?

23. Which current British army regiment was founded as the First Regiment of Foot Guards in 1656?

24. The name of which preserve comes from the Portuguese for 'quince', the fruit from which it was originally made?

25. In the Republic of Ireland, what are the Garda Siochana?

26. Which of Batman's enemies was played by Cesar Romero in 1966, Jack Nicholson in 1989 and Heath Ledger in 2008?

27. The phases of the Moon between Full Moon and New Moon are known as waning; what name is given to the phases between the New Moon and the Full Moon?

28. Mombasa is the principal port of which African country?

29. The name of which precious stone comes from the Greek for 'nail' or 'claw'? The pink and white bands of one of its varieties is said to resemble a fingernail.

30. At the Conservative Party's Annual Conference in 2002 who, as Chairperson, said in a speech, 'You know what some people call us – the nasty party'?

These are all subjects chosen by contenders on *Celebrity Mastermind, but we've muddled up the order – can you match the celebrity to their subject?*

Part One

1. Vic Reeves

2. David Blunkett MP

3. Tanni Grey-Thompson

4. Peter Tatchell

5. DJ Scott Mills

6. Rageh Omaar

7. 'Hairy Biker' Dave Myers

8. Michael Howard MP

9. Mick Hucknall

10. Sandie Shaw

A. The Presidency of George W. Bush

B. Malcolm X

C. The Pre-Raphaelite Brotherhood

D. *Prisoner Cell Block H*

E. The *Star Wars* films

F. Nichiren Buddhism

G. The life and work of Matisse

H. The Harry Potter novels

I. The Golden Age of Piracy 1680–1720

J. Liverpool Football Club in the 1980s

Answers: 1 I, 2 H, 3 E, 4 B, 5 D, 6 A, 7 C, 8 J, 9 G, 10 F

Vic Reeves – The Golden Age of Piracy 1680–1720

David Blunkett MP – The Harry Potter novels

Tanni Grey-Thompson – The *Star Wars* films

Peter Tatchell – Malcolm X

DJ Scott Mills – *Prisoner Cell Block H*

Rageh Omaar – The Presidency of George W. Bush

'Hairy Biker' Dave Myers – The Pre-Raphaelite Brotherhood

Michael Howard MP – Liverpool Football Club in the 1980s

Mick Hucknall – The life and work of Matisse

Sandie Shaw – Nichiren Buddhism

Show 13

Specialist Subject 13.1
The Beatles

1. Which group, fronted by John Lennon, was Paul McCartney invited to join after he had seen them play at a church fête in July 1957?

2. In April 1961, the band began a 13-week engagement at the Top Ten club in which city?

3. Who was sacked as The Beatles' drummer and replaced by Ringo Starr?

4. Which record label turned down the Beatles after an audition on 1 January 1962?

5. In April 1964, which Beatles single became the first record to top the British and US charts simultaneously?

6. Who played the memorable guitar solo on 'While My Guitar Gently Weeps' on The Beatles' 'White Album'?

7. On which album were 'Nowhere Man', 'Norwegian Wood' and 'In My Life' first released in the UK?

8. In December 1967, the Apple boutique opened on the corner of Paddington Street and which other London street?

9. What was the title of the band's first UK number one hit single, which spent seven weeks at the top of the charts in 1963?

10. On whose show did The Beatles make their American television debut in February 1964, performing to a record audience of more than 70 million?

11. The lyrics of which Beatles track refer to a work 'based on a novel by a man named Lear'?

12. At which event were the group performing in November 1963, when John Lennon asked those in the cheaper seats to clap, and everybody else to 'just rattle your jewellery'?

13. Which single was credited to 'The Beatles with Billy Preston'?

14. In which country did an international incident occur in July 1966, when the group reputedly refused an invitation to the Presidential Palace after playing a concert?

15. According to the lyrics of the song 'I Am The Walrus', what is the 'Elementary Penguin' singing?

16. Who directed the group's first feature film, *A Hard Day's Night*?

17. At which New York stadium did The Beatles play the first concert of their 1965 American tour, in front of a crowd of over 55,000?

18. The sound effects on which Beatles chart-topper were produced partly by John blowing through a straw while the group's chauffeur, Alf Bicknell, rattled chains in the bath?

19. 'She Loves You' knocked which group off the top of the UK charts? Their song 'Bad To Me' had also been written by Lennon and McCartney.

20. In the Beatles song 'When I'm Sixty-Four', where did the elderly couple hope to rent a cottage every summer 'if it's not too dear'?

21. What was the title of John Lennon's first literary work, a book of nonsense verse and rhyme published in 1964?

22. Which disc jockey, then working on the pirate ship Radio London, was invited to accompany The Beatles on their final American tour in August 1966?

23. The *Twist and Shout* EP, released in the UK in July 1963, consisted of which other track in addition to 'A Taste Of Honey', 'There's A Place' and the title track?

24. On what date in 1967 was *Magical Mystery Tour* first shown on British television?

25. Which of the band's UK number one singles doesn't feature the title anywhere in the lyrics?

26. In which city did the band play their last proper concert on 29 August 1966?

27. Mick Jagger and Keith Richard took part in the live recording of which Beatles chart-topper, broadcast for the first TV global link-up, *Our World* from the Abbey Road studios?

28. Which group reached number one in the UK with a cover of the Beatles' 'Ob-La-Di Ob-La-Da', knocking Paul McCartney's brother Mike McGear and his group Scaffold off the top of the charts in the process?

29. For a quarter of a century, The Beatles and Elvis shared the record for the most UK chart-topping singles. How many number ones did they each have until an Elvis remix topped the charts in 2002?

30. When the Beatles were awarded the MBE, what did they think the letters stood for, according to a quote from Princess Margaret in the *Jewish Chronicle*?

General Knowledge 13.1

1. In the Bible, who interpreted the Pharaoh's dreams as meaning seven years of plenty followed by seven years of famine?

2. Which London road, now renamed Milton Street was traditionally associated with writers and journalists?

3. The Powell Street cable car goes up and down Russian Hill in which American city?

4. What name is given to the mark on the floor that a player stands behind to throw his darts?

5. Limestone and chalk are both carbonates of which element?

6. Which stringed musical instrument takes its name from the Hawaiian for 'jumping flea'?

7. In the nineteenth century, which Empire became known as the 'Sick Man of Europe'?

8. What English surname indicates that an ancestor was a maker or seller of arrows?

9. On which so-called 'island' in the Fens did Hereward the Wake lead resistance against the Normans from 1070 to 1071?

10. In a traditional English pack of playing cards, what does the King of Diamonds have behind his left shoulder?

11. The works of Galen, written in the late second century, were considered the leading authority on which subject until the seventeenth century?

12. What is the name of the traditional Welsh broth normally made with lamb, bacon, leeks, potatoes and cabbage?

13. Who sang with Queen on their 1981 UK number one hit 'Under Pressure'?

14. What name is given to a ring-shaped coral reef which surrounds a lagoon?

15. Which annual film and television awards are made by the Hollywood Foreign Press Association?

16. In ancient Roman gladiatorial contests, a trident and which other weapon was deployed by a retiarius?

17. Who took the title of his 1974 novel *The Dogs of War* from Shakespeare's *Julius Caesar*?

18. What name is traditionally given to the highly corrosive mixture of concentrated hydrochloric and nitric acids which can dissolve gold?

19. The word 'sauna' comes from which language?

20. Which BBC Economics Editor's father was one half of a double act with Donald Swann?

21. What is the name of the government agency founded in 1791 and responsible for providing maps of Britain?

22. In the 1961 film *Breakfast at Tiffany's*, which Oscar-winning song does Audrey Hepburn sing while sitting on the windowsill of her New York apartment?

23. Bismarck said that possible German involvement in which troubled region of Europe was 'not worth the healthy bones of a single Pomeranian grenadier'?

24. Sir Kingsley Amis won the 1986 Booker Prize for which novel about a notable but obnoxious author who retires to Wales, meets up with old friends, and then drops dead?

25. The Po is the longest river in which country?

26. The jazz classic 'Mood Indigo' is particularly associated with whose orchestra?

27. What is the largest British freshwater crustacean? It resembles a small lobster.

28. What game, in which the 'Collegers' play the 'Oppidans', takes place on St Andrew's Day?

29. In Greek mythology, who is the twin sister of Apollo and the Goddess of the hunt, wild animals, chastity and childbirth?

30. Which powerful hallucinogenic agent is derived from ergot, a fungus particularly affecting rye?

Specialist Subject 13.2
British and European Geography

1. Which river is formed by the confluence of the rivers Goyt and the Tame near Stockport in Cheshire?

2. Which mountain range, running down the spine of west central Russia, forms the traditional boundary between Europe and Asia?

3. In which upland area is Dozemary Pool where, according to

tradition, Sir Bedivere threw King Arthur's sword Excalibur after he was mortally wounded at the Battle of Camlan?

4. Which city, once known as Pressburg, became a national capital in 1993?

5. The spire of which cathedral, by far the tallest in England, was added to the main building approximately fifty years after its completion?

6. The headwaters of which major river are two streams, the Breg and Brigach, which rise on the eastern slopes of the Black Forest mountains in Germany?

7. Lee Bank, Lozells and Ladywood are all suburbs of which English city?

8. Which region forms the 'toe' of Italy?

9. Formerly known as Old Beverly Street, in which English city is there a street called the Land of Green Ginger?

10. Which strait separates the Sea of Azov from the Black Sea?

11. Striding Edge and Swirral Edge are narrow ridges on which mountain in the Lake District?

12. Which lake that has an international border running through it has western arms known as the Überlinger See and the Untersee?

13. The twin peaks of Pen-y-Fan, standing 2,906 feet above sea level, and Corn Ddu, at 2,863 feet above sea level, are the highest points in which range of Welsh hills?

14. Leitrim, Roscommon, Sligo and Mayo are four of the five Irish counties that make up the traditional province of Connacht; which is the fifth and southernmost?

15. The waterfalls Cauldron Snout and High Force lie on which major English river?

16. In which modern country is the bulk of the ancient regions of Volinia and Podolia located?

17. Rising to a height of 1,250 feet above sea level, Will's Neck is the highest point of which range of Somerset hills?

18. A large part of which peninsula that formerly belonged to Italy was incorporated into Yugoslavia by the settlements of 1947 and 1954?

19. In which English county are the towns of Malmesbury, Marlborough and Melksham situated?

20. Which mountain range that lies between the Elbe and Weser rivers was divided by the former border between East and West Germany?

21. Which model industrial village in Yorkshire, created between about 1851 and 1876, is named after its founder and the nearby river?

22. What is the name of the dense scrubland vegetation of the Mediterranean? The name was also given to a French resistance movement.

23. In which British cathedral city does a medieval gateway, called the Bishop's Eye, straddle the approach to the moat-ringed Bishop's Palace?

24. Which country's highest point is Mount Musala, in the section of the Rhodopi massif known as the Rila Planina?

25. Lying off the coast of the island of Jersey, which group of rocks form the southernmost point of the British Isles?

26. The Liffey, and which other river, are at opposite ends of the 90-mile-long Royal Canal?

27. Which English city has three railway stations called Central, St David's and St Thomas?

28. Which oblast or province of Russia is an enclave lying between Poland and Lithuania and is completely separated geographically from the rest of the Russian Federation?

29. The rivers Dochart and Lochay, whose confluence is just east of the town of Killin, are the principal headwaters of which river?

30. Rising to a height of 10,964 feet, what is the highest mountain in the Dolomites?

General Knowledge 13.2

1. In *The Importance of Being Earnest*, what was Jack Worthing found in, as an infant, at the Victoria Station cloakroom?

2. Which French engineer designed the steel framework supporting the Statue of Liberty?

3. Which 2006 film has the subtitle 'Cultural Learnings of America for Make Benefit Glorious Nation of Kazakhstan'?

4. The adjective 'otic' refers to which part of the body?

5. Sebastian Coe and which other athlete broke the Mile World Record three times in a ten-day period in August 1981?

6. Which administrative region of Canada, whose name means 'great river' in the indigenous languages, was the scene of a Gold Rush in 1896?

7. In which board game are four dice and a doubling cube used to control the movement of the counters?

8. What word of Greek origin is used for overconfidence that invites disaster or ruin and is often cited as the flaw in the characters of tragic heroes?

9. In mathematics, the Sieve of Eratosthenes is used as a method of finding what sort of number?

10. What common salad ingredient is combined with yoghurt and garlic to make the Greek dish *tzatziki*?

11. Edward IV, Edward V and Richard III were the three monarchs of which royal house, a branch of the House of Plantagenet?

12. Which Johnny Cash song shares its title with a name given to the active volcanoes encircling the Pacific Ocean?

13. What general term, often associated with the Scottish philosopher David Hume, is used for the doctrine that all knowledge and beliefs are to be accepted only if based on personal experience?

14. Which plants that were famously painted by Monet belong to the genus Nymphaea?

15. Which Indian holy city's name means 'Pool of Nectar' and was founded in the 1570s by Ram Das, the fourth Sikh Guru?

16. Which science fiction series was created by Gene Roddenberry in the 1960s? The first broadcast episode was called 'Where No Man Has Gone Before'.

17. What does the word 'Croeso' mean on a Welsh road sign?

18. What now common metal was introduced to the public at the Paris Exposition of 1855 where it was regarded as a new precious metal?

19. Many characteristics of human fingerprints are shared with those of which marsupial?

20. Which of Shakespeare's tragedies was described by the physician Thomas Bowdler as 'unfortunately little suited to family reading' because of its themes of adultery and murder?

21. What name, referring to its historic location, is given to the battle of July 1798 at which Napoleon's army routed an Egyptian force led by Murad Bey?

22. What is the surname of the brothers Auguste and Louis, who were pioneers in the film industry due to their invention of an early motion-picture camera and projector?

23. Amman is the capital city of which Middle Eastern kingdom?

24. What term, from the Italian for 'to touch', is given to a keyboard piece intended to display the dexterity of the performer?

25. Who finally won the Grand National at the fifteenth attempt, when he rode Don't Push It to victory in 2010?

26. In biology, what word for a minute body or cell in an organism, especially a red and white blood cell, comes from the Latin for 'little body'?

27. The words schlock, schmaltz and schmooze come from which language?

28. In physics, what name is given to the phenomenon in which waves appear to bend or spread out as they pass through a small aperture or round the edge of a barrier?

29. In the Middle Ages, which plant with a long, forked root was thought to utter a shriek when pulled from the ground?

30. What did General de Gaulle say was 'Too serious a matter to be left to the politicians'?

These are all subjects chosen by contenders on Celebrity Mastermind, *but we've muddled up the order – can you match the celebrity to their subject?*

Part Two

1. Bill Oddie   A. The Solar System

2. Bernard Cribbins   B. Japanese Motorbikes

3. Sir Tim Rice   C. Australian Rainforests

4. John Bishop   D. Muhammad Ali

5. Lembit Opik MP   E. The History of the County
                                    of Middlesex

6. Adrian Edmondson   F. American Jazz

7. David Lammy MP   G. 18th-Century English Art
                                    and Artists

8. Loyd Grossman   H. The Art of Angling

9. Germaine Greer   I. The Sex Pistols

10. Russell Grant   J. The Irish Potato Famine

Answers: 1 F, 2 H, 3 A, 4 J, 5 B, 6 I, 7 D, 8 G, 9 C, 10 E

Bill Oddie – American Jazz

Bernard Cribbins – The Art of Angling

Sir Tim Rice – The Solar System

John Bishop – The Irish Potato Famine

Lembit Opik MP – Japanese Motorbikes

Adrian Edmondson – The Sex Pistols

David Lammy MP – Muhammad Ali

Loyd Grossman – 18th-Century English Art and Artists

Germaine Greer – Australian Rainforests

Russell Grant – The History of the County of Middlesex

Show 14

Specialist Subject 14.1
Snakes

1. Which snake that can be up to five metres long is the world's longest poisonous snake?

2. Members of which family of snakes, containing about 1,500 species, are noted for having elongated bodies and large eyes?

3. What is regarded as the world's most widespread terrestrial poisonous snake? Its range extends through most of Europe and northern Asia, to the Pacific coast.

4. Sea Snakes use a specialised gland under the tongue in order to expel what substance?

5. Which deadly viper, named after an eighteenth-century Scottish naturalist, is known as 'Tic Polonga' in Sri Lanka where it is the cause of many serious snakebites?

6. The six species of the family 'Dasypeltis' specialise in eating which particular items?

7. Which snake shares its common name with a city in southern France and produces a special secretion to polish its scales?

8. The Colubrid 'boiga irregularis' has eaten various native bird

species to extinction since being introduced accidentally to which Pacific island on a US military airplane?

9. What is the only family of Sea Snakes that contain species which come ashore to lay eggs?

10. When a snake is under attack, it may shed which part of its body in a process known as 'caudal autotomy'?

11. Which snake has the longest fangs, measuring up to five centimetres long, and has a remarkable camouflage among leaves on the ground?

12. The colour of the black mamba is actually more olive green or grey; which is the one part of its body that can be described as truly black?

13. Which highly poisonous snake that can be fatal to man has an Afrikaans name meaning 'tree snake'?

14. Snakes belong to which Order within the Class *Reptilia*, which also includes lizards and worm lizards?

15. Which common name for the 'Bitis arietans' derives from its method of giving a warning by inflating its body and hissing loudly? It is also believed to have the largest litters of any snake, with recorded broods of over 100 offspring.

16. The true fer-de-lance, 'Bothrops lanceolatus', is only found on which Caribbean island?

17. What general name is given to the New World snakes, mostly of the genus 'Micrurus', which are notable for their brightly marked bands of red, black and yellow or white?

18. What name is given to the venom-producing salivary, or parotid, gland of certain rear-fanged snakes such as the Boomslang?

19. How is the snake family 'Crotalinae' generally known, because of the orifices between each eye and nostril that contain heat-sensitive membranes?

20. Which continent's snake population does not include an indigenous species of viper?

21. Which type of snake was pictured on the early American flags with the slogan 'Don't tread on me'?

22. What is the defence mechanism of the West African Royal Python that gives rise to its alternative common name?

23. What alternative name for the Indian Cobra, a favourite of snake charmers, comes from the marking on the back of its hood?

24. In which country was an entirely new species, the three-horned pit viper recently discovered?

25. What common name for the rattlesnake 'Crotalus cerastes' is derived from the way it moves across its desert habitat?

26. In addition to spitting venom, which other last-resort defence mechanism is used by some snakes, including the South African cobra, the Rinkhal?

27. Which North American snake has sub-species that include the Eastern, the Red-Sided and the San Francisco?

28. There are two main categories of snake venom: neurotoxic, typically secreted by cobras and which other, typically secreted by vipers?

29. What is the common name of 'Natrix natrix', which is one of Britain's three native species of snake and is noted for playing dead when it is threatened?

30. Which fish forms the principal diet of the yellow-lipped sea krait, 'Laticauda colubrina'?

General Knowledge 14.1

1. Who did nightclub owner Jack Ruby shoot while he was being transferred to Dallas County Jail on 24 November 1963?

2. Which city in Mali, located on the southern edge of the Sahara, was a major centre of Islamic culture from about 1400 until 1600?

3. Which Greek hors d'oeuvre consists of smoked fish roe mixed with olive oil, lemon and soaked breadcrumbs?

4. Dido was the legendary founder of which ancient Phoenician city on the Gulf of Tunis?

5. With which 1956 play did John Osborne first achieve theatrical success?

6. Romney Marsh and Cheviot are breeds of which farm animal?

7. Which British artist's so-called Spot paintings include Pharmacy and Valium?

8. Encephalitis is the inflammation of which organ of the body?

9. The Kemp brothers, Gary and Martin, were two of the founder members of which 1980s group?

10. Which English city is home to the Fitzwilliam Museum?

11. In two films in the 1960s, which actor played Doctor Dolittle and taught elocution to Eliza Doolittle?

12. Vanilla is obtained from a climbing member of which family of plants?

13. Which aria does Lauretta sing to her father, Gianni Schicchi, in Puccini's opera, begging to be allowed to marry Rinuccio?

14. In the Bible, what is the name of Abraham's concubine and the mother of his son, Ishmael?

15. In horseracing, which is the last and oldest of the five classics of the English season on the flat?

16. What name is given to a pair of stars orbiting a common centre of gravity?

17. Which American comedy series featured the shock-haired Cosmo Kramer, who lived in the same apartment block as the title character?

18. The group of eight colleges and universities in the northeastern United States, including Harvard, Princeton and Yale, are known collectively by what name?

19. By what name, meaning 'little dyer', was the sixteenth-century Venetian painter Jacopo Robusti better known?

20. The Great Bear Lake is the largest lying entirely within which country?

21. A woman on a pedestal, wearing classical drapery and with a torch held high in her right hand, is the trademark of which Hollywood film studio?

22. Which King of England was taken prisoner in a battle at Lincoln in 1141?

23. The name of which alcoholic spirit comes from the Dutch for 'burnt wine'?

24. Which species of crab, found in the UK, uses empty shells or other hollow objects to protect and shelter its body?

25. At which prison did Johnny Cash perform the concert in February 1969 that included the song 'A Boy Named Sue'?

26. Tobermory is the principal town on which Hebridean island?

27. Which Swedish novelist created detective Inspector Kurt Wallander?

28. Which adopted son of Augustus became the second Roman Emperor in AD 14?

29. Toxicophobia is a morbid fear of what?

30. Of which American President did the political comedian Mort Sahl supposedly say, 'Would you buy a second-hand car from this man'?

Specialist Subject 14.2
The Archers since 1970

1. In the 10,000th episode of *The Archers* in 1989, which actress finally gave voice to Pru Forrest after the character had been silent for many years?

2. When Tamsin Gregg is unavailable for recordings, her character Debbie Aldridge manages a farm in which country?

3. In 1982, who emerged unscathed following the car accident in which Sid Perks' wife Polly was killed?

4. Which property did Lilian Bellamy sell in 1994 in order to raise money for her son James, who wanted to buy a house of his own?

5. Which character was born on New Year's Eve 1975?

6. The Parish Church of Ambridge, established in 1281, is dedicated to which Saint?

7. Susan Carter's brother carried out an armed raid on the village Post Office in 1993, which led to both him and Susan being imprisoned. What was his name?

8. What nationality was Debbie Aldridge's husband Simon Gerrard, whom she discovered in the arms of a colleague at the college where he lectured?

9. Although his voice was never heard, who was Jack Woolley's chauffeur and handyman for many years?

10. After the death of the actor George Hart, how was his character Jethro Larkin killed off in *The Archers*?

11. William Grundy's godfathers are Sid Perks and Neil Carter; who is his godmother?

12. When Marjorie Antrobus moved into the village in 1985, where did she live until forced by old age to move into the Laurels nursing home?

13. What was the name of village gossip and shopkeeper Martha Woodford's husband, who died in 1983?

14. Dr Richard Locke, the GP who arrived in Ambridge in 1992, was an enthusiastic member of which historical organisation?

15. What was the name of the horse that Brian bought Alice as a replacement for her old pony Chandler?

16. After starting the conversion in 1984, what was the name of the first farm in Ambridge to go fully organic?

17. Which businessman, formerly involved with Caroline, got Elizabeth pregnant and then deserted her at a motorway service station?

18. What is the name of Ambridge's nearest railway station, lying about six miles west of the village?

19. Tony Archer married Pat in December 1974, but who had he become engaged to earlier that year?

20. What was the occupation of Nelson Gabriel's daughter Rosemary, whom he had not known about until her sudden arrival in Ambridge at the age of twenty?

21. What was the name of the Borchester-based estate agents that Shula joined in the 1970s?

22. Which musical instrument did George Barford play?

23. What is the name of Eddie Grundy's ne'er-do-well elder brother?

24. Which country did Lucy Gemmell, daughter of Sid and Polly Perks, emigrate to on her marriage?

25. Who took Shula and Mark's official wedding photos, one of which appeared on the cover of the *Radio Times*?

26. After Jerry Buckle left the vicarage, Robin Stokes was appointed as a non-stipendiary minister; what was his other job?

27. In 2010, whom did Alice Aldridge marry in Las Vegas while on vacation, before her final year studying engineering at Southampton University?

28. Where did the recording of Princess Margaret's appearance at the Grey Gables charity fashion show in 1984 actually take place?

29. The actress Moir Leslie has played two major characters in *The Archers*. One was the Reverend Janet Fisher; who was the other?

30. What unusual gift did Lynda Snell present to her husband Robert for his sixtieth birthday?

General Knowledge 14.2

1. Which film about a poor Mumbai teenager who wins a fortune on a TV quiz show won the Best Film Oscar at the 2009 ceremony?

2. Which animal's tree home is known as a drey?

3. Which artist painted *The Fighting Temeraire, tugged to her last berth to be broken up* in 1838?

4. What city at the mouth of the River Tawe is known in Welsh as Abertawe?

5. In which of Shakespeare's plays are the title character's last words 'The rest is silence'?

6. Who, along with her husband, opened Britain's first birth control clinic, called the Mothers' Clinic, in Holloway, London, in 1921?

7. Which garden herb with varieties such as Lemon and Silver Queen is used with parsley and breadcrumbs to make a stuffing for veal and poultry?

8. In 596, who was sent from the Benedictine monastery of St Andrew in Rome to England by Pope Gregory the Great to convert the country to Christianity?

9. 'The Great Gate of Kiev' is the last part of which piano work by Mussorgsky?

10. What term is used for a fruit with a thin skin, fleshy interior and a hard, stony inner layer?

11. In snooker, what is the value of the green ball?

12. Which of the Dodecanese islands is the most easterly in the Aegean Sea?

13. 'I'll Be There For You' by The Rembrandts was the theme tune for which American TV comedy series?

14. Who served as Chancellor of the Exchequer from 1947 to 1950, when he retired because of ill health? He was noted for his 'austerity' policies.

15. Which word for a gleeful laugh was invented by Lewis Carroll in 1872, apparently a combination of chuckle and snort?

16. In classical mythology, what name was given to the food which gave the gods immortality?

17. The title track of Michael Jackson's album *Thriller* features a rap from which horror movie star?

18. In the human body, what is the medical name for the breastbone?

19. Which director, famed for his sci-fi films, began his career as a set designer for the BBC before going on to direct episodes of programmes such as *Z Cars*?

20. The name of which American general became synonymous with traitor in America, after he switched sides to the British in 1779 during the War of Independence?

21. Pak Choi is a Chinese variety of what vegetable?

22. The 'Mappa Mundi', a circular map of the world drawn on vellum and dating back to the thirteenth century, is housed at which cathedral?

23. *The Bell Jar*, published under the name of Victoria Lucas, was the only novel by which American female poet, who died in 1963?

24. In Egyptian mythology, the god Thoth is usually shown with the head of which wading bird?

25. Which British artist's 1977 painting *My Parents* shows his mother watching him while his father is reading?

26. On which of the Hawaiian islands is the capital Honolulu?

27. *I Put a Spell on You* was the title of the autobiography of which singer, who died in April 2003?

28. The order Lepidoptera consists of moths, skippers and which other insects?

29. In physics, what term is used for the transference of heat through a fluid or gas by the actual movement of the fluid itself?

30. What did the writer Cyril Connolly say was 'imprisoned in every fat man wildly signalling to be let out'?

Pronunciation

Magnus Magnusson could read Old Norse, and he translated Icelandic novels into English, but he dreaded having to pronounce French on *Mastermind*. When a 'spoof' episode of the programme was recorded for April Fool's Day 1987, its writer Stephen Fry naturally capitalised on Magnus's Achilles heel by having him read out the opening lines from *The Count of Monte Cristo* in the book's original language... and then read them out again when the 'contestant' asked him to repeat the question.

Ironically, once John Humphrys had taken over, a contender in the 2005 final chose as his specialist subject 'Icelandic Family Sagas'! I'm sure Magnus was delighted to see one of his passions on the show – among the sources used to check the questions was his own 1969 translation of the Laxdæla Saga – and he must have been relieved that it was John and not himself who had to quiz another of that year's finalists on the French poet and singer Georges Brassens... not to mention Guillaume Apollinaire, Raymond Queneau *and* the 'Wines of the Loire Valley', all of which had appeared as subjects earlier in the same series.

Whether a contender has chosen the Geography of the UK or of Croatia (as in 2006), British History or Polish History (from 2007), *Mastermind* can call upon the invaluable assistance of the dedicated and professional linguists at the BBC Pronunciation Unit – without whom, tackling questions on the Čičarija mountains, Grk wine from Korkula, Kazimierz the Great, the Synod of Łęczyca and Władisław Łokietek would have been rather daunting to say the least.

Even seemingly straightforward questions, however, can require the help of the Pronunciation Unit. For instance: In which play does Jaques deliver the speech that begins: 'All the world's a stage, and all the men and women merely players'? (See Plays of Shakespeare in Show 3 for the answer.) For those unfamiliar with the play, Jaques is pronounced 'Jaykweez' though an alternative is 'Jaykiss', which gives you an idea of the difficulties involved, not to mention that in the very same play there is another character called Jaques (sometimes spelt Jacques)... One authoritative source advises readers that 'his name *may* [my emphasis] have been pronounced "Jakes".'

Show 15

Specialist Subject 15.1
Sherlock Holmes

1. In which publication did the inaugural Sherlock Holmes story *A Study in Scarlet* first appear in 1887?

2. Where does Holmes immediately perceive Watson to have been, when they meet for the first time in *A Study in Scarlet*?

3. What type of creature is the 'lion's mane' that kills Fitzroy McPherson?

4. According to 'The Adventure of the Dying Detective', which long-suffering landlady has to put up with Holmes's 'incredible untidiness … addiction to music at strange hours … and occasional revolver practice within doors'?

5. In which case concerning a missing racehorse does Holmes draw attention to 'the curious incident of the dog in the night-time' (which doesn't bark because it knows the intruder)?

6. Who is the leader of the Baker Street Irregulars?

7. Which of the Crown Jewels is Holmes asked by the Prime Minister to recover, although Lord Cantlemere opposes his involvement?

8. What is the name of Holmes's brother, who is mentioned for the first time in 'The Adventure of the Greek Interpreter'?

9. Rodger Baskerville dies of which disease in Central America?

10. In *The Sign of Four*, what is Doctor Watson expecting to find when he opens the Benares metalwork box?

11. For what form of transport are the 'Bruce-Partington Plans' a jealously guarded government secret?

12. In 'The Creeping Man', what creature does Professor Presbury begin to both mimic and resemble after injecting himself with Lowenstein's serum?

13. The house at which Ronald Adair is shot dead at long range by Colonel Sebastian Moran, 'the second most dangerous man in London', is in which London street?

14. In 'The Adventure of the Illustrious Client', how does Baron Adelbert Gruner ensure that his fiancée rejects any scurrilous rumours that she might hear about him?

15. The distinctive appearance of Sherlock Holmes, and in particular the legendary deerstalker hat (that was never mentioned by name in the stories) was created by which artist, who illustrated many of the original stories in the *Strand* magazine?

16. In 'The Man with the Twisted Lip', Neville St Clair gives up journalism in favour of which profession that he finds far more lucrative?

17. Mycroft Holmes was a founding member of which club 'for the most unsociable and un-clubbable men in town'?

18. In 'The Adventure of Black Peter', with what was Captain Peter Carey killed?

19. At which Swiss Falls did Conan Doyle intend to kill off Holmes, though after a public outcry his hero was resurrected?

20. In 'The Adventure of the Empty House', the first of his adventures after his supposed death, Holmes visits Watson in the disguise of an old man who claims that he is in what trade?

21. What part of his anatomy does the hydraulic engineer Victor Hatherley leave behind at the house where Colonel Lysander Stark is operating an illegal coin-press?

22. In 'The Adventure of the Three Students', a chapter of which ancient Greek historian's work must be translated in the examination for the Fortescue Scholarship?

23. Wilhelm Gottsreich Sigismond von Ormstein was King of which country?

24. In 'A Case of Identity', why does Mary Sutherland's stepfather want to prevent her from marrying?

25. Which story, set just before the Great War, details Holmes's efforts to capture a German spy called Von Bork?

26. Which species is the snake that features in 'The Adventure of the Speckled Band'?

27. Which international agent blackmails Lady Hilda Trelawney Hope into stealing a confidential document from her husband's dispatch box?

28. What did the red-headed London pawnbroker Jabez Wilson have to copy out when he was duped by John Clay into accepting a position with the spurious Red-Headed League?

29. It is claimed that only two people addressed Holmes by his first name. One was Mycroft; which bird-stuffer in *The Sign of Four* is the other?

30. Which was the last Sherlock Holmes case to be published? It appeared in *Liberty* magazine in March 1927.

General Knowledge 15.1

1. According to an obituary supposedly published in *The Times*, Monique Delacroix was the mother of which fictional secret agent?

2. The American capital, Washington D.C., stands on which river that rises in the Allegheny Mountains and eventually flows into Chesapeake Bay?

3. Ansel Adams, Henri Cartier-Bresson and Yousuf Karsh are famous names in what artistic field?

4. Which class of creatures that begin life in water breathing through gills, but usually live as adults on land using lungs, has a name that comes from the Greek for 'double life'?

5. Which famous gin-based cocktail is said to have been invented in the Long Bar of Raffles Hotel in 1915?

6. In 1948, the Attlee government abolished the twelve seats in the Commons allocated to which institutions?

7. In Holst's suite *The Planets*, which planet was the 'Bringer of War'?

8. Which metallic element is commonly used with nickel in batteries and in control rods for nuclear reactors?

9. In film-set jargon, what name is given to the assistant, or apprentice, to the gaffer or key grip?

10. In 1866, there was a famous race between clipper ships to be the first home with what cargo from China?

11. Muhammad Ali's first professional fight outside America took place at Wembley in June 1963, when he was still known as Cassius Clay. Which British Heavyweight Champion was his opponent?

12. What do the suffixes 'chester', 'cester' or 'caster' in British place names indicate?

13. Whose first book, *A Bear Called Paddington*, was published in 1958?

14. Which wild flower takes its name from the French for 'lion's teeth' because its pointed leaves resemble them?

15. Peter Sellers, Leo McKern and Lionel Jeffries were all offered which television role ultimately taken by Warren Mitchell?

16. What name, now used for a fanatic, originally meant a member of a Jewish sect uncompromising in opposition to the polytheism of Ancient Rome?

17. 'It's still the same old story, a fight for love and glory' is a line from what classic song?

18. In which constellation is Rigel the brightest star and Betelgeuse the second brightest?

19. The surrealist poet Andre Breton referred to which painter as 'Avida Dollars', an anagram of his name which referred to his perceived greed for money and fame?

20. What word, originally used for an inhabitant of an ancient Greek town on the Italian mainland, has come to mean anyone who is devoted to luxury?

21. What is the traditional symbol of pawnbrokers?

22. Which volcano in the Sunda Strait between Java and Sumatra erupted in 1883? The effects were felt for thousands of miles around.

23. In the 1960s, which building on Broadway was an important centre of popular music songwriting, with offices for artists like Carole King, Gerry Goffin and Neil Sedaka?

24. What do people suffering from trichotillomania have a compulsion to pull out?

25. In the film *The Third Man*, Harry Lime says that all that Switzerland has managed to produce after 500 years of democracy is… what?

26. What is the usual translation of the Russian word 'tovarishch'?

27. In furniture construction, for what do the initals M.D.F. stand?

28. Which character from Greek mythology was 'Bound' according to the title of a play by Aeschylus and 'Unbound' according to a poem by Shelley?

29. In Italian cuisine, which pasta has a name meaning 'feathers' or 'quills'?

30. Which Kentish town is the home of the proverbial angry letter writer who signs himself 'Disgusted'?

Specialist Subject 15.2
The Life and Reign of Queen Elizabeth I

1. Where did Elizabeth deliver the words 'I know that I have the body of a weak and feeble woman, but I have the heart and stomach of a king'?

2. At which royal palace did Elizabeth set up her household in 1548, after the death of her stepmother Katherine Parr?

3. Under the terms of which treaty, signed in July 1560, did France recognise Elizabeth as Queen of England?

4. Who was recalled from France in 1573 and became a principal secretary of state in December of that year?

5. What is the only Oxford college to have been founded by Elizabeth? It received its royal charter in June 1571.

6. In the autumn of 1562, Elizabeth fell seriously ill at Hampton Court and, despite the absence of marks on her skin, was correctly diagnosed by her doctor as having which disease?

7. Elizabeth appointed Edmund Grindal to which post in 1575, then suspended him two years later?

8. Which of Elizabeth's courtiers married Lettice Knollys in September 1578 but managed to keep it secret from the Queen for 14 months afterwards?

9. By the terms of the 1559 Act of Supremacy, instead of becoming the Supreme Head of the Church of England Elizabeth became its Supreme... what?

10. Which Florentine banker instigated the plot of 1571 that aimed to put Mary, Queen of Scots on the English throne instead of Elizabeth, with the help of a Spanish invasion?

11. The Treaty of Troyes, agreed between England and France in April 1564, obliged Elizabeth to give up her claim to which overseas territory?

12. Which Pope issued the bull 'Regnans in Excelsis' that excommunicated Elizabeth in 1570?

13. Immediately after acceding to the throne, Elizabeth appointed Robert Dudley as Master of... what?

14. Which ship did Elizabeth purchase from Sir Walter Raleigh in 1587 and rename? It sailed at the head of the Queen's fleet against the Armada a year later.

15. Which member of the council was promoted to the peerage by Elizabeth in 1571, and made 1st Baron of Burghley?

16. Elizabeth's favourite Sir Christopher Hatton, whom she nicknamed 'her lids', was promoted to which position in April 1587?

17. In 1587, at which Spanish port did Francis Drake enter the harbour and destroy tons of Philip II's shipping, before moving on to Portugal?

18. Which Archbishop of Canterbury had been one of Elizabeth's godparents at her christening?

19. Which artist and goldsmith painted a number of miniatures or limnings of Elizabeth from the early 1570s, as well as designing the great seal of the realm?

20. When Lord Chancellor Nicholas Heath announced Elizabeth's accession, he said that her 'most lawful right and title to the crown, we need not...' what?

21. Which spy, arrested by Walsingham's men in November 1583, was executed after confessing that the Duke of Guise was planning an invasion to install Mary, Queen of Scots as Queen of England?

22. Who burst into Elizabeth's private chambers at Nonsuch Palace following his sudden return from Ireland, where he had agreed a truce with the Earl of Tyrone in contradiction of her orders?

THE MASTERMIND QUIZ BOOK

23. Whose death, in suspicious circumstances, led to Robert Dudley being suspended from court by Elizabeth?

24. Members of Essex's faction paid Shakespeare and his players to perform which play on the day before the attempted coup against Elizabeth?

25. The Duke of Medina Sidonia commanded the Armada; who commanded the army in the Netherlands that it was supposed to transport to England?

26. During the reign of her half-sister Mary I, where was Elizabeth imprisoned before being moved to Woodstock?

27. What affectionate nickname did Elizabeth give to her suitor, François, the Duke of Alençon and Anjou?

28. In August 1598, Sir Henry Bagenal was defeated and killed by rebel Irish forces under Tyrone at which battle?

29. What was the name of the Norfolk landowner who was Elizabeth's gaoler while she was imprisoned at Woodstock?

30. Elizabeth died in which palace on 24 March 1603, bringing the Tudor dynasty to an end?

General Knowledge 15.2

1. Which battle is depicted on the final surviving section of the Bayeux tapestry?

2. Whose first novel was *Decline and Fall* in 1928?

3. Bank, Field and Water are three species found in Britain of which small rodent?

4. What is the longest river entirely in England?

5. Lee J. Cobb, Karl Malden and Rod Steiger were all nominated for Best Supporting Actor Oscars for their roles in which classic 1954 film?

6. Which people, whose civilisation reached its height in the sixth century BC, inhabited the part of Italy between the Tiber and the Arno?

7. Carl Andre's *Equivalent* series of sculptures are all made up of a rectangular arrangement of 120... what? The last sculpture, *Equivalent Eight*, was purchased by the Tate Gallery in 1972.

8. What name is given to the Assembly of the Holy Roman Empire that outlawed Martin Luther following his excommunication in 1521?

9. A type of bass tuba with circular coiling is named after which American composer who developed it in the 1890s?

10. What is the name of the hormone that regulates the level of glucose in the blood?

11. Which Michelin three-starred chef is noted for his snail porridge?

12. The principle of Ahimsa, common to both Buddhism and Jainism, has what meaning?

13. Who was appointed as England Test and One Day cricket captain in August 2008, but held the post for less than five months?

14. By area, what is the smallest state in mainland Australia?

15. Which television presenter began his career as the reporter Mike Channel on *Radio Active* and later on *KYTV*?

16. In a plant, what is the name of the single main root from which lateral roots develop?

17. Which left-handed ex-paratrooper usually played a right-handed guitar upside-down?

18. In computing, what term is used for the form of logic which is based on a notion of degrees of truth rather than something being either wholly true or wholly false?

19. Who directed the controversial 1988 film *The Last Temptation of Christ*?

20. On 1 December 1955, who was arrested after refusing to give up her seat on a bus in Montgomery, Alabama. The resulting boycott by passengers ended with the city's buses being desegregated.

21. The blue pigment ultramarine was originally obtained from which semi-precious stone?

22. What was the name of the series of American space stations, the first of which was launched in 1973?

23. Which Scottish philosopher published his first major work, *A Treatise of Human Nature*, in 1739?

24. Which Home Secretary created the Metropolitan Police Force in 1829?

25. Which French word is used to describe wine brought to room temperature?

26. Which term for a measure of length equal to 600 feet in Ancient Greece or Rome, is now applied to many sporting venues?

27. 'Love Changes Everything', which was a hit for Michael Ball, is the opening number from which Lloyd-Webber musical?

28. Which city is shown as being at the centre of the world on the medieval 'Mappa Mundi' housed in Hereford Cathedral?

29. How old did you have to be to qualify for the receipt of an old age pension when they were first introduced in the UK in 1909?

30. In Cockney rhyming slang, what is a 'tea leaf'?

Prime Time

The first series of *Mastermind* was broadcast late at night, but the second unexpectedly ended up in primetime, replacing *Casanova '73*, a sitcom starring Leslie Phillips as Henry Newhouse, a '20th-century libertine' – which had to be moved to after the watershed. *Mastermind* itself once ran into issues with its pre-watershed slot in 1996, when the BBC had to bleep out one of the words used in a set of specialist subject questions on 'The Sex Pistols and Punk Rock'... although anyone who had the subtitles on *did* see the full title of the Pistols' first album, uncensored!

Show 16

Specialist Subject 16.1
Mammals

1. Derived from the Latin 'mamma', what does the word 'mammal' mean?

2. Which creature hunts in family groups called pods and is the largest and fastest member of the dolphin family?

3. Although they also eat slugs and insect larvae, what is the principal diet of the mole?

4. Along with Borneo, which other island is the natural habitat of the arboreal great ape the Orang-utan?

5. Known locally as 'el Tigre', what is the largest species of big cat in the Americas?

6. The male of which of which species of white whale develops a long, twisted tusk that projects through its upper lip?

7. The greatest population of Giant Pandas is found in which Chinese province?

8. Which nuts are the favourite food of the common dormouse, giving it its alternative name?

9. The two species of which African mammal are distinguished by the shape of their upper lip, one of which is pointed and prehensile, while the other is straight?

10. Which mammals of the New World rainforests have coats that often appear green because of the algae growing among the hairs?

11. The Asiatic lion, which was once widespread, is now only found in the wild in which national park in Gujarat, India?

12. Which pig with a distinctive reddish-brown coat, and named after a town in Staffordshire, is reckoned to be the oldest pure English breed?

13. Which Japanese primate is the most northerly species of monkey, inhabiting latitudes where the winter temperatures drop below zero Celsius?

14. The only species of seal to live exclusively in fresh water is found in which lake?

15. In 1971, Philip and Jeanne Wayre founded a charity whose main aim is to promote the conservation of which animal throughout the world, and particularly in Britain?

16. Derived from the malay word meaning 'to roll', what is the alternative name for the seven species of scaly anteater found in tropical Asia and Africa?

17. In what way is the rare banded anteater or numbat distinct from all other Australian marsupials?

18. What is the alternative name for 'Pan paniscus', the black-faced pygmy chimpanzee that inhabits the rainforests of the Congo?

19. Which partially web-footed, semi-aquatic mammal of the South

American forests, sometimes called the water pig, is the largest member of the rodent family?

20. A herd of reindeer was reintroduced into Britain in 1952 in which Scottish mountain range?

21. Which marine mammal, one of the two species of the order Sirenia, can be found in the coastal waters of the West Pacific Ocean, Indian Ocean and Red Sea?

22. Derived from an Arabic word for a fur-bearing animal, what is the name of the smallest of the wild canids? It lives in the Sahara and has extremely large ears that assist with thermo-regulation.

23. What is the shape of the outgrowth of naked skin around the nostrils which gives the bat family, Rhinolophidae, its common name?

24. Which baleen whale that has a Latin specific name meaning 'sharp-snouted' is the most common whale species in British waters, especially in Scotland?

25. Which jackal-sized black and fawn striped member of the family Hyaenidae is unlike the other three species of hyena in that its jaws are weak and its diet consists mainly of termites?

26. The books and list compiled by the IUCN, which contain information on endangered mammals, are known by what colour?

27. The gliding colugas or cobegos of the south-east Asian forests are better-known by as 'Flying...' what?

28. Which antelope-like animal of the family Antilocapridae is the fastest mammal in North America, attaining speeds of up to 90 kilometres per hour?

29. What name is given to the specialised skin that nourishes the growth of deer antlers and guides the formation and development of the tines?

30. So-called because of its distinctive markings, what is the descriptive name of the ucamari, the only South American species of bear?

General Knowledge 16.1

1. Who presented the BBC television series *Life on Earth*, about the origins of living species?

2. Which historic east coast Scottish county is traditionally prefaced by the title 'the Kingdom of'?

3. Which Wagner opera is based on the legend of the Knight of the Swan?

4. The fungus Malassezia globosa is thought to cause which common medical condition of the scalp?

5. Which Italian word, meaning 'fresh', is given to a mural painting technique using water-based paint on lime plaster?

6. Which explorer, along with the crew of his ship, landed on Elephant Island in the South Shetlands in 1916, after they had been trapped in Antarctic pack ice for around ten months?

7. The tulip-shaped glass known as a 'copita' is traditionally used for serving which fortified wine?

8. In Greek mythology, who was the goddess of retribution or vengeance, especially upon those who roused the indignation of the gods?

9. Which Booker Prize-winning author wrote the novel *On Chesil Beach*, which was published in 2007?

10. Dendrochronology is the technique of dating artefacts and events by using what?

11. In the original 1969 film of *The Italian Job*, in which city does the classic car chase take place?

12. In 1965, who became the first leader of the Conservative party to be chosen by a ballot of his fellow MPs?

13. In which seven-a-side team sport do players' positions include Goal Keeper, Wing Attack and Goal Shooter?

14. What name that literally means 'my master' but is usually translated as 'teacher', is given to the spiritual leader of a Jewish congregation or community?

15. Which musical by Lerner and Loewe was an adaptation of George Bernard Shaw's play *Pygmalion*?

16. Which Swedish word, meaning 'representative', is used for an official who investigates complaints against public bodies?

17. Which spice was known in the Middle Ages as Indian saffron, because of its colour?

18. Which town that was the site of a Battle in the Wars of the Roses, lies at the confluence of the Rivers Avon and Severn?

19. In which Scott Fitzgerald novel does the title character fall in love with a married socialite, Daisy Buchanan, the cousin of the narrator Nick Carraway?

20. Greenfly and Blackfly are two members of which family of soft-bodied insects that feed on plant sap?

21. Which architectural feature can be dog-leg, straight, open well or circular?

22. Which shipping forecast area, in the North Sea, is directly north of German Bight?

23. In the 1984 film *Splash*, what does Daryl Hannah's character Madison become again if she gets her legs wet?

24. What name is usually given to the process of coating iron or steel with zinc to protect it against corrosion?

25. Whose biggest hit in Britain was 'Wonderful World', which reached Number Two in the charts when it was re-issued in 1986, more than twenty-one years after his death?

26. Which early Greek mathematician is best known for his thirteen-volume work *Elements*, on geometry and related subjects?

27. What is the surname of the footballing brothers who played for England in the 1966 World Cup final?

28. What is the meaning of the nautical term 'avast'?

29. Opened in 1837, which was London's first main-line railway terminus?

30. Which television programme habitually ended with the co-stars saying 'So it's goodnight from me... and it's goodnight from him'?

Specialist Subject 16.2
Pop Music of the 1980s and 1990s

1. Which group's song, 'Brass In Pocket', was the first single to reach number one in the UK charts in the 1980s?

2. Despite becoming the bestselling album of all time, only one of the songs on Michael Jackson's *Thriller* reached the top of the UK singles charts; what was its title?

3. Which group reached the UK top 10 with 'Smells Like Teen Spirit', released in 1991?

4. Before forming the Pet Shop Boys, Neil Tennant was the assistant editor of which pop magazine?

5. What was the title of Madonna's first UK number one single in 1985? The song featured in the film *Desperately Seeking Susan*?

6. What were the group Vapors 'turning' according to the title of their 1980 top ten hit single?

7. Which guitarist with The Smiths co-wrote most of the band's songs with Morrissey?

8. 'She came from Greece, she had a thirst for knowledge. She studied sculpture at St Martin's College' is a line from which Pulp hit single?

9. Which British actress appeared as the Fairy Godmother in the video of Adam and the Ants' 'Prince Charming'?

10. What was the title of the only UK top ten single by the Australian band INXS? The song was released in 1988 and reached number two in the charts.

11. Which Birmingham-based band, fronted by lead singer Dennis Seaton, had six top 40 singles in the 1980s?

12. Which singer's bestselling album *Diva*, released in 1992, was her first as a solo artist?

13. After the break-up of The Jam, what was the name of the band that Paul Weller formed in 1983 with the keyboard player Mick Talbot?

14. In the mid-1980s, Frankie Goes to Hollywood, Jennifer Rush and Huey Lewis and the News all had hits with different songs that shared the same title. What was it?

15. Who sang with a group called the Sunsets, popular as a live attraction in Europe, before his solo career took off after he appeared as the title character in the stage musical *Elvis*?

16. Professor Brian Cox was a member of which chart-topping band of the 1990s?

17. Which American singer wrote UB40's 1983 number one hit 'Red Red Wine'?

18. Which group had a top ten hit with 'Driving In My Car' in 1982?

19. Which model appeared in the video for Billy Joel's 'Uptown Girl', and later married the singer?

20. The cover of which Blur album shows Walthamstow dog-track?

21. Which group's first UK top ten hit single was 'Gimme All Your Lovin' in 1984?

22. 'You make the sun shine brighter than Doris Day' is a line from which Wham! hit?

23. Who sang the line 'Tonight, thank God, it's them instead of you' on the original Band Aid single 'Do They Know It's Christmas' in 1984?

24. What was the stage-name of Oasis guitarist Paul Arthurs?

25. Which group's first chart success was with 'Johnny Come Home' which got to number eight in 1985?

26. In 1987, Aretha Franklin topped the UK singles charts in collaboration with which male singer?

27. Underworld's hit 'Born Slippy' was rereleased and reached number two in the UK charts after featuring in which cult film?

28. Which female vocalist sang with Peter Gabriel on 'Don't Give Up', a top ten hit in 1986?

29. Which band returned to the top of the UK charts in 1999 with 'Maria', more than 18 years after their previous chart-topper, 'The Tide Is High'?

30. Which former Buggles vocalist produced Frankie Goes To Hollywood and Seal?

General Knowledge 16.2

1. Soldiers of the United Nations peacekeeping forces wear berets of what colour?

2. The award-winning Swiss Re building in the City of London, designed by Norman Foster, is commonly known by what name?

3. Which legendary Irish hero is said to have built the Giant's Causeway and lived in a cave on the island of Staffa?

4. In the SI system of units, which prefix is used to denote one thousand millionth of one unit?

5. Which actor plays Withnail's Uncle Monty in the cult 1987 film comedy *Withnail And I*?

6. Which city lies on the River Usk, a few miles above its entry into the Severn estuary?

7. Which author based his stories about the spy Ashenden on his

experiences in the British Secret Service during the First World War?

8. The dried leaves of which plant that is the only member of the genus Lawsonia produce a red-orange dye that has been used since ancient times for body art and hair dye?

9. At the Grammys in 2012, which British singer won all six awards for which she was nominated?

10. Which country's 'perpetual neutrality' was recognised at the Congress of Vienna, in 1815?

11. Which word for merry comes from the belief that those born under the sign of Jupiter are of a cheerful disposition?

12. Which famous actress stood as the Workers' Revolutionary Party candidate for Manchester Moss Side, at the 1979 General Election?

13. Orange pekoe, Lapsang Souchong and Oolong are all varieties of what?

14. Which Spanish monk, whose name became a byword for a sadistic interrogator, instituted the Inquisition in 1478, and was the first holder of the post of Grand Inquisitor?

15. Which Scottish golfer won the European Order of Merit a record eight times between 1993 and 2005?

16. In which country are the Spanish enclaves of Ceuta and Melilla?

17. Which quiz show was the first programme to be transmitted on Channel Four, when the channel began broadcasting in November 1982?

18. What name was given to the cliff face at the southern end of the

Capitoline Hill in Rome, from which traitors were flung to their death?

19. Which song, written by Irving Berlin, first appeared in the 1942 film *Holiday Inn* and went on to become one of the bestselling singles of all time?

20. What is the medical name for a continuous ringing or buzzing in the ears?

21. Who painted a famous picture of the Marquess of Rockingham's racehorse, Whistlejacket, in around 1762?

22. Which term, meaning a strict disciplinarian, is taken from the name of Louis XIV's Inspector General of Infantry, who devised a rigorous system of drill?

23. Which metal was produced in India and China from about the thirteenth century? The first smelting works in Europe didn't appear until about 1740 in Bristol.

24. What is the name of the British equivalent of the German savoury dish Blutwurst?

25. Roseate, Sooty and Arctic are among the species of which sea bird?

26. Which conductor, composer and pianist was the first American to conduct at La Scala, Milan, in 1953?

27. Which city is the capital of the American state of Georgia?

28. Which American player won the first of her six Wimbledon Women's Singles titles in 1966?

29. Which insects of the order 'Isoptera' that dwell in large colonies are sometimes called 'white ants', because of their similarity in lifestyle to ants, to which they are actually unrelated?

30. Which anti-war novel begins, 'It was love at first sight. The first time Yossarian saw the chaplain, he fell madly in love with him'?

Mastermind on location

For its first quarter of a century, *Mastermind* was filmed at locations all over the UK – from the very first at the University of Liverpool in 1972 to what at the time appeared to be the very last: appropriately recorded at the Cathedral of St Magnus in Kirkwall, Orkney. In between, the programme visited venues as splendid as Coventry Cathedral and Blenheim Palace, and as diverse as Chatham Dockyard, the Science Museum and the Commonwealth Institute (the venue for the 1993 final, won by Gavin Fuller who was just 24 years old at the time).

These days, a single series of *Mastermind* comprises no fewer than 31 programmes, not to mention additional Celebrity versions; this sometimes requires the filming of over a dozen shows in a single week and has meant that the modern-day *Mastermind* production team travel the country solely for the purpose of auditioning potential contenders... who invariably ask, 'Why don't you make *Mastermind* on location any more?'

Just occasionally, though, the programme manages to escape from a TV studio and head out into the big wide world – most poignantly in 2007, when the final was recorded at Glasgow Caledonian University in tribute to Magnus Magnusson, who had been the university's Chancellor until his death earlier that year.

Show 17

Specialist Subject 17.1
Formula One Motor Racing

1. On 13 May 1950, on which circuit did Nino Farina win the first Formula One Grand Prix race?

2. In 2008, who became the youngest ever Grand Prix winner when he won for Toro Rosso?

3. Which British car, driven by Stirling Moss, gained its first Formula One victory at Monaco in 1960?

4. Which driver took the 1982 world title despite only winning one Grand Prix that season?

5. All but three teams withdrew from which 2005 Grand Prix over a tyre safety issue?

6. Who claimed Pole Position on his Formula One debut at the 1996 Australian Grand Prix?

7. In 1971, Peter Gethin won which race by one hundredth of a second from Ronnie Peterson, in the closest ever Formula One finish?

8. Who became the Ferrari's Technical Director in 1997? He later won the world title with his own team?

9. Which team won seven drivers' titles in eight seasons from 1984 to 1991?

10. Which former world champion overtook Michael Schumacher and Ricardo Zonta in the same manoeuvre, to take victory at the 2000 Belgian Grand Prix?

11. In 1976, Niki Lauda returned to Formula One and finished 4th in the Italian Grand Prix only six weeks after suffering horrific burns and receiving the Last Rites after an accident at which circuit?

12. During the 2008 season, Rubens Barrichello broke the record for the most Grand Prix entries; whose total of 256 did he beat?

13. On which circuit did Jenson Button and Lewis Hamilton both secure their first Grand Prix victories, in 2006 and 2007 respectively? Nigel Mansell had secured the world title at the same track in 1992.

14. Which world champion was kidnapped by Fidel Castro's July 26 Movement but was released unharmed? His kidnappers even made him breakfast in bed.

15. Which team returned to Formula One in 1989 after a one-year absence, during which Bernie Ecclestone sold his controlling interest?

16. Which driver gave Benetton both their first and last Grand Prix victories?

17. Which city began hosting the European Grand Prix in 2008?

18. Which driver competed in Formula One for twelve years but only managed one victory, at the 1995 Canadian Grand Prix?

19. In 2000, his first season in Formula One, Jenson Button drove for which team?

20. In 1989, at the age of 42, who won the Indy 500 fifteen years after winning his second Formula One world title?

21. Which British circuit staged its first Formula One Grand Prix in 1993? The race was won by Ayrton Senna, who lapped all but one of the other drivers despite having started only fourth on the grid.

22. Which world champion survived an accident at Monaco in 1955, when he drove off the circuit and into the harbour, only to die while testing a new Ferrari four days later?

23. Damon Hill secured which team's first Formula One victory at Spa in 1998, ahead of teammate Ralf Schumacher?

24. Who ended Michael Schumacher's five-year reign as world champion by taking the title in 2005?

25. Which Grand Prix was held from 1950 to 1954, after which motor-racing was banned in its host country?

26. Which Ligier driver was the surprise winner of the 1996 Monaco Grand Prix, when only three other cars made it to the finish?

27. What was the Spyker team renamed as, after being sold in 2007 to Vijay Mallya?

28. British drivers finished 1st, 2nd and 3rd in the World Championships of 1964 and 1965. Jim Clark took the title in 1965 ahead of Graham Hill and Jackie Stewart; who had beaten Hill and Clark to the championship the previous year?

29. What was the name of the mile-long straight on the Paul Ricard circuit, which for many years was the venue for the French Grand Prix?

30. What was unusual about the Tyrrell car in which Jody Scheckter won the 1976 Swedish Grand Prix?

General Knowledge 17.1

1. Which King abdicated the British throne in December 1936?

2. Like Rome, which city in Yorkshire is said to be built on seven hills?

3. What is the better-known title of Franz Hals' painting *Portrait of a Gentleman*, which can be seen at the Wallace Collection in London?

4. Which country on the Arabian peninsula was formed in 1990 by the union of two neighbouring states, one of which was the former British colony of Aden?

5. What name of Afrikaans origin is given to lean meat that is cut into strips and dried in the sun?

6. According to the Oxford English Dictionary, the earliest use of which acronym, describing local opposition to an undesirable development, occurs in an article about landfill sites that appeared in the *Christian Science Monitor* in 1980?

7. 'Nobody's perfect' are the last words of which 1959 film, in which Joe E. Brown's character discovers that the 'girl' he has proposed to is actually a man?

8. On which plants did Gregor Mendel perform the experiments that laid the foundation of the science of genetics?

9. Which semi-autobiographical novel by Jack Kerouac describes the wanderings across America of a writer named Sal Paradise and his friend Dean Moriarty?

10. What is the capital of the Canadian province of Ontario?

11. Which member of England's 2003 Rugby World Cup-winning team was only the third player to have represented England at Rugby Union after having done so at Rugby League?

12. Which pig-like mammal, whose natural habitat ranges from the southern deserts of the USA to Patagonia, has three species called 'Collared', 'White-lipped' and 'Chacoan'?

13. Which 1970s soul singer provided the voice of Chef in the television series *South Park* until 2006, when he resigned because an episode satirised Scientology?

14. Xanthippe, who was notorious for her bad temper, is believed to have been the wife of which Greek philosopher?

15. The ballet *Gayaneh*, which includes the famous Sabre Dance, is by which composer?

16. Which disease, caused by a deficiency of vitamin C, was once common in sailors and characterised by swollen bleeding gums and bleeding into the skin and joints?

17. Part of the Biblical book of Daniel was originally written in which language that is closely related to Hebrew and is said to have been Jesus's mother-tongue?

18. The drink slivovitz is distilled from which fruit?

19. In grammar, which tense denotes an action that was completed before a past point in time and is formed in English by the use of the word 'had' and the past participle of a verb?

20. Susan Philipsz, the 2010 winner of the Turner Prize with works including *Lowlands Away*, was the first person to win using which medium?

21. What is the name of the pass that links Innsbruck in Austria with Bolzano in Italy?

22. Paul Newman won a Best Actor Oscar for his role in which film that was the sequel to his earlier picture *The Hustler*?

23. From 1948 until 1967, the Mandelbaum Gate was the only border crossing point in which divided city?

24. In the novel by Cervantes, what is the name of Don Quixote's manservant?

25. In Hinduism and Buddhism, what term is used for the influence of a person's past actions on their future lives and incarnations? In the West it has come to mean 'destiny'.

26. Who played his last competitive tennis match in September 2007, when he partnered Jamie Murray to victory in a doubles match against Croatia in a Davis Cup tie?

27. In mathematics, what name is given to the number system whose base is two; so only the digits zero and one are needed to specify a number?

28. Which company was first incorporated in 1916 as the Pacific Aero Products Company, and was renamed after its founder in 1917?

29. What name was given to the pouch-like addition to the crotch of men's hose, which was first worn in the fifteenth century but was being derided as indecent by the 1580s?

30. Which 1970s pop group featured the Construction Worker, the Biker, the Cowboy, the Native American, the GI and the Cop?

Specialist Subject 17.2
The Great War and the Second World War

1. Which battle raged from 1 June to 18 November 1916, resulting in over a million killed or injured, and all for an Allied advance of just seven miles?

2. Who, before leaving the Philippines in March 1942, told his successor, Major-General Jonathan Wainwright, 'Hold on. I shall return'?

3. What was codename of the British intelligence system, based at Bletchley Park, which succeeded in tapping into the very highest-level communications of the German and later the Japanese armed forces?

4. Which German victory of late August 1914 was regarded as revenge for the battle of the same name in 1410 at which the Teutonic Knights had been routed by Poles and Lithuanians?

5. Which Marshal of the Soviet Union personally commanded the final assault on Berlin in April 1945 and went on to serve as Minister of Defence from 1955 to 1957?

6. What codename did Nazi Germany give to its planned invasion of Britain, for which victory in the Battle of Britain was a necessary precondition?

7. Which British colonel commanded the Arab force that captured the Red Sea port of Aqaba on 6 July 1917?

8. Shortly before the German surrender at Stalingrad, Hitler promoted their commander von Paulus to what rank, in the mistaken expectation that he would commit suicide rather than be captured by the Soviets?

9. The RAF used two main fighter planes in the Battle of Britain; the Spitfire was one, what was the other?

10. In June 1919, at which naval base in the Orkneys did the Germans scuttle their high seas fleet under orders from Rear-Admiral von Reuter?

11. Which German Field Marshal was put in charge of the defence of the French Channel coast against a possible Allied invasion in 1944?

12. On which island is Mount Suribachi, where the US Marines famously hoisted the Stars and Stripes in February 1945, during one of the bloodiest battles in their history?

13. The treaty ending the Great War was signed in June 1919, in the Hall of Mirrors of which palace?

14. Which famous 1942 invention by Barnes Wallis was codenamed 'Upkeep'?

15. Which British soldier was appointed military advisor and leader of the guerrilla campaign in Ethiopia in November 1940 and led the forces that liberated Addis Ababa from the Italians in May 1941?

16. The Third Battle of Ypres is more commonly known by the name of which Belgian village that was the scene of the last of the fighting?

17. What nickname did the British Seventh Armoured Division adopt during the North Africa campaign in the Second World War?

18. On 28 November 1943, Churchill, Roosevelt and Stalin held their first meeting together in which capital city?

19. Before facing a firing squad in Brussels on 12 October 1915, who stated, 'I realise that patriotism is not enough. I must have no hatred or bitterness towards anyone'?

20. Which island was finally captured by American troops on 21 June 1945, after 82 days of fierce fighting against the Japanese?

21. Who was head of RAF Fighter Command during the Battle of Britain, but was effectively removed from his post in November 1940?

22. Where, in December 1917, were negotiations held and a treaty later signed which ended the war between the Bolsheviks and the Central Powers?

23. Who commanded 242 Squadron during the Battle of Britain, and later became a German prisoner after a mid-air collision over France in August 1941?

24. On D-Day, the Allies suffered the greatest number of casualties on which of the beaches, which was given the epithet 'Bloody'?

25. Who, during his speech to the House of Commons on 11 November 1918, said 'I hope we may say that thus, this fateful morning, came to an end all wars'?

26. What name was given to the series of air raids on British towns and cities of cultural interest that were launched by the Germans between April and October 1942?

27. The capture of the bridge over the Rhine at which city was the ultimate objective of Operation Market Garden, launched on 17 September 1944?

28. Who became Architect to the Imperial War Graves Commission after the Great War, and designed the Cenotaph in Whitehall?

29. The controversial raids on which German city took place on 13 and 14 February 1945, as part of Operation Thunderclap?

30. Who signed the capitulation of the German armed forces to the Allies in an upstairs room of the Rheims Collège Moderne de Garçons on 7 May 1945?

General Knowledge 17.2

1. Whose first fantasy novel, *The Hobbit*, was published in 1937?

2. Moths and butterflies belong to which order of insects?

3. In which opera by Verdi does the Duke of Mantua sing 'La Donna è Mobile'?

4. Which republic that declared its independence in June 2006 has borders with Croatia, Bosnia and Herzegovina, Serbia and Albania?

5. In painting using tempera, what is most commonly used to mix the powdered pigment instead of oil?

6. Diego Colon, who eventually inherited the title of Viceroy of the Indies in 1511, was the eldest son of which explorer?

7. 'Kitten Kong', 'Planet of the Rabbits' and 'Bun Fight at the O.K. Tea Rooms' were episodes of which 1970s television comedy series?

8. What name for a papal edict comes from the Latin word for the lead seal used on the document?

9. Which of Charles Dickens' characters says that 'every idiot who goes about with "Merry Christmas" on his lips should be

boiled with his own pudding, and buried with a stake of holly through his heart'?

10. What is the name of the American astronomer who proved, in the 1920s, that large star systems exist beyond the Milky Way? He also showed that the universe was expanding.

11. In which Tuscan city are the Palio horse races that take place on 2 July and 16 August? They are part of a pageant dating back to the fifteenth century.

12. Who returned from his wanderings after the Trojan War but, at first, was only recognised by his dog Argos?

13. What is the name of the famous apple brandy that is a speciality of Normandy?

14. Which airbase near Newbury became a centre for anti-nuclear protests in September 1981 after the intention to site Cruise missiles there was announced?

15. The works of which composer of ragtime music include 'Maple Leaf Rag' and 'The Entertainer'?

16. Which palm tree is native to tropical Africa and Madagascar and gives its name to the fibre made from its leaves, which is used to make hats and baskets?

17. In a novel by Anne Brontë, Helen Graham is the tenant of which hall?

18. Which resort in the Cairngorms is the major ski centre of the Scottish Highlands?

19. John Constable wrote of which of his fellow artists that 'he seems to paint with tinted steam, so evanescent, so airy'?

20. In Islam, what name from the Arabic for 'story' is given to the traditions and sayings of the prophet Muhammad?

21. Which sauce that's often served with fish consists chiefly of mayonnaise, with chopped gherkins, capers and herbs?

22. Which word for a mental condition typically characterised by delusions of persecution comes from the Greek for 'beyond' or 'beside' and 'mind'?

23. Who starred with her real-life husband, Michael Williams, in the TV comedy series *A Fine Romance*?

24. In which city are New Street and Snow Hill railway stations?

25. In the UK, RoSPA is the Royal Society for the Prevention of what?

26. The Pharos, which was the most celebrated lighthouse in antiquity, stood in the harbour of which city?

27. Who was the lead singer and chief songwriter of the pop group The Kinks?

28. Only two species of mammal hatch from an egg. The echidna, or spiny anteater, is one; what is the other?

29. What is the literal meaning of the Latin expression 'tempus fugit'?

30. In which 1979 film does Terry Jones' character say the line 'He's not the Messiah, he's a very naughty boy'?

Life after the Black Chair

Over the past few years, anyone who fancied testing their memory and intellect against a *Mastermind* champion would have been positively spoilt for choice: from tackling one of Gavin Fuller's quizzes in the *Telegraph*, to Fred Housego on *Round Britain Quiz*, Shaun Wallace on *The Chase*, or *Eggheads*' Kevin Ashman, Chris Hughes and Pat Gibson.

Other champions who returned to the small screen include the actor Stephen Tomlin, who won in 1991 under his real name of Stephen Allen, while his predecessor David Edwards made one extremely lucrative television appearance in 2001, when he scooped the top prize on *Who Wants to be a Millionaire?*

In 2012, *Mastermind* winners were to be found everywhere from the blogosphere (David Clark's 'lifeaftermastermind') to the Romantic Novelists' Association – 1997 champion Anne Ashurst, a prolific author for Mills and Boon under her pen name of 'Sara Craven', was elected its Chair in 2011. In the same year David Beamish, the 1988 champion, was appointed as Clerk of the Parliaments, with responsibility for running the administration in the House of Lords.

Show 18

Specialist Subject 18.1
Great Scientists:
Galileo, Newton, Darwin and Einstein

1. While studying medicine at Edinburgh University, Charles Darwin was introduced to whose evolutionary theories by Dr Robert Grant?

2. In which work of 1686–1687 did Isaac Newton put forward his laws of gravitation and motion?

3. Where was Albert Einstein employed in 1905, when he published his Theory of Special Relativity?

4. Galileo Galilei's *Dialogue on the Two Chief World Systems* compared traditional 'Aristotelian' cosmology with whose theories, which Galileo himself supported?

5. In 1831, Darwin undertook a five-year voyage on which ship, captained by Robert Fitzroy?

6. Why was Newton forced to leave Cambridge in 1665, and again in 1666? On both occasions he returned to the family home at Woolsthorpe Manor in Lincolnshire.

7. Einstein's Theory of Special Relativity is based on two

fundamental postulates. One is that the laws of physics are the same for all observers moving at constant velocity relative to one another; the other is that what remains constant, regardless of the motion of the source relative to the observer?

8. In 1589, Galileo took the chair of mathematics at which university, where he allegedly demonstrated that the speed at which objects fall is not proportional to their mass?

9. Who was the author of *Principles of Geology*, which Darwin made frequent use of during his voyage around the world?

10. Which of his Newton's 'laws' can be summarised as 'For every action, there is an equal and opposite reaction'?

11. In his 'annus mirabilis' of 1905, Einstein provided an explanation for which phenomenon that had been first observed by Robert Brown in the 1820s?

12. In 1610, using the newly invented telescope, Galileo discovered that which planet had moons, implying that not all celestial bodies orbited the Earth?

13. While in Patagonia, what was Darwin doing when he realised that he had found an example of a rare species of Rhea that was subsequently renamed rhea darwinii?

14. In 1669, Newton became the second holder of what Chair of Mathematics at Cambridge University?

15. Einstein famously claimed that 'God is subtle but he is not...' what?

16. Galileo and Christoph Scheiner had a long and bitter debate regarding the nature of what solar phenomenon, that both had discovered independently?

17. In 1858, from whom did Darwin receive a manuscript entitled 'On The Tendency of Varieties to Depart Indefinitely from the Original Type', leading to a joint presentation of their theories of natural selection?

18. In his 1693 treatise 'Praxis', Newton attempted to summarise his lengthy studies of... what?

19. Einstein was awarded the Nobel Prize for his services to Theoretical Physics, and especially for his discovery of the law explaining what effect?

20. Which Pope permitted Galileo to write the *Dialogue*, but condemned him to life imprisonment after its publication for supporting the heliocentric model?

21. At a meeting of the British Association for the Advancement of Science in 1860, who attempted to ridicule Darwin's *Origin of Species* by asking Darwin's supporter Thomas Huxley 'whether he'd rather be descended from a monkey through his grandmother or grandfather'?

22. In 1696, Newton left Cambridge after thirty-five years to become warden of which organisation?

23. Einstein was appointed a professor at which American educational institution in 1932?

24. Galileo is credited with inventing a primitive version of which piece of measuring equipment in around 1593?

25. Which work of 1871, a sequel to *Origin of Species*, included Darwin's famous declaration that 'Man still bears in his bodily frame the indelible stamp of his lowly origin'?

26. A Royal Society report of 1713 found in Newton's favour in his long-running priority dispute with which mathematician over the invention of calculus?

27. In 1952, Einstein was offered which political office, but declined?

28. While under house arrest, Galileo's *Dialogues Concerning Two New Sciences* was smuggled out of Italy and published in which country in 1638?

29. What was the name of the house in Kent that Darwin bought in 1842 and lived in for the rest of his life?

30. In 1703, Newton succeeded which of his rivals as President of the Royal Society?

General Knowledge 18.1

1. Which film includes the lines 'Close your eyes and tap your heels together three times. And think to yourself "There's no place like home"'?

2. Which desert occupies most of the country of Botswana, in southern Africa?

3. Glenn Miller co-wrote which piece of music that was recorded by his Orchestra in 1939, and was adopted as their signature tune?

4. Which sixteenth-century Flemish cartographer is famous for his map projection in which lines of latitude and longitude are represented by parallel lines?

5. What generic name is commonly given to French aperitifs such as Pernod and Ricard that are flavoured with aniseed, and turn a cloudy yellow when water is added?

6. In a speech on nuclear disarmament in 1987, which Labour

politician said, 'I would die for my country... but I would not let my country die for me'?

7. Which British architect designed the new Wembley stadium, which opened to the public in 2007?

8. What is the name given to the highest point on a horse's back from where its height is measured?

9. In which Charles Dickens novel does the title character go to America to seek his fortune, accompanied by his servant Mark Tapley?

10. In Norse mythology, which god, who could change his shape and sex, was chained to a rock as punishment for slaying Balder?

11. The Leonids and the Perseids are among the best-known examples of which phenomenon, marked by a large number of 'shooting stars' appearing over a relatively short period of time and seeming to come from the same place?

12. What is the name of the principal town on the island of Guernsey?

13. What piece of sporting equipment has limbs, a belly and a nocking point?

14. The Scottish plant collector, David Douglas, has given his name to a primrose, and also to a species of which coniferous tree?

15. Which singer was at the top of the UK charts for 10 consecutive weeks in 2007 with the song 'Umbrella'?

16. In the Anglican Church, the Sunday before Ascension Day is sometimes known by what name that is derived from the Latin for 'to ask'?

17. Cliff Barnes becomes President of America in the last episode of which television series?

18. Endorphins, which are found naturally in the brain, have the ability to relieve... what?

19. Which Renaissance artist had the surname of Sanzio, though he is sometimes referred to as Santi?

20. The Battle of Navarino, which is believed to be the last major sea battle involving only wooden sailing ships, was fought in 1827 as part of which country's war of independence?

21. What name is given to a large-scale musical work, typically on a religious subject, for solo voices, chorus and orchestra that is normally performed without scenery, costumes or acting?

22. At 1,072 metres above sea level, Landi Kotal, in Pakistan, is the highest point on which pass?

23. Who wrote the poem 'Islanders' at the end of the Second Boer War, in which he refers to 'flannelled fools at the wicket' and 'muddied oafs in the goals'?

24. What name for the group of mainly aquatic animals such as crabs, lobsters and shrimps comes from the Latin word for 'shell'?

25. Which boxer was voted the 2007 BBC Sports Personality of the Year? His father Enzo won the Best Trainer award at the same ceremony.

26. In September 490 BC, at which battle did the Athenians, under Miltiades, win a decisive victory over the Persians?

27. The Indian delicacy known as Bombay Duck is actually a dried form of... what?

28. Poison and Water are two deadly kinds of which herbaceous plant that's a member of the parsley family?

29. Which city in Northern Ireland stands on the River Foyle?

30. Ken Russell described which of his films as 'the story of the marriage between a homosexual and a nymphomaniac'?

Specialist Subject 18.2
The Films of Alfred Hitchcock

1. The trailer to which Alfred Hitchcock film described it as 'The picture you must see from the beginning or not at all'?

2. On which American landmark does the climax of *North by Northwest* take place?

3. Who plays the dual parts of Madeleine Elster and Judy Barton in *Vertigo*?

4. Which Hitchcock movie is said to be the only film ever made using only the 'ten-minute take'?

5. *Rebecca* and *The Birds* in 1963 were both based on stories by which writer?

6. What nickname does Jeff give to the ballet dancer in the apartment block opposite him in *Rear Window*?

7. In which of his films did Hitchcock make his traditional cameo appearance as a bus passenger sitting next to Cary Grant's character John Robie?

8. Which actress made her first screen appearance in *The Trouble with Harry*, as Jennifer Rogers?

9. The surrealist artist Salvador Dalì designed the dream sequences for which film?

10. Who composed the music for several Hitchcock films, including the shrieking violins in *Psycho*?

11. Which 1943 Hitchcock film, based on a story by John Steinbeck, tells of the desperate struggle for survival of a group of people whose vessel has been torpedoed?

12. In *Rebecca*, what is the name of the sinister housekeeper who eventually burns down Manderley rather than see Maxim and his bride happy there?

13. Which 1956 film starring Henry Fonda and Vera Miles was billed as the first Hitchcock film based on a true story?

14. In *The Trouble With Harry*, what was Harry?

15. Whose roles in Hitchcock's films include Lisa Fremont in *Rear Window* and Frances Stevens in *To Catch a Thief*?

16. Which 1956 Hitchcock film was a remake of a film he had made in England in 1934?

17. In *Psycho*, what is the full name of Janet Leigh's character, who checks into the Bates Motel with almost $40,000 of stolen money?

18. Which Hitchcock film starred Peggy Ashcroft and John Laurie as Margaret and John Crofter, and Wylie Watson as Mr Memory?

19. Hitchcock made *Rebecca*, *Spellbound* and *The Paradine Case* for which legendary Hollywood producer?

20. What important job was performed by Ray Berwick, part of the production crew on *The Birds*?

21. What name did Hitchcock give to the device that triggers the plot, such as stolen papers or missing uranium?

22. In which Hitchcock film does Marlene Dietrich sing Cole Porter's 'The Laziest Gal In Town'?

23. How is the murder of Miriam Haines seen in *Strangers on a Train*?

24. Who played the sailor killed by the young Marnie, in the film of the same name?

25. In which Hitchcock film is a bishop kidnapped in the middle of saying Mass?

26. Who appeared as the second Mrs de Winter in *Rebecca* and went on to win an Oscar for playing Lina in *Suspicion*?

27. Which film features the cricket-loving Charters and Caldicott, played by Basil Radford and Naunton Wayne?

28. Hitchcock based *Marnie* on which author's 1961 novel?

29. In *Dial M for Murder*, what does Margot Wendice use to kill her assailant as he is trying to strangle her?

30. In his cameo appearance in *Torn Curtain*, what is Hitchcock holding on his lap in the hotel lobby?

General Knowledge 18.2

1. What name is given to the process by which sunlight is used by green plants to manufacture carbohydrates from carbon dioxide and water?

2. Which small market town in Powys is famous for its annual literary festival and its many second-hand book shops?

3. By what must the diameter of a circle be multiplied to calculate its circumference?

4. Lieutenant John Chard commanded the defence of which supply depot in 1879, during the Anglo-Zulu war?

5. In an early work by Van Gogh, which vegetables are being eaten by peasants in the light of an oil lamp? The painting is on view at the Van Gogh museum in Amsterdam.

6. Members of which order of mammals are characterised by a single pair of continually growing incisors on each jaw?

7. What is the original surname of the actor Nicolas Cage, whose uncle is a famous film director?

8. Which European capital city stands on the River Tagus?

9. 'Anitra's Dance' and 'Solveig's Song' are part of Grieg's incidental music to which play by Ibsen?

10. In Greek mythology, who gave Theseus the thread that enabled him to escape from the Labyrinth after he slew the Minotaur?

11. In Middle Eastern cookery, what type of seeds are crushed to make the oily paste known as Tahini?

12. The upper house of the Isle of Man's Parliament is known as the Legislative Council; what is the name of the Lower House?

13. What is the title of the play by Sheridan, in which Captain Absolute and Bob Acres are both in love with Lydia Languish?

14. The Hindu festival Janmashtami, meaning 'birth on the Eighth day', celebrates the birth of which god in the town of Mathura?

15. Which television character used to travel on crowded commuter trains that habitually arrived late for a variety of reasons, including 'escaped puma at Chessington North'?

16. The nineteenth-century surgeon, Joseph Lister, pioneered the use of which acid as an antiseptic?

17. Which awards for urban music were established in 1996 by Kanya King, while she was working as a television researcher?

18. Which Duke led the army that defeated the Jacobites at the Battle of Culloden?

19. What term is used for a timber or stone beam over a doorway or window?

20. Which Scottish city has three cathedrals – St Machar's, St Mary's and St Andrews – all of which are made of granite?

21. What was the name of Dante's beloved, whom he immortalised first in *The New Life* and later in *The Divine Comedy*?

22. Which tropical Asian fig tree has aerial roots, which develop from its branches and descend to the ground to become new trunks?

23. Which sport is played in three periods of twenty minutes, each of which starts with a face-off?

24. In AD 313, who was the co-emperor of Rome with Licinius, when they issued the Edict of Milan that removed all obstacles to the practice of Christianity and other religions in the Roman Empire?

25. Which film musical was originally written by Jim Jacobs and Warren Casey, and is set at Rydell High School in the 1950s?

26. The northernmost point of the continent of South America lies in which country?

27. Which Liverpool pop group topped the charts for the first time in April 1963 with 'How Do You Do It'?

28. In zoology, what term is used for a limb or tail that is capable of grasping or holding?

29. The tank-like casing of which famous television aliens was created by the BBC designer Raymond Cusick?

30. In 2003, what name for French Fries was adopted temporarily in the cafeterias serving the US House of Representatives, because of France's opposition to the war in Iraq?

'You have two minutes on...'

During *Mastermind*'s original incarnation, contenders tackled subjects ranging from 'The Moomin Saga', to 'British Poisoners', while 'The Life-Cycle and Habits of the Honey Bee' appeared twice. Since the programme returned, there hasn't been a year without at least one set of questions on something unexpected...

John Humphrys' first series featured two minutes on 'the History of Video Games', while the year after included 'Murders and Murderers' *and* 'Capital Punishment in the UK since 1945', although 'Unicorns' provided some light relief. For enjoyable revision, few subjects surely can match 'the History of Spirits and Liqueurs' from series three, while the year after provided even more good cheer with such original offerings as 'Civic Heraldry of the Russian Empire', 'Enclaves and Exclaves', 'Existentialism', 'Arabic Dance' and 'Firearms'.

The following year, pub quizzers across the land raised a glass to 'Real Ale Breweries of Britain'. In the next series, it was finally the year of 'British Trotskyism' – well its history from 1932 to 1949, anyway. Since then, successive series have seen contenders choose 'Angels', 'Witches (of Pendle)', 'Human Parasites' and 'Alchemy'!

Show 19

Specialist Subject 19.1
The TV Series *Blackadder*

1. Which character takes the salute in the opening credits of *Blackadder Goes Forth*?

2. When Blackadder's aunt and uncle, 'the two most fanatical puritans in England', come to dinner, what vegetable does Baldrick serve them, even though the only one he can find is 'exactly the same shape as a... thingy'?

3. In 'The Black Seal', who is dismissed from Blackadder's service because he 'would bore the leggings off a village idiot'?

4. What is the name of the book written by Blackadder under the pseudonym Gertrude Perkins, which has taken him seven years to write?

5. What has Baldrick been using as a sugar substitute in his 'coffee' (that's actually made of mud), since New Year's Eve 1915?

6. Who co-wrote the first series with Rowan Akinson, and then the next three with Ben Elton?

7. What is Percy wearing that leads Blackadder to comment that he looks 'like a bird who's swallowed a plate'?

8. *Who's Who* lists Sir Talbot Buxomly's interests as 'flogging servants, shooting poor people, and the extension of slavery to anyone who hasn't got a...' what?

9. Kate, who almost marries Blackadder in Series Two then reappears as Melchett's driver in Series Four, uses what male pseudonym?

10. In 'The Queen of Spain's Beard', what has caused the marks on Blackadder's neck, which he originally says are lovebites?

11. In the final episode of *Blackadder Goes Forth*, Edmund points out to George that while the British Empire covers a quarter of the globe, the German Empire consists only of what?

12. After firing Baldrick in 'Beer', how does Blackadder reply when Baldrick says that he has been in his family since 1532?

13. What is the name of the character who runs the coffee shop in the third series?

14. Which character does Edmund behead after seeing him trying to steal his horse, in the first episode to be broadcast?

15. For what offence is Blackadder charged at his court martial, along with 'disobeying some orders as well'? General Melchett, who is also the witness for the prosecution, sentences him to death.

16. Who visits Blackadder at 4 o'clock in the morning to try and recover a thousand pounds lent to him by the Bank of the Black Monks of St Herod – 'Banking with a Smile and a Stab'?

17. On St Juniper's Day, the King strips Blackadder of the title Duke of Edinburgh, leaving him as Warden of what?

18. Who produced all four series of Blackadder?

19. Who does Baldrick impersonate for the concert party, though his costume consists solely of a bowler hat and a dead slug which he attempts to use as a false moustache? General Melchett assumes he's a 'slug balancer'.

20. In the first series, Blackadder is appointed to which post after the previous incumbent was killed by being butted in the stomach with a spiked helmet? One of his predecessors had been hit by a falling gargoyle and another was impaled on the spire of Norwich cathedral?

21. Baldrick is elected MP for which rotten borough – or 'robber button' as the Prince Regent refers to it – by 16,472 votes to nil, even though there is only one voter… who happens to be Blackadder… who is also the returning officer!

22. Before they are disturbed by the Bishop of Bath and Wells, Blackadder tells Mollie (an 'inexpensive prostitute') that he'd have gone to bed with whom if he'd 'wanted a lecture on the Rights of Man'?

23. While he's in the Field Hospital, Blackadder uncovers which character as a spy when she fails to notice that only two out of Oxford, Cambridge and Hull are great universities, though General Melchett thinks the odd one out is Oxford?

24. How did Doctor Samuel Johnson's father attempt unsuccessfully to attract his attention while Johnson was writing his Dictionary?

25. In the first series, who plays the Witchsmeller Pursuivant?

26. What was Percy savaged by when he was a baby, making him terrified of going on the sea voyage around the Cape of Good Hope, or 'the Sea of Certain Death' as Sir Walter Raleigh refers to it?

27. Blackadder is commissioned by General Melchett to find an artist to paint a morale-boosting cover for which magazine, and ends up sitting in No Man's Land 'painting pictures of the Germans'?

28. What is the name of the interpreter played by Jim Broadbent, in 'The Queen of Spain's Beard'?

29. In Series Four, which actor plays the Red Baron von Richthoven, who intends to send Blackadder and Baldrick to teach home economics in a convent school as punishment for spilling 'the precious German blood of many of my finest and blondest friends'?

30. How does Blackadder respond when Prince Ludwig 'the Indestructible' asks if he has been 'inconweenienced' by the interrogator from the Spanish Inquisition (who is armed with a scythe)?

General Knowledge 19.1

1. In the words of a well-known saying, 'it is a waste of time to carry coals to...' which city?

2. Which mammals belong to the order chiroptera, which literally means 'hand-wings'?

3. What French name is given to the white sauce, made from seasoned milk and a roux of flour and butter, which can be used as the basis for other sauces such as Mornay?

4. Caracas is the capital city of which South American country?

5. The works of which twentieth-century American Realist

painter include *August in the City*, *Cape Cod Afternoon* and *Drugstore*?

6. In Ancient Greece, the common people were referred to as 'hoi polloi'; what was the equivalent in ancient Rome?

7. What is the name of the nineteenth-century English philosopher who was a disciple of Jeremy Bentham's Utilitarian movement? His works included the treatises *On Liberty* and *The Subjection of Women*?

8. What name is given to the visible surface of the Sun, which emits most of the light that reaches the Earth?

9. Who finally won an Oscar in 2007 for directing *The Departed*, after seven previous unsuccessful nominations?

10. What is the name of the punctuation mark used to indicate possession, or the omission of letters?

11. In which Puccini opera does Rodolfo sing the aria 'Che gelida manina', or 'your tiny hand is frozen', to Mimi?

12. In Chapter Three of the Book of Exodus, God promises to bring the Israelites to a land flowing with what two things?

13. Argentina are the reigning Olympic champions in which equestrian sport that last featured at the Summer Games in 1936?

14. Which American state was the first to secede from the Union, and was also the site of the first engagement in the Civil War, when Fort Sumter was surrendered to the Confederates?

15. In architecture, what name that is derived from the Greek for 'arch' or vault' is given to a semicircular or polygonal recess in a church, typically at its eastern end?

16. Osier, whose flexible twigs are used in basket-making, is a shrubby member of what genus of trees?

17. In a musical score, which direction is used for playing notes on a stringed instrument by plucking the strings instead of using the bow?

18. Which Irish seaport is situated near the mouth of the River Lee?

19. Which playwright's autobiography *Untold Stories* begins with an account of his childhood in Leeds?

20. What name was given to the prefabricated harbours that were towed across the Channel for use in the 1944 Normandy landings?

21. In 1951, Kiki Haakonson became the first winner of which international contest?

22. What collective name, meaning 'knowledge', is given to the sacred scriptures of Hinduism?

23. Which former member of The Libertines later became the lead singer of Babyshambles?

24. Which British architect was jailed in 1974, having been found guilty of bribing public figures to win contracts?

25. What name, taken from the German for 'a splash', is given to a drink consisting of equal parts of white wine and soda-water, or sparkling mineral water?

26. The Little, Great Crested and Black-necked are species of which water bird?

27. Which style of trousers did the British Royal Navy replace with flares in 1977?

28. The Trans-Siberian railway runs from Moscow to the port of Nakhodka, which lies around 100 miles east of which city?

29. Which acid can build up in the muscles during strenuous exercise, causing cramp-like pains?

30. In which film does Michael Palin slay the dragon that is menacing the medieval kingdom of King Bruno the Questionable, played by Max Wall?

Specialist Subject 19.2
The Nobel Prize

1. In 2007, the Intergovernmental Panel on Climate Change and which American politician were the joint winners of the Nobel Peace Prize?

2. On which date, the anniversary of Alfred Nobel's death, do the award ceremonies for the Nobel Prizes take place?

3. Who was the first British woman to become a Nobel Laureate, when she won the 1964 Chemistry Prize?

4. Which of the prizes can be divided between two, but not three, candidates?

5. John Nash, who was the subject of the film *A Beautiful Mind*, was a joint recipient of the 1994 Economics Prize for his work on which theory?

6. Henry Labouisse, who received the 1965 Peace Prize on behalf of UNICEF, was the son-in-law of which Laureates?

7. Henrik Dam and Edward Doisy shared the 1943 prize for Physiology or Medicine for their discovery of and work on which vitamin?

8. When Antony Hewish and Sir Martin Ryle shared the 1974 Physics Prize they became the first winners from which branch of science?

9. Which Swedish poet was awarded the 2011 Prize for Literature?

10. In 1990, the Peace Prize award ceremony moved to which venue, having previously been held in the auditorium of the University of Oslo?

11. What is the surname of the brothers Jan and Nikolaas, who won Nobel Prizes in 1969 and 1973 respectively?

12. What term is commonly used for the economic theory of which 1976 Economics Prize winner Milton Friedman was a leading exponent?

13. Which Italian-born physicist emigrated to America immediately after receiving the 1938 Nobel Prize? Four years later his experiments led to the first controlled nuclear chain reaction.

14. In 1904, Ivan Pavlov became the first physiologist to win a Prize, for his work on the physiology of which bodily function?

15. In 1902, Theodor Mommsen became the first person to be awarded the Literature Prize for a historical work; who was the second?

16. What do Nobel laureates Erik Axel Karlfeldt, Dag Hammarskjöld and Ralph Steinman have in common?

17. Which 1908 Chemistry laureate discovered the existence of a positively charged atomic nucleus? His model of the atom was later validated by the work of fellow laureate Niels Bohr.

18. Stanley Prusiner won the 1997 Prize for Physiology or Medicine

for his discovery of which agent, thought to be responsible for degenerative brain diseases such as BSE?

19. Which head of state was nominated controversially for the Peace Prizes of 1945 and 1948, for his 'efforts to end World War Two'?

20. In 1896, future Physics laureate Guglielmo Marconi had received the first patent to be granted for what system that he had developed? A year later he founded a company of the same name.

21. What is the penname of the American author Chloë Anthony Wofford, who was awarded the 1993 prize for Literature?

22. In 1968, which organisation, on the occasion of its 30th anniversary, established the Prize in Economic Sciences in Memory of Alfred Nobel?

23. What name was given to the anti-particle whose mass is equal to that of the electron, but has the opposite electric charge; its existence was predicted by Nobel laureate Paul Dirac in 1930?

24. Who shared the 1962 prize for Physiology or Medicine with James Watson and Maurice Wilkins?

25. What name, after an architect, did Harold Kroto give to the compound, comprising 60 carbon atoms bound together, for the discovery of which he, Robert Curl and Richard Smalley shared the 1996 Chemistry Prize?

26. Which institution, along with its director Mohamed El Baradei, were the joint winners of the 2005 Peace Prize?

27. Which writer's omission from the list of nominees for the 1901 Literature Prize led to a public letter signed by forty-two Swedish authors and artists who called him 'the revered patriarch of contemporary literature'?

28. The names of those who were nominated unsuccessfully for Nobel Prizes are not revealed for how many years afterwards?

29. In 2010, British physiologist Robert Edwards was awarded the prize for his pioneering work in which field? The medical procedure he helped develop was first performed successfully in humans in 1978.

30. What circumstance connects the German pacifist and journalist Carl von Ossietzky, Burmese politician Aung San Suu Kyi and Chinese human rights activist Liu Xiaobo, at the time they were awarded the Nobel Peace prize?

General Knowledge 19.2

1. Which Scots Gaelic word is used for a lake, or a narrow inlet of the sea, in the Scottish Highlands?

2. Which future Prime Minister first entered Parliament in 1979, as the Conservative MP for Huntingdonshire?

3. Which word of Italian origin is used for a bell tower, particularly a free-standing one?

4. During the period known as the Great Schism, between 1378 and 1417, there were a series of Popes based in Rome and another series, known as the antipopes, who were based in which French city?

5. What is the principal flavouring of the Greek drink ouzo?

6. What term, meaning an 'entrance hall' in Latin, is used for the two upper cavities of the heart?

7. The opening line of which nineteenth-century Russian novel is

'All happy families resemble each other; each unhappy family is unhappy in its own way'?

8. What is the name of Europe's largest wading bird, which is noted for its distinctive bubbling call and long, downward-curving bill?

9. According to tradition, a true Cockney must be born within the sound of… what?

10. Which term for an expert in a particular field, especially one called on to explain the subject to the general public, comes from the Sanskrit for 'learned'?

11. In the film *Chariots of Fire*, which Olympic Gold medallist is portrayed by Ben Cross?

12. Which islands in the Atlantic take their name from the Portuguese for 'goshawks', although it is now believed that the early explorers who reached the islands misidentified buzzards instead?

13. Who wrote the music for the opera-oratorio 'Oedipus Rex', which was performed for the first time in Paris in 1927?

14. The city of Ise contains an important shine to Amaterasu, a sun goddess in which religion?

15. The sequel to the BBC drama series *Life on Mars* had what title that was also taken from a David Bowie song?

16. In the Roman calendar, the calends was the name given to which day of each month?

17. Which band topped the UK singles charts for the first time in May 1995 with 'Some Might Say'?

18. Which shrub that's noted for its attractive flowers and handsome foliage has a name meaning 'rose tree' in Greek?

19. Which American-born British sculptor created the 'brutalist' religious works *Genesis* and *Ecce Homo* in the 1930s?

20. Which Earl, who died in 1731, gave his name to a mechanical model of the solar system that was designed to show the motions of the planets around the Sun?

21. Which author of detective novels was thought to have died in a car crash in 1926, but was later discovered staying in a Yorkshire hotel, where she had registered as 'Mrs Neele'?

22. According to Islamic tradition, which angel dictated the Koran to the prophet Muhammad?

23. Which musician was known as the 'King of Skiffle' and enjoyed hits including 'Rock Island Line' and 'My Old Man's A Dustman'?

24. In which English county are the Quantock Hills?

25. Which British cyclist won a Gold, a Silver and a Bronze medal at the 2004 Olympics?

26. Parsley, Marsh, Common and Edible are European species of which amphibian?

27. How is the Spanish fashion designer Francisco Rabaneda y Cuervo better known; he is famed for his use of materials such as metal, paper and plastic, and also for his work on the film *Barbarella*?

28. The god Mimir, who is renowned for his knowledge and wisdom, is part of which people's mythology?

29. What was the name of the pirate radio DJ from the 'Brixton Broadcasting Corporation', who was created and played by Lenny Henry?

30. What name is given to the seasoned, jellied loaf made from the boned meat of the head of a pig or calf?

Are you smarter than a 10-year-old?

Some of the brightest 10- and 11-year-olds have taken on the Black Chair in Junior Mastermind *and demonstrated a depth of knowledge that would put many adults to shame. See how you get on with some of the questions posed to the contestants...*

Capital Cities

1. Which European capital city stands on the River Tagus and hosted the final of Euro 2004?

2. Which North African capital stands near the site of the ancient city of Carthage?

3. The name of which capital city combines the names of its two main parts, on either side of the Danube?

4. The capital of which Commonwealth country, with a Pacific coastline, was named Port Moresby by Captain John Moresby after his father, Admiral Fairfax Moresby?

5. Which capital city is known as Helsingfors in Swedish, one of the country's two official languages?

6. The American capital, Washington DC, stands on which river?

7. In which capital city's harbour is there a statue of Hans Christian Andersen's 'Little Mermaid'?

8. Which South American capital city is the nearest to the Equator?

9. Kyoto was the capital of which Asian country for over a thousand years?

10. The Rhodesian capital Salisbury was given what new name, after the country achieved independence as Zimbabwe?

11. Káthmandu is the capital of which Himalayan kingdom?

12. Piraeus is the chief port of which European capital city?

13. Which South American capital city has a Spanish name meaning 'Good Winds'?

14. What is the name of Ethiopia's capital city, which means 'new flower'?

15. Wenceslas Square is a popular boulevard in which European capital?

16. Cape Town is the legislative capital of South Africa, but which city is its administrative capital?

17. Which capital is known as 'the Eternal City', to which 'all roads lead'?

18. The capital of The Gambia was formerly known as Bathurst; by what name is it now known?

19. Which capital city in the far north of Europe has a name meaning 'Smoky Bay'?

20. Which Middle Eastern capital is believed to be the oldest continuously inhabited city in the world?

Answers

1. Lisbon

2. Tunis

3. Budapest

4. Papua New Guinea

5. Helsinki

6. Potomac – accept Anacostia

7. Copenhagen

8. Quito (capital of Ecuador)

9. Japan

10. Harare

11. Nepal

12. Athens

13. Buenos Aires

14. Addis Ababa

15. Prague

16. Pretoria or Tshwane

17. Rome

18. Banjul

19. Reykjavik

20. Damascus

THE MASTERMIND QUIZ BOOK

Show 20

Specialist Subject 20.1
Winston Churchill

1. Winston Churchill was born prematurely in which building, in 1874?

2. In his first speech to the Commons as Prime Minister, Churchill said, 'You ask, what is our aim? I can answer that in one word…' What word was it?

3. For which newspaper did Churchill write as a war correspondent, while serving as an officer in the South African Light Horse in 1900?

4. For which constituency did Churchill serve as a Liberal Member of Parliament for fourteen years from 1908 to 1922?

5. When Churchill became Prime Minister in May 1940, whom did he appoint as Lord President of the Council?

6. In January 1911, while serving as Home Secretary, Churchill controversially insisted on witnessing personally a confrontation between the police and anarchists, led by 'Peter the Painter', who were under siege in a house in which street?

7. What event of the Second World War prompted Churchill to

make his 'we shall fight on the beaches' speech in the House of Commons?

8. During the Boer War, Churchill was captured and imprisoned in which city, but escaped by climbing over the prison wall?

9. What was the name of Churchill's wife, whom he married in 1908?

10. What is the title of Churchill's only novel, a Ruritanian romance published in 1900?

11. According to Churchill's speech of March 1942, the fall of which city was 'the greatest disaster to British arms which our history records'?

12. Whom did Churchill appoint as Commander in Chief of the First Fleet at the start of the Great War, replacing Sir George Callaghan?

13. In 1922, Churchill bought which house in Kent as a family home and renovated it extensively, even taking up bricklaying to work on the property himself?

14. At which university was he collecting an honorary degree in 1943 when he gave his speech that included the line 'the price of greatness is responsibility'?

15. After returning to the Conservatives and Parliament in 1924, Churchill was immediately appointed to which Cabinet position that his father Lord Randolph had once held?

16. Churchill appointed two Labour MPs to his first war cabinet in 1940; Clement Attlee was one, who was the other?

17. Parliament finally passed a bill concerning the government of which then-colony in 1935, although Churchill had maintained

a vehement campaign against it?

18. As Chancellor, what important policy did Churchill enact in 1925? It is now generally regarded as one of his biggest mistakes.

19. About which Labour minister did Churchill quip, 'There but for the grace of God, goes God'?

20. In April 1948, which American magazine began serialising Churchill's war memoirs?

21. In a speech to the Commons made on 16 August 1945, Churchill said there were few virtues that which people did not possess, and few mistakes they had ever avoided?

22. Whom did Churchill appoint as his scientific adviser in 1940? He was a leading advocate for the heavy bombing campaign against Nazi Germany.

23. What name did Churchill give to the political party he tried to build in support of Edward VIII during the abdication crisis?

24. How old was Churchill when he resigned as Prime Minister for the last time?

25. At a dinner party, who reproached Churchill for being drunk? He replied that she was ugly but that he would be sober in the morning?

26. In 1959, Churchill was re-elected as an MP for the final time, retaining his seat in which constituency?

27. What did Churchill call for in his speech of September 1946 to the University of Zürich?

28. In 1898, Churchill took part in the famous cavalry charge at which battle in Sudan?

29. In 1963, what distinction was bestowed on Churchill, whose mother was American, by the US Congress?

30. Defending his decision to leave the Liberals and rejoin the Conservatives, Churchill claimed that 'anyone can rat, but it takes a certain amount of ingenuity to…' what?

General Knowledge 20.1

1. The name of which small breed of chicken is also used as a weight category in boxing?

2. What is the proper name, derived from Latin, for the thick, colourless, opalescent fluid that is constantly in the mouths of humans and other vertebrates?

3. Which sauce is known as crème anglaise in French?

4. What is the common name for trees of the genus Morus? The alba or white species is cultivated for the raising of silkworms, while the black and red species are raised for their fruits.

5. Which British sculptor's major works include the massive reclining figures outside the UNESCO Headquarters in Paris and the Lincoln Center in New York?

6. What was the name of the British working-class movement that was established in 1838, whose demands included votes for all men?

7. The novels of which American science fiction writer have formed the basis of films including *Blade Runner*, *Total Recall* and *Minority Report*?

8. Which word, of Old Norse origin, is used in Scotland to refer to

a narrow inlet of the sea, or a river estuary such as that of the Clyde?

9. What was the name of the all-star rock group, formed in 1988, which featured Bob Dylan, Jeff Lynne, Tom Petty, Roy Orbison and George Harrison?

10. What is the common name for the small, striped squirrel of the genus Tamias, which is found mainly in North America?

11. What is stored in a Leyden jar?

12. Which pressure group, formed by young Conservatives, takes its name from the location in the East End of London where they held their first meeting in February 1951?

13. For most of his professional basketball career, Michael Jordan played for which team?

14. Which Roman Emperor had his mother, Agrippina, put to death in AD 59, and did the same to his wife Octavia three years later?

15. In music, what English term that is derived from the Latin for 'against note', describes the art of combining two or more melodies that sound simultaneously?

16. According to John's Gospel, in which town did Jesus miraculously turn water into wine at a wedding feast?

17. In 2008, who won an Oscar for his role as the ruthless assassin Anton Chigurh in *No Country for Old Men*?

18. In humans, the word 'foetus' is used for the unborn child from the ninth week after conception. What word is usually used by medical professionals for the earlier stage?

19. John Sullivan took the name of which television sitcom from the title of an episode in his earlier series *Citizen Smith*?

20. What is the name of the group of seven islands in the southern Pacific Ocean that are an unincorporated territory of America, and which include Tutuila, on which the capital Pago Pago is situated?

21. The French literary historian René Étiemble is generally credited with popularising which word as a description of the intrusion of English into the French language?

22. Smooth, palmate, and warty are all species of which amphibian that's native to Britain?

23. What name is usually given to a small gabled window, projecting from a sloping roof?

24. Which province of Ireland includes Dublin and the south-eastern counties?

25. Which grape is the main component of the wine Chianti and is widely thought to take its name from an Italian phrase that literally means 'blood of Jupiter'?

26. In Rastafarianism, the name of which ancient city is used to denote evil?

27. The children's author Theodor Geisel, whose rhyming picture books feature a number of different anthropomorphic characters, was better known by what name?

28. What name, derived from the Dutch for 'to mumble', was given to the followers of the fourteenth-century English religious reformer John Wycliffe?

29. Which American businessman was involved in perfecting an electronic keyboard instrument that was patented in 1934 and named after him?

30. In a famous television series, which character tells his wife that her specialist subject on *Mastermind* should be 'the bleedin' obvious'?

Specialist Subject 20.2
The Novels of Charles Dickens

1. 'Whether I shall turn out to be the hero of my life, or whether that station will be held by anybody else, these pages must show' is the opening line of which Dickens novel?

2. In *Great Expectations*, how does Mr Jagger's clerk, Mr Wemmick, refer to his old father, to whom he is devoted?

3. In which novel does the title character go to seek his fortune in the USA?

4. What is the relationship between Oliver Twist and the villainous Monks, who bribed Fagin to keep Oliver in the gang?

5. In which Dickens novel is Christmas spent at Dingley Dell, the home of hospitable Mr Wardle?

6. Which Dickensian headmaster 'had but one eye, and the popular prejudice runs in favour of two'?

7. What is the subtitle of *Barnaby Rudge*? It refers to the events and the date which form the novel's backdrop?

8. In *A Tale of Two Cities*, what is Jarvis Lorry's three-word reply to the mysterious message that he receives while he is travelling to Paris as an agent for Tellson's Bank?

9. Which of the novels is narrated in parts by Esther Summerson?

10. The supposedly ten-year-old Ninetta Crummles appears on stage under what theatrical title, in *Nicholas Nickleby*?

11. In *The Mystery of Edwin Drood*, in which ancient Cathedral city is the Nuns' House Seminary for Young Ladies, of which Miss Twinkleton is the Principal?

12. In which novel is the establishment mentioned in the title taken over by the hideous dwarf, Daniel Quilp?

13. What is the name of Mr Pickwick's manservant?

14. Which novel features the fictional government department, the Circumlocution Office, whose principle is 'How not to do it'?

15. At the beginning of *Barnaby Rudge*, in which inn near Chigwell does the Parish Clerk, Solomon Daisy, tell a story of twenty-two years earlier?

16. Which novel, published in 1864–1865, was the last work that Dickens completed?

17. In *David Copperfield*, what is the first name of Mr Micawber?

18. Which Dickens novel was condemned by Thomas Macauley for its 'sullen socialism'?

19. What is the name of the rigorously strict Principal of the Brighton Boarding Academy that Paul Dombey attends from the age of six?

20. Which alternative word for an umbrella comes from the surname of the nurse in *Martin Chuzzlewit*?

21. In *Great Expectations*, which sulky enemy of Pip marries Estella?

22. Which debtors' prison formed part of the setting for *Little Dorrit*?

23. Which of Dickens' villains has daughters who are ironically

named Charity and Mercy?

24. In *Pickwick Papers*, a memorable by-election was fought between the Blue Party and the Buff Party, in which town?

25. In *The Old Curiosity Shop*, what is the name of the errand boy to the shop, who is devoted to Nell and tries to find her and her grandfather when they flee from Quilp to the country?

26. Tommy Traddles is described as the 'merriest and most miserable of all the boys' at which school, in *David Copperfield*?

27. In *Our Mutual Friend*, what is the name of the schoolmaster who takes up Charley Hexam as his special pupil and falls in love with Charley's sister, Lizzie?

28. In *Hard Times*, what is the occupation of Sleary, who helps Mr Gradgrind Senior arrange for his son Tom to flee abroad?

29. What is the name of the Manor House in which Miss Havisham has shut herself away after being jilted on her wedding day, many years earlier?

30. What unusual death befalls the eccentric scrap dealer Mr Krook in *Bleak House*?

General Knowledge 20.2

1. In medieval times, the tusk of the narwhal was prized as it was thought to be the horn of which creature?

2. In the Roman Republic, what title was held by the two chief magistrates, who were elected by the comitia centuriata and held power for one year?

3. In a comic opera by Rossini, which character introduces himself by singing the aria 'Largo Al Factotum'?

4. The island of Taiwan was historically known by what name, that means 'beautiful' in Portuguese?

5. Which brand of champagne takes its name from the married name of Nicole-Barbe Ponsardin? She took over her husband's business after his death in 1805.

6. The whooping and the demoiselle are two species of which tall wading bird that resembles a heron?

7. The Media Centre at which British sports ground won the Stirling Prize for Architecture in 1999?

8. What name was given to the series of American space probes that were launched from 1958 onwards? The first was intended to study the Moon, while the eleventh passed Neptune in 1990.

9. *Existentialism and Humanism* and *Being and Nothingness* are among whose philosophical works?

10. What term derived from Latin is used for the part of the human skull that encloses and protects the brain?

11. Which country won three consecutive Eurovision Song Contests between 1992 and 1994?

12. Which fragrant white spring flower that is used in France as a symbol of May Day, has just one species, whose scientific name is 'Convallaria majalis'?

13. What is the title of the last film that James Dean starred in before his death? For part of it, he appears as a middle-aged man with grey hair.

14. What name was given to the area of English settlement in

Ireland, around Dublin, that was originally established during the reign of Henry II?

15. Who first achieved UK chart success in 2000 with the album *White Ladder*?

16. The old Norse word 'foss' is used to refer to what type of geographical feature, such as Janet's Foss in the Yorkshire Dales?

17. Which acid gives oranges, lemons and limes their sharp taste?

18. Ulema is the name used for a group of religious and legal scholars in which religion?

19. In the final episode of the television series *The Young Ones*, the title characters are singing which Cliff Richard hit, when their double decker bus topples over the edge of a cliff?

20. What is the common name of the mammal that's also known as a pangolin?

21. Which spoof Western stars Cleavon Little, who is appointed as the Sheriff of Rock Ridge, and Gene Wilder, whose character is the only inmate of the town jail?

22. What name is given to the fibrous protein contained in hair and nails?

23. In 1990, which British golfer emulated the American Jack Nicklaus by successfully defending the US Masters title?

24. Which three-letter word for an evil spell or a curse is derived from a Pennsylvania Dutch word meaning 'to practise witchcraft'?

25. The artist Grayson Perry, who has a female alter-ego called 'Claire', won the 2003 Turner Prize for his works in which medium?

26. The Inca god creator Viracocha, who is said to have taken Inca culture to Polynesia, was also known by what name that was later given to a famous sailing craft?

27. Which of Shakespeare's plays features two pairs of twins? One pair are both called Antipholus, while the other pair are both called Dromio?

28. Which animal appears on the flag of California?

29. In AD 325, which city was the venue for the first ecumenical council of the Church, summoned by the Emperor Constantine to deal with the Arian controversy, and gave its name to a Creed that was formulated later?

30. Whose speech attacking Denis Healey's 1978 Budget was described, by Healey himself, as 'rather like being savaged by a dead sheep'?

Are you smarter than a 10-year-old?

Harry Potter

1. According to the Sorting Hat's song in *The Philosopher's Stone*, in which house 'dwell the brave at heart'?

2. In *The Goblet of Fire*, which country does Ireland beat in the Quidditch World Cup Final?

3. What does Dobby the house elf wear as a symbol of his enslavement?

4. What do the Dursleys give Harry, in addition to a note about the summer holidays, when he spends Christmas at Hogwarts in *The Chamber of Secrets*?

5. What is the name of the quill shop in the village of Hogsmeade?

6. Which two words are needed to make the Marauder's Map go blank after it has been used?

7. What is the name given to the type of bat-winged horses in *The Order of the Phoenix*, which Harry and Luna Lovegood can both see?

8. In *The Chamber of Secrets*, whose full name is an anagram of 'I AM LORD VOLDEMORT'?

9. What do the letters N, E, W and T stand for in NEWTs, the highest academic qualification that Hogwarts offers?

10. What is the first name of Mrs Dursley, Harry Potter's Muggle aunt?

11. According to Snape, which stone taken from the stomach of a goat will save you from most poisons?

12. When Harry asks Cho Chang to the Yule Ball, she tells him that she is already going with whom?

13. What creature is Hagrid's pet, Buckbeak, which is saved from execution when Hermione's Time-Turner takes her and Harry back three hours in time?

14. According to *The Order of the Phoenix*, which of the Death Eaters murdered the Prewetts?

15. What is the name of the three-headed dog that guards the entrance to the place where the philosopher's stone is being kept?

16. When Hedwig's wing is injured in *The Order of the Phoenix*, to whom does Harry take her for help?

17. In *The Chamber of Secrets*, Draco Malfoy calls Hermione which word for someone who is Muggle-born?

18. Who takes over from Oliver Wood as Gryffindor's Quidditch captain?

19. What noise is fatal to basilisks, according to the page of a book found in the hand of the petrified Hermione in *The Chamber of Secrets*?

20. What is the name of the cat that Hermione buys in *The Prisoner of Azkaban*?

1. Gryffindor

2. Bulgaria

3. Pillowcase

4. Toothpick

5. Scrivenshaft's (Quill Shop)

6. 'Mischief Managed'

7. Thestrals

8. Tom (Marvolo) Riddle

9. Nastily Exhausting Wizarding Tests

10. Petunia

11. Bezoar

12. Cedric Diggory

13. Hippogriff

14. Antonin Dolohov

15. Fluffy

16. Professor (Wilhelmina) Grubbly-Plank

17. Mudblood

18. Angelina Johnson

19. The Crowing of the Rooster

20. Crookshanks

Show 21

Specialist Subject 21.1
Frank Sinatra

1. Francis Albert Sinatra was born in which town in New Jersey, in 1915?

2. With which bandleader did Sinatra fight a legal battle to break his contract, in order to pursue a solo career?

3. Which of his LPs was number one on the first UK album chart, in July 1956?

4. Which famous actress became Sinatra's second wife?

5. Which record label, founded by Sinatra in 1961, was acquired by Warner Brothers two years later?

6. Which duet did his character Mike Connor perform with Liz Imbrie, played by Celeste Holm, in the 1956 film *High Society*?

7. With which actress did Sinatra have an affair while he was in New York in 1946, filming *It Happened in Brooklyn*?

8. Frank and his daughter Nancy had a number one hit in 1967 with which song?

9. Which honorary member of Sinatra's 'Rat Pack' was known as 'Chicky Baby'?

10. Which 1966 song was the first single released by Sinatra's own Reprise label to top the UK charts?

11. Barbara, the fourth Mrs Sinatra, had been married previously to which of the Marx Brothers?

12. What physical defect lead to him being classified 4-F by the military, keeping him out of active service during the Second World War?

13. Which pivotal film role did he supposedly get through Mafia influence? The scenario was repeated in *The Godfather*, with Al Martino playing a character loosely based on Sinatra?

14. Which of his songs spent more than two years on the UK singles charts?

15. In the late 1950s, after the death of her husband, Sinatra proposed to which actress but then humiliated her by rescinding the offer after Louella Parsons had leaked it?

16. Sinatra starred in which 1964 film that also featured Sammy Davis junior, Bing Crosby, Dean Martin as Little John, and Peter Falk as Guy Gisborne?

17. After his move to Capitol, whose arrangements on the 1954 album *Young at Heart* helped revive Sinatra's singing career?

18. What was the unfortunate title of the film Sinatra was shooting with his daughter Nancy, when her first husband, Tommy Sands, walked out on her?

19. As well as his future fiancée Juliet Prowse, Sinatra also met which world leader on the set of the 1960 film *Can-Can*?

20. What was the title of Sinatra's 1973 comeback album, which was released just over two years after he had announced his 'retirement' in June 1971?

21. With whom did he re-record the classic Cole Porter song 'I've Got You Under My Skin' as a duet in 1993?

22. Two years after winning an Academy Award for *From Here to Eternity*, he was nominated for Best Actor after playing Frankie Machine in which film?

23. What was the name of the accompanist and guitarist who arranged and conducted the 1962 album *Sinatra and Strings*?

24. The Reverend Jesse Jackson and the UN Special Committee on Apartheid criticised Sinatra for appearing in which city in August 1981?

25. What nickname, borrowed from a cartoon character, did Sinatra's third wife Mia Farrow use for him?

26. With which Oscar-winning song did he first top the British charts in 1954?

27. Which of the Rat Pack played Jimmy Foster in the original version of *Ocean's Eleven*, in which Sinatra starred as Danny Ocean?

28. Which talent agency had dropped Sinatra in 1952 when his throat haemorrhaged and his career seemed over?

29. Sinatra collaborated with which jazz musician on the 1964 album *It Might as Well Be Swing*?

30. Which 1988 cartoon film used an archive recording of Sinatra for the voice of the Singing Sword?

General Knowledge 21.1

1. Igneous, metamorphic and sedimentary are the three main classifications of... what?

2. In August 1939, the Government Code and Cypher School moved from London to which house in Buckinghamshire, which was the former home of the London financier Herbert Samuel Leon?

3. Ananas comosus is the botanical name for which tropical fruit that was found by Columbus on the island of Guadeloupe?

4. Britain's largest seabird, which was formerly called the solan goose, is now commonly known by what name?

5. According to Mark Antony in Shakespeare's *Julius Caesar*, who was 'the noblest Roman of them all'?

6. The historic region of Mesopotamia forms the greater part of which modern-day country?

7. Which British film company, noted for its low-budget horror movies, has its origins in companies set up in the 1930s by the cinema chain owner Enrique Carreras and the jewellery store owner William Hinds?

8. According to the Bible, the walls of which city fell down when the Israelites, led by Joshua, blew their trumpets?

9. Which opera by Gounod, about a scholar who sold his soul to the devil, was based on a dramatic poem by Goethe?

10. Which word for a meeting, at which candidates in an election address potential voters, comes from an Old Norse word meaning 'household assembly held by a leader'?

11. Which group of British artists, formed in 1911, took their name from an area of Greater London that was often used as the setting for paintings by Walter Sickert?

12. What name is given to a chemical or nuclear process which yields products that initiate further processes of the same kind, such as in a nuclear reactor?

13. Andy Bell and Vince Clarke were the members of which chart-topping pop act?

14. In ancient times, which sea was referred to as the Pontus Euxinus, or 'Hospitable Sea', apparently in an attempt to placate the powers that were believed to control the elements?

15. In the television series *Star Trek*, which character's mother is Amanda Grayson, a schoolteacher from Earth?

16. Which tubes that are named after a sixteenth-century Italian anatomist, connect the ovaries to the uterus in mammals?

17. Which London football team won their first trophy for nine years, by defeating Chelsea in the 2008 Carling Cup final?

18. What term is used to describe a stag with twelve or more points on its antlers?

19. Leslie Ash, Toyah Wilcox and Sting all appeared in which cult 1979 film about Mods and Rockers?

20. Which English cathedral features what is believed to be the UK's oldest working clock, dating from medieval times?

21. In grammar, what name is given to a word that is placed before a noun or pronoun to express the relation between it and another word?

22. Lakshmi, the Hindu goddess of wealth and fortune, is known by what name in the Ramayana, where she is the wife of Rama?

23. Which planet's deep blue colour is due to the absorption of red and infra-red light by methane gas in its atmosphere?

24. Which tropical plant of the pea family was once widely cultivated for the dark blue dye that can be produced from its leaves?

25. What was the name of the land of giants that Gulliver visited in the second part of his Travels?

26. In 1759, which British General was killed on the battlefield of the Plains of Abraham, during the victory which ended French rule in Canada?

27. In the cocktail known as a Rusty Nail, Scotch whisky provides one part of the alcoholic content; which liqueur that is also of Scottish origin provides the other?

28. Port of Spain is the capital of which Caribbean island?

29. Which American singer, who had originally been a jazz pianist, had UK top ten hits with 'Somewhere Along The Way' and 'When I Fall In Love'?

30. What is the usual name given to the statue of a small boy urinating, which was erected in Brussels in 1619?

Specialist Subject 21.2
Leonardo da Vinci

1. Leonardo's painting, widely held to be a portrait of the wife of Francesco del Giocondo, is best known by what name?

2. What was the first name of Leonardo's mother, who was never married to his father, Piero da Vinci?

3. The novelist Matteo Bandello described Leonardo painting which of his works 'from sunrise until the dusk of evening, never laying down the brush, but continuing to paint without remembering to eat or drink'?

4. In the mid to late 1460s, Leonardo was apprenticed to which Florentine sculptor and painter?

5. In 1503, Leonardo was involved in plans to change the course of the river Arno so that which nearby rival city of Florence would be cut off from the sea?

6. Leonardo was commissioned to decorate one wall of the Florentine Council Chamber with scenes from the Battle of Anghiari; which artist and arch-rival was invited to decorate the opposite wall?

7. Leonardo painted his fresco *The Last Supper* in the refectory of which Church and Dominican Convent?

8. For which powerful Milanese family did Leonardo work around 1483, with one commission being for an equestrian monument to the former Duke of Milan?

9. What is the popular name for Leonardo's portrait of Cecilia Gallerani painted in the 1480s?

10. In 1481, Leonardo was commissioned to paint which biblical scene for the high altar of the San Donato a Scopeto monastery just outside?

11. From 1502 to 1503, Leonardo worked as a military engineer for which infamous son of Pope Alexander VI?

12. In which city was the court of Isabelle d'Este where Leonardo stayed briefly around 1500?

13. To which student and long-time companion did Leonardo bequeath his notebooks, drawings and instruments?

14. Leonardo and his friend, the accomplished mathematician Luca Pacioli, collaborated on which book, first published in 1509?

15. In Leonardo's 1478 painting *Benois Madonna*, the infant Jesus is reaching for what object in the Virgin Mary's hand?

16. Which emissary of the Florentine republic and author of a famous work on politics became a close friend of Leonardo during their service with Cesare Borgia?

17. What name, from the Greek for 'bird' and 'wings', is given to a flying machine with flapping wings, of which Leonardo, with his apparent obsession with the possibility of man-powered flight, drew many detailed diagrams?

18. In 1994, which businessman and philanthropist bought the collection of Leonardo's scientific work known as the 'Codex Leicester'?

19. In a letter found in the 1950s, believed to have been written by Leonardo in around 1503, he offers to design what major structure for the Ottoman Sultan, Bayezid II?

20. What is the bearded ascetic on the left-hand side of Leonardo's *The Madonna of Foligno* carrying in his left hand?

21. Leonardo helped his student Rustici to make a large bronze sculpture of which biblical figure teaching, over the north door of the Baptistery in Florence?

22. Leonardo's last major project was to design a new palace and town at which location in the centre of France?

23. In which branch of science did Leonardo reputedly collaborate

with Marcantonio della Torre in around 1510?

24. According to a popular legend, now disproved, Leonardo died in the arms of which king?

25. His study of the proportions of the human form, *Homo ad Circulum*, has what alternative name, after a Roman architect?

26. Which architect and author, and great exponent on Brunelleschi, had written a pioneering treatise called *On Painting* in 1435? It was a major influence on Leonardo.

27. What was the name of the manor-house, near Amboise on the River Loire, which was Leonardo's last home? It was provided for him by the French king, Francis I.

28. In 1476, Leonardo and others were accused anonymously of engaging in homosexual acts with which 17-year-old artist's model?

29. What was Leonardo commissioned to design for the Florentines in 1515? They used it to greet the French king on his entry to Lyons on 12 July that year.

30. Whose work, now generally known as *Lives of the Artists* was first published in 1550? It is a major biographical source on Leonardo?

General Knowledge 21.2

1. In 1988, which examination replaced O-levels and CSEs?

2. In a notorious speech in Birmingham in April 1968, who said, 'Like the Roman, I seem to see the River Tiber foaming with much blood'?

3. Which singer sculpted the statue of Eleanor Rigby, situated in Stanley Street, Liverpool?

4. What is the name of the model village on the banks of the Clyde, which was created in 1785 by David Dale, but later taken over by his son-in-law Robert Owen?

5. Coburg, Vienna and Bloomer are all types of which food?

6. The name of which Celtic people, who inhabited northern Scotland, comes from the Latin for 'painted' because of their custom of painting or tattooing their bodies?

7. The title of which John Steinbeck novel is a four-word phrase taken from a Robert Burns poem?

8. Red, silver, sugar, Norway and Japanese are all species of which tree?

9. Which playwright's works for television included *Blackeyes* and *The Singing Detective*?

10. Which Cardinal was effectively the Chief Minister to Louis XIII of France from 1624, until his death in 1642?

11. Which island nation's language has its roots in Arabic, but is written in a Latin script?

12. Which term for a Hindu or Sikh spiritual leader is derived originally from the Sanskrit for 'venerable'?

13. Which Scottish group's album *Screamadelica* was the first winner of the Mercury Music Prize, in November 1992?

14. In humans, which gland is situated in the throat below the larynx, and controls the rate of metabolism?

15. Which flightless Australian bird derives its name from the

Portuguese for 'ostrich'?

16. Which river flows in a generally easterly direction for around 1,770 miles before emptying into the Indian Ocean, but is believed to have only six major crossing points?

17. In 2008, who hosted a television series and published a book both called *How to Cheat at Cooking*?

18. What name is given to the branch of chemistry that is concerned with the study of compounds of carbon?

19. In Spanish, what name is given to a wine-shop, or a place for storing and maturing wine?

20. In anatomy, what name is given to a tiny opening, especially in the skin, through which sweat and other substances pass to the surface?

21. Which highly stylised art form, associated with the Eastern Roman Empire and noted for its icons and mosaics, was eventually challenged by artists such as Giotto and Duccio?

22. Some species of which brightly coloured small marine fish are particularly known for clearing parasites from larger fish, and even cleaning their teeth for them?

23. In a standard modern symphony orchestra, the first violins appear immediately to the left of the conductor; which stringed instruments appear immediately to the right of the conductor?

24. People born on which island, off the coast of England, are referred to as Caulkheads? Residents of the island who were not born there are known as Overners.

25. Which play by Oscar Wilde is subtitled 'A Trivial Comedy for Serious People'?

26. Who succeeded his relative Trajan as the Roman Emperor in AD 117?

27. Which race was first held in 1903? It was originally sponsored by the magazine *L'Auto*, which was noted for being printed on yellow paper.

28. Whom did Paul famously describe as 'the beloved physician' in his Epistle to the Colossians?

29. Which Gaelic word is used for a social gathering involving traditional music and dancing?

30. Victor Mature refused to wrestle with a lion in which Biblical epic, even when he was told that it had no teeth, on the grounds that he didn't wish to be gummed to death?

Are you smarter than a 10-year-old?

Queen Victoria

1. In 1824, Louise Lehzen was appointed to which post? She was an important influence during Victoria's childhood.

2. What was the name of the dog that was Victoria's favourite pet from when she was 14 until it died in 1840?

3. Which Prime Minister flattered Victoria and referred to her as 'the Fairy Queen'?

4. What important event in Victoria's life took place in the Chapel Royal of St James's Palace on 10 February 1840?

5. Which Scottish castle, later to become the Royal family's summer home, did Victoria and Albert first visit in 1848?

6. How many of Victoria's nine children were girls?

7. Which European language that Victoria spoke fluently helped when she first met Prince Albert?

8. What was the name of the glass structure built in Hyde Park, where Victoria opened the Great Exhibition on 1 May 1851?

9. In 1865, which of Victoria's servants was given the official title 'the Queen's Highland Servant'?

10. On 13 June 1842, what form of transport did Victoria use for the first time, to travel from Slough to Paddington?

11. Of which illness did Prince Albert die at Windsor Castle on 14 December 1861?

12. In which wooden cottage, built in the grounds of Osborne House, were the Royal children taught manual and housekeeping skills?

13. Which Prime Minister did Victoria so dislike that, at first, she refused to send a letter of condolence to his widow in May 1898?

14. Which anaesthetic did Victoria use for the first time to ease the pain during the birth of Prince Leopold in 1853?

15. Which nurse recounted her stories of the Crimean War to Victoria during a dinner at Balmoral in 1856?

16. What royal title did Victoria bestow on her husband Albert by letters patent on 25 June 1857?

17. Victoria's eldest son, the future King Edward VII, was christened Albert Edward; by what name was he known to his family?

18. To which literary post was Alfred Lord Tennyson appointed by Victoria in November 1850?

19. From 1841 onward what did Prince Albert have imported from Germany every year for the family's festive celebrations?

20. Which Jubilee was celebrated in 1897 to mark Victoria's sixty years on the throne?

Answers

1. (Victoria's) Governess

2. Dash

3. (Benjamin) Disraeli

4. She married (Albert)

5. Balmoral

6. Five

7. German

8. Crystal Palace

9. John Brown

10. Train or Railway

11. Typhoid (fever)

12. Swiss Cottage

13. (William) Gladstone

14. Chloroform – accept Trichloromethane

15. Florence Nightingale

16. Prince Consort

17. Bertie

18. Poet Laureate

19. Christmas trees

20. Diamond

Show 22

Specialist Subject 22.1
The Life and Reign of Henry VIII

1. What was the name of Henry VIII's older brother, who was married to Catherine of Aragon in 1501 but died shortly afterwards, making Henry heir to the throne?

2. In 1530, who died at Leicester Abbey while under arrest, during his journey to London?

3. Which form of address, derived from the Latin for 'greatness', was used for the King during Henry's reign, in addition to the traditional 'Your Grace' or 'Your Highness'?

4. In the late 1520, Wolsey presented which palace that he had begun building in 1515 to Henry?

5. In 1513, which battle between the English and the Scots led to the death of the Scottish King James IV?

6. To which woman did Henry give the title Marquess of Pembroke?

7. On which date in 1511 did Queen Catherine give birth to Henry's first son, Henry Prince of Wales, who died soon afterwards?

8. Which book of the Bible warns of the consequences 'if a man takes his brother's wife', which Henry used to justify his divorce from Catherine of Aragon?

9. Who told Solicitor General Sir Richard Rich, 'I am sorrier for your perjury than mine own peril,' after he had been condemned to death on the basis of evidence produced by Rich?

10. The 1533 Act in Restraint of Appeals began by stating that the realm of England was... what, and therefore not subject to the authority of Rome?

11. By the Treaty of Greenwich in July 1543, Henry's five-year-old son, the future Edward VI, was betrothed to which six-month-old baby girl?

12. Henry wrote the *Defence of the Seven Sacraments* as a response to which author's treatise *De Captivitate Babylonica*?

13. In July 1545, Henry witnessed personally the sinking of which of his ships off the coast of Portsmouth?

14. Henry met which of his wives for the first time at the Bishop of Rochester's Palace?

15. In January 1536, Henry was knocked unconscious during what type of sporting contest?

16. In 1535, Henry granted which of his ministers the title of Vice-Gerent (meaning Deputy) in Spirituals?

17. Which heraldic bird featured on the badge of Anne Boleyn?

18. Henry was a patron of which German artist, who settled in England in 1532 and painted a number of portraits of Henry and his prospective wives?

19. In 1519, Henry sent Richard Pace on an unsuccessful mission to

obtain which title for him?

20. Which noble family was accused of being involved in a treasonous plot that led to the execution of one of its members, and the condemnation of another, at the end of Henry's reign?

21. Which act of March 1534 declared Henry's marriage to Catherine to be 'utterly void and annulled'?

22. To which scholar and humanist was Henry introduced by Thomas More in 1499?

23. In 1540, Thomas Cromwell was granted which earldom shortly before he was executed for treason?

24. What Latin name was given to the survey made in 1535 to determine the revenues of the church in England and Wales?

25. What was the emblem depicted on the badge and banner of the Pilgrimage of Grace, an uprising against Henry's religious policies, led by Robert Aske?

26. Henry was buried in 1547 in St George's Chapel, Windsor, alongside the body of which of his six wives?

27. Which of his counsellors did Henry omit from the executors of his will because of his 'troublesome nature'?

28. What was the name of Jane Seymour's family home in Savernake in Wiltshire?

29. Who did Catherine Parr marry after Henry's death?

30. Built on Henry's orders in the 1530s, what type of building was Hampton Court's Great House of Easement?

General Knowledge 22.1

1. Which tree-dwelling lizard is noted primarily for its ability to change colour?

2. The name of which English county was restored to the map as a Unitary Authority on 1 April 1997? The area had been incorporated into Leicestershire for the previous twenty three years.

3. Which cartoon character was portrayed as the Sorcerer's Apprentice in the 1940 film *Fantasia*?

4. Which word means a fixed number of people who are required to attend a meeting for its proceedings to be regarded as valid?

5. Which painting by John Everett Millais was used in a famous advertisement for Pear's Soap? It was originally called 'A Child's World'?

6. Which Athenian law-giver of the seventh century BC, whose penal code punished even trivial offences with death, has given his name to any system of repressive legal measures?

7. Which French literary heroine of the nineteenth century is seduced by Rodolphe Boulanger?

8. What name is given to the technique of growing plants in a liquid nutrient solution, instead of soil?

9. Who wrote the music and lyrics for *A Funny Thing Happened on the Way to the Forum*, which was first performed on Broadway in 1962?

10. In physics, which standard or SI unit of pressure is equal to one Newton per square metre?

11. What was the surname of the brothers Adolphe and Edouard-Jean, who began producing an orange liqueur in Angers in 1849?

12. Which holy book consists of 114 chapters known as surahs?

13. What deliberately ironic name was chosen for the band co-formed by Paul Heaton in Hull in 1989, after his former group The Housemartins split up?

14. Which city stands at the western end of the Canadian Pacific Railway?

15. Which word for a waterproof jacket is also used colloquially for an unfashionable person with obsessive interests?

16. In human anatomy, what name is given to the large muscle group in the front of the thigh, consisting of four muscles that act to extend the legs at the knee?

17. Which play by Anthony Schaffer was filmed in 1972 and 2007, with Michael Caine in one of the leading roles each time?

18. During the Second World War, the Home Secretaries Sir John Anderson and Herbert Morrison, gave their names to... what?

19. Which piece of sporting equipment was invented in 1902 by a London dentist called Jack Marks? It was first used by the boxer Ted 'Kid' Lewis.

20. Which butterfly takes its name from the small white patch on the underside of each wing that resembles a punctuation mark?

21. Which German composer, whose most famous work is his First Violin Concerto in G Minor, was the conductor of the Liverpool Philharmonic Society from 1880 to 1883?

22. Stibium is the Latin name for which chemical element that has been given the symbol Sb as a result?

23. Which type of curry has a name that can be roughly translated from Hindi as 'onions twice'?

24. In which county is Britain's deepest cave, known as Titan, which is around 460 feet deep?

25. In painting, what Italian term is used for thick, opaque oil paint applied with a brush, knife or fingers for textural effect?

26. Who succeeded his father, Vespasian, as the Emperor of Rome in AD 79 and directed the restoration of Campania after the eruption of Vesuvius?

27. In which cult television series was 'the Village' patrolled by a white balloon called Rover?

28. According to a well-known proverb, which King of Israel was renowned for his furious chariot driving?

29. Which novel by C.S. Lewis takes the form of a series of letters between a senior devil and his novice nephew Wormwood, giving him advice on how to secure the damnation of an earthly man known as 'the Patient'?

30. Which British political party's 2007 manifesto advocated giving McDonald's the contract for prison catering, and selling socks in packs of three for when one gets lost?

Specialist Subject 22.2
The England Football Team since 1945

1. Which England player scored at the World Cup finals of 1998, 2002 and 2006?

2. Haitian-born Larry Gaetjens scored the goal that gave which country a shock victory over England at the 1950 World Cup?

3. Who scored England's third penalty in the shoot-out against Spain in the quarter finals of Euro '96, six years after seeing his spot-kick saved in the 1990 World Cup semi-final?

4. Which England player won his 74th international cap in the 1966 World Cup final, making him the most-capped player in the team that day?

5. To which country did England lose out in qualification for the 1978 World Cup finals on goal difference?

6. Who scored for England after only 27 seconds of a World Cup match against France in 1982?

7. Whose shot squirmed through goalkeeper Robert Green's hands for the USA's equaliser in England's opening match at the 2010 World Cup?

8. In the 1966 World Cup finals, which was the only one of England's opponents that they failed to beat?

9. Who kept goal for England in the 3-2 defeat to West Germany, in the 1970 World Cup quarter-final?

10. Polish goalkeeper Tomaszewski, who played superbly in the 1-1 draw that stopped England from qualifying for the 1974 World Cup, was dubbed a... what by Brian Clough before the game?

11. Against Italy in 1948, who became the first goalkeeper to captain England in the twentieth century?

12. Who were England playing in the 1982 World Cup finals, when Kevin Keegan came on as a substitute to make his final international appearance?

13. Gary Lineker scored six goals for England in the 1986 World Cup finals; who scored England's other goal?

14. Who was the only England player to score during the penalty shoot-out against Portugal, in the quarter-final of the 2006 World Cup?

15. Who did England beat in their first-ever game at a World Cup finals tournament, in 1950?

16. Who scored England's first goal against Brazil in a 2-0 win at the Maracana in 1984; it was the first time England had won away against the Brazilians?

17. Which Nottingham Forest midfielder became the 1,000th player to be capped by England when he replaced Glenn Hoddle in a friendly against West Germany in September 1987?

18. On which Italian island did England play their first round group matches in the 1990 World Cup finals?

19. Which striker, who scored 44 international goals, won the last of his 57 England caps against Austria in Vienna in 1967?

20. Against Morocco in 1986, who became the first England footballer to be sent off at the World Cup finals?

21. In which Japanese city, which had an indoor stadium with a retractable pitch, did England beat Argentina 1-0 at the 2002 World Cup finals?

22. Gary Lineker's final game for England, against Sweden at Euro '92, ended prematurely when he was substituted after 61 minutes. Which player replaced him?

23. Billy Wright and which other player appeared for the team in the 1950, 1954 and 1958 finals tournaments?

24. How many players did Sven Goran Eriksson substitute during a friendly against Australia in 2003?

25. Who made one appearance for England in the 1966 World Cup and was not picked again for over 11 years, until Ron Greenwood selected him along with five other Liverpool players for a match against Switzerland?

26. Who scored West Germany's equaliser in the last minute of the 1966 World Cup final, to send the match into extra time?

27. By what score did Hungary beat England at Wembley in 1953 (before winning the return 7-1 the following year)?

28. Whose goal against Belgium, in the last minute of extra time, took England through to the 1990 World Cup quarter-finals?

29. During a European Championship game against Yugoslavia in 1968, who became the first England player to be sent off in a full international?

30. In which city did England win a World Cup qualifier, away to Germany, by five goals to one in September 2001, with Michael Owen scoring a hat-trick?

General Knowledge 22.2

1. Which 1977 film was later tag-lined 'May the Force be with you'?

2. In human biology, what substances derive their name from the Greek for 'first', because of their primary importance to the body?

3. Raymond Chandler's novel *The Big Sleep* featured which private investigator?

4. The raven is the largest member of which family of birds?

5. The name of which county in Kentucky has become a generic term for whiskey made principally from maize?

6. Which religious faith was founded in mid-nineteenth-century Iran, by Mirza Hoseyn Ali Nuri?

7. The artist Jerome von Aeken, who was born in s'Hertogenbosch in the Netherlands around 1450, is better known by what name?

8. Slieve Donard, the highest point in Northern Ireland, is in which mountain range?

9. *The Minister of Divine* is an American version of which BBC television comedy series?

10. In French history, what name is given to the period from 20 March 1815, when Napoleon re-entered Paris after escaping from his exile on Elba, until 29 June, when he abdicated as Emperor?

11. Which future Prime Minister wrote his first novel, *Vivian Grey*, in an attempt to pay off his debts? It was originally published anonymously in 1826?

12. What name is given to the number one, followed by one hundred zeroes? It is said to have been coined by the nine-year-old nephew of the American mathematician, Edward Kasner.

13. Which chart-topping Beatles' single begins with the lines 'Standing in the dock at Southampton, trying to get to Holland or France'?

14. Which large coniferous tree is the only species of pine that is native to Britain?

15. Who was the only player to beat Bjorn Borg in a Wimbledon Men's Singles final?

16. When Czechoslovakia split into two separate countries in 1993, which city became the capital of Slovakia?

17. The ballad opera *Polly* by John Gay was the sequel to which of his earlier works?

18. Which place on the slopes of Mount Parnassus was the site of the most important temple dedicated to the god Apollo, and to his oracle?

19. What term was coined in 1952 by the art critic Harold Rosenberg, to describe paintings created by activities such as riding a bicycle over the canvas?

20. Renal calculus is the medical term for what painful human ailment?

21. Which bungling magician used to come on stage to the tune 'The Sheikh Of Araby'?

22. What term is used for the procedure by which an MP who is persistently disobedient can be suspended from the Commons' chamber?

23. Which cartoon character was usually shown at the beginning of each episode operating a dinosaur powered crane at the Rockhead and Quarry Construction Company?

24. Which company was formed in 1600, during the reign of Elizabeth I, to compete with Spain, Portugal and the Dutch for the spice trade?

25. Which pasta is made in the form of narrow ribbons, and takes its name from the Italian for 'little tongues'?

26. The Republic of Suriname, on the north-east coast of South America, was a colony of which country before gaining independence in 1975?

27. Pelham and Grenville were the forenames of which novelist?

28. Which word, from the Latin for a wild beast, is used to describe an animal that has run wild after being domesticated?

29. Which percussion instrument (consists of tuned metal bars, and) takes its name from the German for 'bell' and 'play'?

30. Which of the Apostles is the Patron Saint of tax collectors and accountants?

Are you smarter than a 10-year-old?

The Simpsons

1. What was Marge Simpson's surname before she married?

2. According to Marge, in the episode 'Lisa's First Word', what were the first words ever spoken by Bart?

3. What is the name of the legendary saxophone player who teaches Lisa how to express her sadness through music?

4. In the episode 'The Regina Monologues', Homer mistakes Tony Blair for which TV comedy character?

5. The Simpsons' family dog is Santa's Little Helper, but what is their pet cat called?

6. Which platoon, described as 'the fightingest squad in the fightingest company in the third fightingest battalion in the army' did Grampa Simpson command during the Second World War?

7. In 'The Joy of Sects', which sect promises to take the Simpsons away in a spaceship to a cosmic paradise known as Blisstonia?

8. In which episode does stunt motorcyclist Lance Murdock crash while attempting to jump over Homer at Nero's Palace, Las Vegas?

9. What is the surname of Krusty the Clown's former sidekick Sideshow Bob?

10. What is the name of the nearby town with which Springfield has a great rivalry in all things?

11. When Bart is about to be murdered by Sideshow Bob in the episode 'Cape Fear', his last request is to ask Bob to sing the whole of which Gilbert and Sullivan operetta?

12. In 'A Fish called Selma', who talks Selma into illegally letting him pass his driver's license vision test in exchange for a dinner date?

13. What type of food franchise does Marge buy after being voted out of the Springfield Investorettes?

14. In 'You Only Move Twice', Homer Simpson accepts a job with which corporation when he moves the family from Springfield to live at Cypress Creek?

15. Homer took Marge to see a psychiatrist named Dr Zweig to cure her fear of what?

16. In a parody of a famous *Dallas* storyline, who was finally revealed to have shot Mr Burns?

17. Which composer does Bart play in the episode 'Margical History Tour'?

18. How did the town of Springfield commemorate Lisa's achievement in finishing second in the National Spelling Bee?

19. In the episode 'I am Furious Yellow', which internet cartoon series does Bart create, based on Homer?

20. Which trademark saying of Homer's entered the Oxford English Dictionary in June 2001?

1. Bouvier

2. 'Aye Carumba'

3. Bleeding Gums Murphy

4. Mr Bean

5. Snowball (II)

6. The Flying Hellfish

7. The Movementarians

8. 'Viva Ned Flanders'

9. Terwilliger

10. Shelbyville

11. *HMS Pinafore*

12. Troy McClure

13. Pretzels

14. Globex Corporation

15. Flying

16. Maggie (Simpson)

17. Mozart

18. They carved her face or head into the mountain

19. 'Angry Dad'

20. D'oh!

Show 23

Specialist Subject 23.1
Stanley Kubrick

1. Vincent d'Onofrio was asked to gain over 60 pounds in order to play a leading part in which of Kubrick's films?

2. Which film director played Victor Ziegler in Kubrick's last film, *Eyes Wide Shut*?

3. Kubrick shot a sequence featuring Scatman Crothers crossing a road 96 times during the making of which film?

4. What was the name of the renegade general played by Sterling Hayden in *Dr Strangelove*?

5. The title sequence of *A Clockwork Orange* is accompanied by an electronic version of which English composer's *Music for the Funeral of Queen Mary*?

6. Which Kubrick film, based on historical fact, dealt with the corrupt mechanisms by which three French soldiers in the First World War came to be executed as an example to their peers for refusing to follow orders?

7. Which actor's role in *Full Metal Jacket* was scripted largely from his foul-mouthed improvisations?

8. What was the name of fictional snowbound hotel in Colorado that was the setting for the novel and film *The Shining*?

9. Which of Kubrick's films received seven Oscar nominations?

10. Later to become famous for parts including a TV detective, which Oldham-born actor's first credited film role was as gang-member Dim in *A Clockwork Orange*?

11. In *Dr Strangelove*, the message on one bomb in the bay of the B-52 Alabama Angel is 'Dear John'; what greeting is on the other?

12. Which actor was approached by Kubrick to play the role of Napoleon in a film project that was never realised?

13. What is the subtitle of the first part of *2001: A Space Odyssey*, set among herbivorous apelike creatures that evolve into modern man?

14. Which virtuoso of the Moog synthesizer provided the electronic music and sound effects in *A Clockwork Orange*, and later worked on *The Shining*?

15. Kubrick replaced Anthony Mann as the director of which film, after just one week's shooting?

16. Who played the title role in Kubrick's controversial adaptation of Nabakov's novel *Lolita*?

17. From *A Clockwork Orange* onwards, all of Kubrick's films were produced by which film studio?

18. Which British character actor provided the narration for *Barry Lyndon*?

19. In *A Clockwork Orange*, what is the name of the technique employed to turn Alex against violence by a form of aversion therapy?

20. In *Spartacus*, in which press baron's mansion did Kubrick shoot the scenes set in Crassus' villa?

21. Ted de Corsia, who appeared uncredited as a legionnaire in *Spartacus*, had a much larger role as Patrolman Randy Kennan in which earlier Kubrick film?

22. Who said modestly of *2001: A Space Odyssey*, 'It reflects 90 per cent on the imagination of Stanley Kubrick, about 5 per cent on the genius of the special effects people and perhaps 5 per cent on my own contribution'?

23. In *Dr Strangelove*, Peter Sellers plays the title character as well as Group Captain Lionel Mandrake and who else?

24. Later to find fame in the Bond films, which actress played Nurse Mary Lore in *Lolita*?

25. A disused gas works in Beckton, East London doubled for which Vietnamese city during the filming of *Full Metal Jacket*?

26. Douglas Rain has what role in *2001: A Space Odyssey*?

27. In which state is Timberline Lodge, the venue that provided the exterior shots of the hotel in *The Shining*?

28. Which sitcom actor played Captain Quinn in *Barry Lyndon*?

29. Who won a Best Supporting Actor Oscar for his performance as Lentulus Batiatus in *Spartacus*?

30. What are the final spoken words of *Dr Strangelove*, spoken by the title character, which are followed by shots of mushroom clouds as the Doomsday machine is triggered?

General Knowledge 23.1

1. What type of headgear takes its name from a battle in the Crimean War?

2. On 29 December 1170, who was murdered by Reginald Fitz Urse, Hugh de Morville, William de Tracy and Richard le Bret, who believed they were fulfilling the wishes of King Henry II?

3. The works of which English painter and engraver, born in 1697, included *A Harlot's Progress* and *A Rake's Progress*?

4. In cows and other ruminants, what are the rumen, the reticulum, omasum and the abomasum?

5. Alan Ayckbourn wrote the lyrics for the unsuccessful 1975 musical *Jeeves*; who wrote the music?

6. Which northern English county is known as the 'Land of the Prince Bishops'?

7. Which novel by George Eliot opens with the line 'Miss Brooke had that kind of beauty which seems to be thrown into relief by poor dress'?

8. In the Roman Catholic church, what name is given to the assembly of cardinals which meets to elect a new pope?

9. Who was the longest-serving Blue Peter presenter? He hosted the show from 1965 until 1978.

10. Lateral Epicondylitis is the medical term for which sporting injury, caused by excessive twisting movements of the hand?

11. What is the name of the Eastern European soup made from beetroot, which gives it a strong red colour?

12. Which publisher and newspaper proprietor was the Labour MP for Buckingham from 1964 until 1970?

13. Which two words are inscribed on the front of the Victoria Cross?

14. In Greek mythology, what name was given to the monstrous whirlpool that lurked opposite the cave-dwelling sea monster Scylla, and was said to swallow unwary travellers in the Straits of Messina?

15. Which private detective was played by Richard Roundtree in a 1971 film, and again in a 2000 film of the same title, in which Samuel L. Jackson starred as his nephew?

16. The two branches of which river meet near the Sudanese city of Khartoum?

17. Which Austrian-born composer wrote over 600 songs, including settings of poems by Goethe and Schiller, before his death at the age of 31 in 1828?

18. In gardening, what term is used for the clipping of trees or hedges into decorative shapes?

19. Victory in a close race in which sport is sometimes referred to as 'winning by a canvas'?

20. In the 1950s, Eugene Polley invented the 'Flashmatic', and Robert Adler came up with the 'Zenith Space Command'; both of these were forerunners of what common household gadget?

21. In architecture, what classical name is used for a column which is carved into the shape of a female figure, clad in long robes?

22. Which group, who were led by Gerrard Winstanley and also called themselves the 'True Levellers', set up farming

communities on former crown and common land from April 1649?

23. Which writer born in Gdansk was the author of *The Tin Drum*? In 1999, he was awarded the Nobel Prize for Literature.

24. What name has been given to England's first natural World Heritage Site, a stretch of coastline that runs for 95 miles from Orcombe Point near Exeter, to Old Harry Rocks near Swanage, and is famed for its fossil-bearing beaches?

25. Who was the Roman god of Fire, and the equivalent of the Greek god Hephaestus?

26. What term describes the way of walking particular to mammals, including humans, in which the whole lower surface of the foot is on the ground?

27. Which Babylonian king gives his name to a size of champagne bottle containing twenty normal-sized bottles?

28. Which international language was devised by Doctor Ludwig Zamenhof in 1887?

29. Which singer released her debut album *Rockferry* in March 2008?

30. In a classic Monty Python sketch, what accompanied 'Lobster thermidor aux crevettes with a Mornay sauce garnished with truffle paté, brandy and a fried egg on top'?

Aircraft and Aerial Warfare of the First and Second World Wars

1. Which bomber flew its first combat mission on 5 June 1944, against the Japanese railway yards in Bangkok?

2. What visual symbol of aircraft identification did the RFC and RNAS adopt in December 1914?

3. The London Blitz lasted from 7 September to 13 November 1940, but which British city was hit the following night with devastating ferocity?

4. On 18 November 1939, Flight Lieutenant 'Shorty' Longbottom flew a specially adapted Spitfire on a sortie over the Siegfried Line to prove the value of what to the Allies?

5. Which was the first British fighter to mount a side by side pair of synchronised forward-firing machine guns?

6. In which Italian port did twenty-one Fairy Swordfish from HMS *Illustrious* severely damage the ships of the Regia Marina in a torpedo attack on 11 November 1940?

7. What official name was given by the US Air Force to the basic transport model of the Douglas C-47 with large side-loading doors and strengthened floors?

8. What type of aircraft was the Messerschmitt Me 321 Gigant, first used on 14 September 1941 in an attack on the Estonia island of Saaremaa?

9. Designed by Henry Royce during 1914, what was the first Rolls-Royce aero engine?

10. From November 1941 to January 1945, who was the Luftwaffe's General in Command of Fighters?

11. Which aircraft began the 8th Air Force's European heavy bombing campaign, with an attack on marshalling yards at Rouen, on 17 August 1942?

12. What nickname did the pilots of the Luftwaffe bestow on the Short Sunderland after a single aircraft had fought off six Ju 88s while on convoy escort duty at the start of the Norwegian campaign?

13. Later to achieve fame for his part in a historic flight, who designed a fighter in 1917 called the A.1 Scout that he put together almost wholly from Sopwith Triplane and Pup parts?

14. During the winter of 1942–1943, the Luftwaffe lost 488 aircraft flying supply missions to which beleaguered army?

15. Which was the last bi-plane fighter to see active service with the RAF?

16. On 11 January 1943, who was appointed Commander-in-Chief, Mediterranean Air Command, subordinate to Eisenhower only?

17. Under what name did the naval version of the Spitfire enter service with the Fleet Air Arm in June 1942?

18. During the Great War, which Norwich-based manufacturing company moved into aircraft construction as part of the war effort? Their first design was the P3 Bobolink fighter.

19. Which Hawker fighter that entered service in April 1944 was one of the main aircraft used to chase V1 flying bombs, accounting for around a third of those destroyed by aircraft?

20. In December 1941, Bomber Command flew two daylight raids against which French Channel port, attempting to sink the

Scharnhorst, Gneisenau and the Prinz Eugen?

21. Which British aircraft easily outflew the Me 109s it encountered on its first reconnaissance missions over France in September 1941?

22. What general term was used to denote biplanes where the propeller was behind the engine and wings of the aircraft?

23. Which aircraft's most famous missions included the low-level raid against the oilfields at Ploesti in Romania, on 1 August 1943?

24. Which motor company built the two-seater biplane the Greyhound, proposed as a replacement for the Bristol fighter?

25. On 24 October 1944, Group Captain D.E. Gillam led an attack on the headquarters of the German 15th Army in Dordrecht killing 70 staff officers; which aircraft were used on the raid?

26. Which American Navy Commander developed the recoilless gun, adopted by the RNAS in 1915?

27. What derisory name did the US Navy give to the Battle of the Philippines sea in June 1944, when over 300 Japanese aircraft where shot down by US carrier-based fighters?

28. What is the family name of the brothers who developed the Gnome engine that powered many aircraft during the First World War?

29. What feature of the DB 601 engines, fitted in the Messerschmitt Bf 109E, allowed negative-g manoeuvres without the engine spluttering or cutting out?

30. Who piloted the modified B-29 bomber *Enola Gay* that dropped the atomic bomb on Hiroshima?

General Knowledge 23.2

1. What sort of fictional creatures are Great Uncle Bulgaria, Tobermory and Madame Cholet?

2. In Arthurian legend, which knight, who was the son of Lancelot and Elaine, was the purest and noblest of the Round Table?

3. Which work did Mozart leave unfinished when he died? It had been commissioned anonymously by Count Walsegg-Stuppach, who may have intended to pass it off as his own.

4. In which South American country is Mount Cotopaxi, which is one of the world's highest continuously active volcanoes?

5. The colouring and flavouring syrup grenadine is made chiefly from the juice of which fruit?

6. What is the name of the stage in a butterfly's development between the caterpillar and the full adult stage?

7. Samuel Beckett's *Waiting for Godot* was published originally in which language, in 1952?

8. Which twentieth-century British Prime Minister had served as Foreign Secretary before forming his administration, and did so again some years afterwards?

9. In architecture, what name is usually given to the upright division between the panes of a window?

10. What name is given to the strictly orthodox grouping of Sunni Muslims that is the dominant form of Islam in Saudi Arabia?

11. In which film is the title character, played by Paul Newman, put on a chain gang as a punishment for cutting the tops off of parking meters?

12. What acid is found in rhubarb leaves, which are generally toxic to humans?

13. Which women's sport was first played in England in 1895, at Madame Martina Bergman-Osterberg's Physical Training College in Dartford?

14. Which royal house ruled France from 1328 until 1589?

15. Garry Shandling played which fictitious television chat show host, who was modelled on David Letterman?

16. Drumochter summit is the highest point on Britain's mainline railway system; it lies on the line between Perth and which city?

17. Whose first UK top ten album as a solo artist was *Off the Wall*, which was released in 1979?

18. Which mineral that is used as a gemstone, has varieties which include emerald, morganite and aquamarine, as well as the colourless goshenite?

19. What is the name of the tall, sweet, yeast-raised fruit cake from Milan, which is traditionally eaten at Christmas and other celebrations?

20. In ancient Mesopotamian religion, who was the goddess of war and love and the equivalent of the western Semitic Astarte?

21. The collective noun for which type of birds is a 'murder'?

22. What is the usual scientific name for Vitamin B2? It is derived from a word for a type of sugar and the Latin for 'yellow'.

23. What three digits do you need to dial before the area code, in order to phone America or Canada from the United Kingdom?

24. According to Greek legend, what was the name of the king

of Cyprus who fell in love with an ivory statue of his ideal woman, which was subsequently brought to life by the goddess Aphrodite?

25. Which painter sued the art critic John Ruskin for describing *Nocturne in Black and Gold: The Falling Rocket* as 'throwing a pot of paint in the public's face'?

26. Cephalonia and Corfu are the largest of which group of Greek islands?

27. Doctor Johnson arranged for the publication of whose novel *The Vicar of Wakefield*, to save the author from being jailed as a debtor?

28. What name for the class of molluscs that includes snails and slugs comes from the Greek for 'stomach' and 'foot'?

29. Which Belgian-born gypsy guitarist was the joint-leader of the Quintette du Hot Club de France, along with Stephane Grappelli?

30. Which film producer is reputed to have said, 'A verbal contract isn't worth the paper it is written on'?

General knowledge

If you did well on the Juniors' specialist subjects, then why not test your general knowledge against David, the champion in 2007, who scored 16 out of 20 in two minutes:

1. What name is used for the feet of mammals such as horses and cattle?

2. A statue of which South African statesman and President was unveiled in Parliament Square in London, in August 2007?

3. Which two animated characters star in the films *A Close Shave*, *The Wrong Trousers* and *The Curse of the Were Rabbit*?

4. Which Greek hero was delayed on his journey home from the Trojan War by the nymphs Calypso and Circe?

5. What term from the French for 'to paste' is used for a picture built up from pieces of paper or fabric stuck onto a backing material?

6. In the novels by J.R.R. Tolkien, whom did Smeagol become after living in a cave in the Misty Mountains for over 400 years?

7. Which Swedish pop group has had hits with the songs 'Waterloo', 'Dancing Queen' and 'Mamma Mia'?

8. What type of reference book did Samuel Johnson write in the mid-18 century?

9. In cricket and rugby, what name is given to a match – usually one of a series – between teams representing two different countries?

10. Romano Prodi and Silvio Berlusconi are two recent Prime Ministers of which European country?

11. Which author has written the books *Mortal Engines*, *A Darkling Plain* and *Larklight*?

12. Which Austrian composer who died in 1791 aged only 35 had the forenames Wolfgang Amadeus?

13. How many strings does a modern guitar normally have?

14. What name is shared by insects and a fault in a computer system or program?

15. Which member of the Royal Family has held the title Princess Royal since 1987?

16. Which of Shakespeare's tragic heroes speaks the words 'To be or not to be, that is the question'?

17. The Sun's energy comes from the conversion of which gas into helium?

18. Near which Australian city are the famous Bondi and Manly beaches?

19. At what time of the day did the armistice come into force that saw the end of the First World War on 11 November 1918?

20. In ancient Roman times what name was given to the open spaces in the middle of towns which were surrounded by public buildings and used generally as meeting places?

Answers

1. Hooves

2. Nelson Mandela

3. Wallace and Gromit

4. Odysseus

5. Collage

6. Gollum

7. Abba

8. Dictionary

9. Test

10. Italy

11. Philip Reeve

12. Mozart

13. Six

14. Bug

15. (Princess) Anne

16. Hamlet

17. Hydrogen

18. Sydney

19. Eleven o'clock or Eleven a.m.

20. Forum

Show 24

Sharks and Whales, Dolphins and Porpoises

1. To which group of aquatic mammals, whose name comes from the Greek, translated as 'sea-monster', do whales, dolphins and porpoises belong?

2. The world's second largest shark, which is a regular visitor to British coastal waters in summer, is commonly known by what name?

3. The Baiji dolphin, which may now be extinct, is or was native to which river?

4. What is the name of the tiny sensory pores around a shark's head and snout that detect electrical currents in the water?

5. There are two main types of whale: odontoceti (toothed whales) and which other group that includes many of the larger whales?

6. Which fish is a favourite food of the Great Hammerhead shark, despite having a sharp, poisonous tail spine?

7. What name is given to the two horizontal flattened fin-like structures that form the tail of cetaceans?

8. 'Squalene', used in medicine and cosmetics, is obtained from the oil of which organ of the shark?

9. Which group of dolphins of the genus Stenella get their general name from their acrobatic displays in which they leap high out of the water and turn rapidly on their own axis?

10. Which part of a shark's body may be defined as 'hetero-circle'?

11. What general name, of Scandinavian origin, is given to the family to which the largest whales belong, such as the Blue and Fin Whales?

12. What is the common name of the fastest known shark, which is also a prized game fish with a spectacular leap?

13. What name is given to the bulbous forehead of many toothed cetaceans, containing oil, muscles and air sacs; it is believed to play an important role in echo-location?

14. Which shark is known as the 'rubbish bin' of the sea because of the items it swallows? It is thought by some to be second only to the Great White shark for attacks on humans.

15. The males of which whale are particularly noted for their long and complex songs during the breeding season to attract females and possibly ward off rivals, regarded as among the most varied in the animal world?

16. The plackoid tooth-like scales that cover a shark's skin are known by what two-word term?

17. The highly endangered porpoise, the Vaquita, is only found at the northern end of which body of water?

18. What common alternative name for the Blue Whale comes from the yellowish colour of its underside caused by algae?

19. Which fish that is also known as 'shark-sucker' or 'sucker-fish', attaches itself to sharks and feeds on scraps while cleaning off parasites?

20. Which large whale lives exclusively in Arctic waters and gets its common name from the distinctive shape of its huge head?

21. What name is most commonly given to the forceful and often repeated tail-slapping on the surface of the water by a whale or dolphin while most of the animal is under water?

22. The Megamouth shark was only discovered in 1976 when one became accidentally entangled in a naval ship's anchor off which island group?

23. Which large whale, also known as the Cachalot, can be identified at a distance by its forward angled blowhole directed to the left?

24. By what alternative name, after a bird, is the Beluga sometimes known because of the variety of sounds it makes which can be heard above and below the surface?

25. Squalidae is the scientific name of which shark family?

26. The Amazon River Dolphin or Boto is also known by what alternative common name because of the colouration of many adults, particularly as they age?

27. What name is generally given to dried shark skin when it is used as an abrasive for smoothing and polishing?

28. Which large whale, known by whalers as the 'devil fish' because of its ferocity when threatened, is the only living member of the family and genus named after the Danish naturalist Daniel Eschricht?

29. The Right Whales got their name because they have been traditionally regarded as the right whales for what?

30. Which bio-luminescent shark gets its common name from the way it clamps its jaws onto its victim, then twists to gouge out a plug of flesh?

General Knowledge 24.1

1. Hydrophobia is an alternative name for which, often fatal, disease?

2. Which sea lies between the Italian and Balkan peninsulas, and is an arm of the Mediterranean?

3. Which Russian dramatist's works include the plays *The Seagull* and *The Cherry Orchard*?

4. What name for a college of religious instruction comes from the Arabic for 'to study'?

5. In 2005, which artist created an installation of 100 cast-iron figures of naked men, at Crosby beach on Merseyside?

6. Which creature's name means 'earth pig' in Afrikaans?

7. Which musical instrument, along with two violins and a viola, makes up a conventional string quartet?

8. Who was the first Holy Roman Emperor, crowned in Rome on Christmas Day, AD 800?

9. What was the last film directed by David Lean, which was released in 1984 and based on a novel by E.M. Forster?

10. Which word for the walking un-dead, was originally the name of a god in West African voodoo cults?

11. What is fermented to make both the Japanese drink, Sake, and the Chinese drink, Samshu?

12. What penname did newspaper columnist Sir William Connor use when he wrote for the *Daily Mirror*?

13. In the Rugby League Challenge Cup final, what is the name of the trophy awarded to the 'Man of the Match'?

14. Who was Britain's second Labour Prime Minister?

15. Which scientist, during an appearance on *The Simpsons*, said, 'Your theory of a donut-shaped universe is interesting, Homer. I may have to steal it'?

16. In which English county does the River Trent rise?

17. Which composer of electronic music, who is renowned for his film scores, was born in Volos, Greece in 1943?

18. Which popular spring flower takes its name from the Turkish or Persian for 'turban'?

19. Since 1833, where in England has a red ball been dropped daily at 1pm precisely, as a public time signal?

20. What was the last pitched battle to be fought on English soil, in July 1685?

21. In the Bible, who was the second wife of Jacob and the mother of Joseph and Benjamin?

22. Which is the only member of the cat family which cannot fully retract its claws?

23. In the novels by Sue Townsend, what is the name of Adrian Mole's girlfriend during his schooldays, who later becomes Labour MP for Ashby-de-la-Zouch?

24. Uhuru Peak, meaning 'Freedom Peak' in Swahili, is the highest point of which mountain?

25. Which sculptor created the gilt-bronze baldachin that stands over the tomb of St Peter in Rome?

26. Which Paul Simon song, written while he was on a tour of English folk clubs, is commemorated by a plaque on Widnes station near Liverpool?

27. To two decimal places, how many centimetres are there in an inch?

28. Which actor was the first to play Doctor Who?

29. What is the traditional topping of a Simnel cake?

30. Margaret Thatcher was born in which town, once voted the most boring in England?

Specialist Subject 24.2
The Hitchhiker's Guide to the Galaxy by Douglas Adams

1. Which two words are 'inscribed in large, friendly letters' on the cover of the Guide?

2. According to Douglas Adams, the title came to him in 1971, while he was 'lying drunk in a field' in which Austrian city?

3. At the beginning of The Hitchhiker's Guide, Arthur Dent's house is knocked down to make way for what, shortly before

the Vogons destroy the Earth for the same reason?

4. What is the name of the creature that, when placed in the ear, 'enables the user to understand anything said to them in any form of language'?

5. Later adopted as the name of the official Hitchhiker's Guide Appreciation Society, in which sector of the universe does the spaceship *Heart of Gold* pick up Arthur and Ford Prefect?

6. What was the translation of the last message from the dolphins before the Earth was destroyed by the Vogons? Douglas Adams later used it as the title for the fourth book in the 'trilogy'.

7. What task does the immortal being Wowbagger the Infinitely Prolonged set himself, so he has a purpose in life?

8. Slartibartfast won an award for designing which country with 'lovely crinkly edges'?

9. At the end of the first book, what does Marvin the Paranoid Android do to the Blagulon Kappa police-craft that makes its computer commit suicide?

10. In *So Long, and Thanks for All the Fish*, the Mid-Galactic Census found that every single person in the galaxy had 2.4 legs and owned what?

11. According to the Guide, what is 'the most massively useful thing an inter-stellar hitchhiker can have'?

12. The second time that Arthur meets Zaphod Beeblebrox, he observes that he now has what extra body parts (and has stopped calling himself 'Phil')?

13. What is the name of Trillian and Arthur's daughter, who was conceived through artificial insemination?

14. Among those who helped to build the *Heart of Gold* was a Hooloovoo, a super-intelligent shade of which colour? For the unveiling ceremony it was 'temporarily refracted into a free-standing prism'.

15. In *The Restaurant at the End of the Universe*, Ford Prefect meets his old friend Hotblack Desiato of the plutonium rock band Disaster Area, and discovers that he is spending a year dead for what reason?

16. What is the name of the main town on the planet of Now-What?

17. The Jatravartid people, who have more than fifty arms each, are the only race to have invented... what, before the wheel?

18. Shortly before alien robots invade Lord's cricket ground, Ford is humming the same note repeatedly, claiming it to be the first note of which Noel Coward song?

19. According to the super-computer Deep Thought, the Answer to Life, the Universe and Everything is 42. What is the question?

20. Why does Rob McKenna's wife always bring the washing in when he rings to say that he is on his way home?

21. Who wrote the 'philosophical blockbusters' *Where God Went Wrong*, *Some More of God's Greatest Mistakes* and *Who Is This God Person Anyway*, as well as the bestselling *Well, That About Wraps It Up for God*?

22. As it is possibly the only thing that can travel faster than the speed of light, the Hingefreel People of Arkintoofle Minor once tried to build spaceships powered by... what?

23. Max Quordlepleen, the host at the Restaurant at the End of the Universe, has just come from which other eating place at the very other end of time?

24. According to the radio series, how did Arthur Dent's only brother meet his unfortunate death?

25. After landing on prehistoric Earth, what 'small problem' do the Golgafrinchams encounter when they adopt the leaf as legal tender due to 'the high level of leaf availability'? They plan to remedy this by 'burning down all the forests'.

26. What phenomenon that renders things virtually invisible relies on people's natural predisposition not to see things they don't want to, weren't expecting or can't explain?

27. According to the radio series, the use of which swear word is beyond the pale, and worse than 'joojooflop', 'swut' and 'turlingdrome'?

28. What is God's final message to his creation, which Marvin reads and then dies happy?

29. According to the Guide, what is the best way to get a drink out of a Vogon?

30. Although the exchange rate of eight Ningis to one Triganic Pu is straightforward, why has nobody collected enough Ningis to exchange for one Pu?

General Knowledge 24.2

1. Whose first chart entry, which got to number one in 1965, was 'It's Not Unusual'?

2. Men from which country are recruited to serve with the Gurkhas?

3. Which innovative design style, popular in the 1920s and 1930s,

takes its name from the Exposition Internationale des Arts Decoratifs et Industriels Modernes, held in Paris in 1925?

4. During the Second World War, which key battle took place between 23 October and 4 November 1942?

5. In the words of a popular First World War song, 'It's a long way to...' where?

6. In Greek mythology, who was the mother of Oedipus and later unwittingly became his wife?

7. In the 1997 film *Mrs Brown*, who played the title role opposite Billy Connolly?

8. The falabella is thought to be the smallest breed of which animal?

9. Which prolific writer of romantic fiction was born at Tyne Dock, County Durham, in 1906, and set many novels in her native North-East?

10. Which Welsh river flows into the Severn estuary at Newport, and has a name with the same origin as the word 'whisky'?

11. Which traditional Christmas treat originally contained meat and was made in the shape of a cradle, as a reminder of the manger in which Jesus lay?

12. For which more serious disease did Gloucestershire surgeon, Edward Jenner, discover a vaccination when he inoculated eight-year-old James Phipps with cowpox in 1796?

13. At which horseracing venue are there two racetracks, the Rowley Mile Course and the July Course, which are separated by the Devil's Dyke?

14. Which device that revolutionised the electronics industry was

patented in 1948 by three American physicists working at the Bell Telephone laboratories?

15. Who subtitled his Fifth Symphony 'A Soviet artist's reply to just criticism'?

16. Ailsa Craig, Sungold and Money Maker are varieties of which common salad ingredient?

17. Which of the Goodies is a qualified doctor and has hosted the BBC medical programme *Bodymatters*?

18. In 1100, which English King was shot and killed by an arrow whilst out hunting in the New Forest?

19. Which toy has a name thought to mean 'come-come' or 'return' in one of the Filipino languages?

20. In Christendom, which title, dating back to the 5th century AD, was originally given to the bishops of the five major episcopal sees, namely Rome, Alexandria, Antioch, Constantinople and Jerusalem?

21. The works of which American novelist, who lived from 1843 to 1916, include *Washington Square* and *The Ambassadors*?

22. Halifax is the capital of which Canadian province?

23. What name is given to the method of printing a design that was originally drawn onto a special plate of flat limestone with a greasy crayon?

24. The ptarmigan is a member of which bird family that is native to the mountains of Scotland?

25. Which cocktail consists of one measure of vodka, to three or four of orange juice, with a half-measure of Galliano floated on top?

26. Which royal residence is overlooked by the hill known as Arthur's Seat?

27. The voice of which ill-tempered cartoon character was provided by Clarence Nash?

28. Who was British Prime Minister at the time of the abdication of Edward VIII in 1936?

29. Which word can mean an apparatus for raising heavy weights, a small flag indicating nationality and a male donkey?

30. In the title of Audrey Eyton's book *The F-Plan Diet*, what does the 'F' stand for?

Questions you could guess, even without…
well, the question!

It is an axiom of quizzing – if you have to guess, go for the most obvious answer. To avoid *Mastermind* becoming a test of guesswork, easily guessable questions have to be strictly rationed but they do pop up here and there (as you'll know if you're doing the quizzes in this book). To test your powers of guesswork, in each case the correct answer is the *most obvious* option available – see how many you can get.

1. Which Parisian landmark…?

2. Which ice dancing pair…?

3. Which internet search engine…?

4. Which Sixties pop group…?

5. Which mountain…?

6. Which South African…?

7. Which fictional secret agent…?

8. Which supersonic plane…?

9. Which playwright…?

10. Which scientific equation…?

11. Which Belgian surrealist…?

12. Which sparkling wine…?

13. Which bagless vacuum cleaner…?

14. Which Brazilian footballer…?

15. Which Mancunian artist…?

16. Which egg-laying mammal…?

17. Which King of Macedon…?

18. Which American astronaut…?

19. Which Italian sports-car manufacturer…?

20. Which Icelandic volcano…?

Answers

1. Eiffel Tower

2. Torvill and Dean

3. Google

4. The Beatles (the Rolling Stones aren't really 'pop'!)

5. Everest

6. Nelson Mandela

(00)7. James Bond

8. Concorde

9. William Shakespeare

10. $E=MC^2$

11. René Magritte

12. Champagne (we'll accept Dom Perignon – clearly you have expensive tastes!)

13. Dyson

14. Pelé (plus a point extra for Edson Arantes do Nascimento if you were answering against the clock.)

15. L.S. Lowry

16. (Duck-billed) Platypus (half a point for the Echidna – or Spiny Anteater… 10 bonus points for any other *correct* answer)

17. Alexander (the Great or III)

18. Neil Armstrong

19. Ferrari

20. Eyjafjallajokull (plus a bonus point if you spelt or pronounced it properly)

THE MASTERMIND QUIZ BOOK

Show 25

Specialist Subject 25.1
Pop Music of the 1950s and 1960s

1. 'Rock Around The Clock' by Bill Haley and his Comets was featured over the credits of which film starring Glenn Ford?

2. Which instrument did Dave Clark of the Dave Clark Five play in the group?

3. What was the title of Tom Jones's second and last number one single to date, which topped the charts in November 1966?

4. In 1967, which double-A side became the first Beatles single since 'Please Please Me' not to top the UK charts?

5. Which actress appeared with Mike Sarne on the 1962 chart-topping single 'Come Outside'?

6. Jeff Beck, Eric Clapton and Jimmy Page were all guitarists at various times in which 1960s rock group?

7. In July 1957, which song gave Elvis Presley his first UK number one single?

8. Which disc jockey had hits in the 1960s with 'So Much Love' and 'Its Only Love', which he complained his fellow DJs refused to play?

9. The Who never topped the UK singles charts but twice reached number two, with 'My Generation' and which other song?

10. Which singer, sometimes referred to as 'Britain's Elvis', was released from the army in 1959 as 'medically unfit' after two months?

11. Which Everly Brothers' single was number one in the UK charts for seven weeks in 1960?

12. Who was lead vocalist on the Spencer Davis Group's number one hit 'Keep On Running'?

13. Which group, led by Gary Brooker, topped the UK singles charts in 1967 with a hit inspired by a Bach suite?

14. Which chart-topping single of 1958 was written by Otis Blackwell and Jack Hammer?

15. Which singer had her only top 20 hit in 1965, when 'Rescue Me' reached number 11 in the charts?

16. Which sixties duo made their first record as Caesar and Cleo before topping the charts with their second, which was released under their more famous name?

17. Which was the third of Gerry and the Pacemakers' three consecutive number one hits?

18. Which creator of the 'twang' guitar style first entered the charts in 1958 with 'Rebel Rouser', which reached number 19 in the UK charts?

19. Which record by the Shangri Las reached number 11 early in 1965, despite being banned by the BBC?

20. Which popular singer was born Arnold George Dorsey in Madras, India, in 1936?

21. The Jimi Hendrix Experience's first single reached number six in the UK charts early in 1967; what was its title?

22. Which member of the Hollies sang, un-credited, about Jennifer Eccles and her terrible freckles on the Scaffold's 'Lily The Pink'?

23. In March 1959, which Paul Anka song posthumously gave Buddy Holly his only solo UK number one hit?

24. In the early 1960s, which singer had a day job as a fitter with the Gas Board and played at night in his brother's skiffle group, The Cavaliers?

25. What was the name of the Soho coffee bar where Tommy Steele and other early British rock 'n' rollers were discovered?

26. Cilla Black, Dionne Warwick and Mary May all took which song into the charts in 1964?

27. Which group, formed in 1969, featured Robert Fripp, Greg Lake and Ian McDonald among its original line-up?

28. Which Rolling Stones record of 1966 only reached number two, ending a string of 5 consecutive number one hits?

29. Which founder member of Fleetwood Mac wrote their number one instrumental hit 'Albatross'?

30. 'Arnold Layne' was the first single released by which group? It reached number twenty in the UK charts in 1967.

General Knowledge 25.1

1. What is the name of the Benedictine monk who, according to popular legend, invented champagne?

2. In the Peloponnesian War, the people of which city-state, noted for its rigid military discipline, were the enemies of the Athenians?

3. What is the profession of a person with the letters R.I.B.A. after their name?

4. The city of Stirling stands on the right bank of which major river?

5. It was widely believed that which crewmember of the Starship *Enterprise*, who first appeared in 1967, had been added to *Star Trek* at the request of *Pravda*?

6. Which political party folded in June 1990, after polling just 155 votes at a by-election in Bootle and finishing behind the Monster Raving Loony Party?

7. Which French painter's works include *The Gleaners* and *The Angelus*, two of the most reproduced paintings of the nineteenth century?

8. A rockhopper is a species of which bird?

9. In a well-known Anglo-Saxon poem, who kills the monster Grendel?

10. What was the name of the garden where Jesus was arrested on the night of the Last Supper?

11. The musical *Blood Brothers* is set in which city?

12. The Aspen or Trembling Poplar belongs to which family of shrubs and trees?

13. In 1844, teams from Canada and the USA played the first international match in which sport?

14. Bubbles of which gas are formed in the blood of divers when they get 'the bends'?

15. Which 2006 Martin Scorsese film starred Jack Nicholson as the gangster Frank Costello?

16. Which city, renowned for its sword-making, was the capital of Spain until 1560?

17. Aurora is the real name of the title character in which ballet, with music by Tchaikovsky?

18. Which Trojan war leader was the son and heir of Priam, the last king of Troy?

19. Which delicately flavoured vegetable was once known as 'sparrow grass'?

20. Cassiterite is the principal commercial ore of which metal that has been mined in Cornwall since ancient times?

21. The term for which figure of speech, where apparently contradictory terms are placed together, comes from the Greek for 'sharp' and 'foolish'?

22. Which creatures form the main part an aardvark's diet?

23. Sir John Tenniel, is particularly remembered for illustrating the works of which nineteenth-century children's author?

24. Which county is said to take its name from the Dumnonii, a Celtic people who lived in the area?

25. Which television programme featured a family business that was based at Oil Drum Lane, Shepherds Bush?

26. Anne Neville, the youngest daughter of the Earl of Warwick, was the wife of which English King?

27. Which word, derived from the Old French for a 'splinter of wood', is used to describe an artist's workshop or studio?

28. Which free-market economist, who died in November 2006, used the phrase, 'There's no such thing as a free lunch' as the title of one of his books?

29. Which band, formed in Sheffield in the 1980s, took its name from a fictional group mentioned in Anthony Burgess' novel *A Clockwork Orange*?

30. What bodily function is also called 'sternutation'?

Specialist Subject 25.2
Astronomy and Cosmology

1. When a star collapses to a size equal to or less than the Schwarzschild radius, what does it become?

2. Which is the southernmost of the two stars that represent the heads of the twins in Gemini?

3. What name is given to a pair of stars rotating about a common centre of mass under their mutual gravitational attraction?

4. What is the furthest celestial object visible to the naked eye? It is 2.3 million light years away from Earth.

5. What name is given to matter, thought to comprise about 90 per cent of the mass of the universe, which is undetectable by the radiation it emits but whose existence is inferred by the motions of certain stellar objects?

6. Which astronomical event, previously observed in 1882, was visible with eye protection in the UK on 8 June 2004?

7. What name is given to the two, relatively small, galaxies visible

to the naked eye from the southern hemisphere, which were first recorded in 1519?

8. Betelgeuse and Rigel are the two brightest stars in the constellation Orion; which second magnitude blue-white giant is the third brightest?

9. The Chandrasekhar limit of around 1.4 solar masses is the maximum theoretical value for stability of what type of star?

10. What term is used for the displacement of spectral lines towards longer wavelengths caused by the doppler effect when a celestial source is moving away from the observer?

11. In 1929, which American astronomer proposed the law, named after him, that the recession velocity of an extra-galactic object is proportional to its distance?

12. What term, similar to 'the Big Bang' is used for the theory that the universe might eventually collapse back on itself and compress to a singularity?

13. In which constellation is the dim red dwarf that is the nearest star to the Earth, apart from the Sun?

14. When viewed from two widely different points in space, a nearby star will appear to have shifted slightly in position with respect to more distant stars. What is this apparent displacement called?

15. In spring in the Northern Hemisphere, the near dawn rising of which star cluster has, since ancient times, marked the beginning of the seafaring and farming season, while its morning setting in the autumn has marked the season's end?

16. What name is given to the phase of the Moon, or of a planet, when it appears more than half, but not completely, full?

17. In which region of the electromagnetic spectrum did Penzias and Wilson detect a cosmic background in the mid 1960s that provided evidence for the Big Bang theory?

18. What name is given to the diagonal band of a Hertzspung-Russell diagram which contains about 90 per cent of the stars?

19. Which is the larger of the two ray craters in the Oceanus Procellarum that are clearly visible to the naked eye when the Moon is full?

20. Which comet, named after the two amateur American astronomers who discovered it, reached its perihelion on 1 April 1997?

21. Which small constellation, found at the foot of Orion, represents the animal that the mythical giant was fond of hunting?

22. Which nineteenth-century English astronomer gives his name to the scale universally in use for measuring the brightness of a stellar object?

23. Which orange giant star represents the so-called 'bull's eye' in Taurus?

24. Which observatory, situated about 40 miles north of San Diego, is home to the 200-inch Hale telescope, which until 1976 was the largest of its type?

25. What is the name of the apparent gap in the Milky Way, seen in the summer months parallel to Cygnus, caused by a thick band of interstellar dust?

26. Schiaperelli's 1877 map of which planet showed lines across its surface that he called 'canali' or channels? This led to the idea that there might be artificial waterways on the planet.

27. What is the popular name for the theoretical tunnels between two black holes or other points in space-time?

28. Which annual meteor shower reaches its maximum in early January?

29. Which term describes the apparent path of the Sun's annual motion through the so-called fixed stars?

30. What name is given to the cluster of galaxies to which our galaxy, the Milky Way, belongs?

General Knowledge 25.2

1. What is Archimedes said to have shouted while running naked in the street, after discovering the principle of buoyancy in his bath?

2. Bornean and Sumatran are the two subspecies of which of the great apes?

3. The name of which style of art and architecture is believed to derive from the French word 'rocaille', meaning 'shell-work', and the Italian word for baroque?

4. The first Anglo-Saxon settlers in Britain were said to be led by two brothers. One was called Hengist; what was the name of the other?

5. Which Spanish soup, generally served chilled, is produced from a mixture of raw salad ingredients that are made into a puree?

6. In November 1963, undersea volcanic action led to the formation of which small island off the southern coast of Iceland?

7. Which actor, better known for his parts in musicals, received an Oscar Nomination for Best Supporting Actor for his role in *The Towering Inferno*?

8. Which post-war American President, who served for over two years, was never elected either to that office or that of Vice-President?

9. According to the title of Shakespeare's play, the nobleman Timon was from which city?

10. The contact process is an industrial method of manufacturing which acid?

11. Johann Strauss the Elder composed a march in honour of which Austrian military hero, in 1848?

12. In Greek mythology, who is the Muse of History?

13. In which European language does 'muito obrigado' mean 'thank you very much'?

14. What is the common name for the eye condition 'hypermetropia'?

15. Which Football League club is named after the day of the week when its original players took a half-day off work in order to participate?

16. Which area of central London, in the borough of Camden, gives its name to the group of writers, artists and thinkers who lived or met there in the early twentieth century?

17. Which classic album by Miles Davis, one of the bestselling jazz records of all time, features the tracks 'So What' and 'Blue In Green'?

18. Glen Moy and Glen Ample are varieties of which soft fruit,

widely grown in Scotland?

19. Which actor, whose first major success was the title role in a television adaptation of *Nicholas Nickleby*, is the son of a former Attorney-General and Lord Chancellor?

20. Which Indian religion, founded in the 6th century BC by Mahavira, lays particular stress on the system of ahimsa, or non-violence to any living things?

21. Which Birmingham band first topped the UK singles charts in 1983 with 'Is There Something I Should Know'?

22. Against which country did the USA fight the so-called War of 1812, which actually lasted until the winter of 1814–1815?

23. Which Russian-born American artist created the series of paintings *Black on Maroon* and *Red on Maroon*, originally intended for a restaurant in the Seagram Building in New York?

24. Turku was the capital of which European country from the 13th century until 1812, while it was under Swedish and then Russian rule?

25. Which author created the character Tarzan?

26. Which seabird got its name because its presence was believed to be a sign that bad weather was coming?

27. Which type of lager takes its name from the town, now in the Czech Republic, where it was originally brewed in 1842?

28. In 2005, David Trimble was succeeded as the leader of which political party by Sir Reg Empey?

29. What number on the pH scale indicates that a solution is neutral; neither acid nor alkaline?

30. Which television quizmaster is played by the *League of Gentlemen* star Mark Gatiss in the film *Starter for Ten*?

Rejected specialist subjects

In its original incarnation, *Mastermind* had a reputation for only allowing contenders to choose 'highbrow' subjects: the lyricist Tim Rice applied, but wasn't even offered an audition as one of his proposed subjects was 'Pop Music'. He did eventually make it onto *Celebrity Mastermind* – see 'Celebrities and their subjects'.

These days the criteria for an acceptable subject are more flexible, although there are still limits. I vividly recall one would-be contender being most upset when we refused to allow him to do 'The History of the World since AD 1' – imagine trying to set that, let alone revise it. 'Routes to Anywhere in Mainland Britain by Road from Letchworth' was also turned down, along with 'Orthopaedic Bone Cement in Total Hip Replacement' and 'Perfect Squares from $99^2 = 9801$'... It must, however, have been a particularly mean-spirited producer who rejected 'Diamonds are a Girl's Best Friend (as Everybody Knows)'!

Show 26

Specialist Subject 26.1
The Civil War and Interregnum

1. What was the name of the bill drawn up by the House of Commons in 1641 listing all the grievances that had occurred during the reign of Charles I?

2. Who commanded the Parliamentary forces at the Battle of Edgehill, in October 1642?

3. Cromwell and the cavalry troops he commanded were a key factor in the Parliamentary victory at Marston Moor. What was their nickname?

4. The King's young sons, Charles and James, narrowly escaped the impact of a cannonball while observing the Battle of Edgehill, in the charge of which famous physician?

5. Which places of popular entertainment were closed by the Puritan Parliament in 1642?

6. During their march on London in November 1642, where were Royalist troops confronted by the Earl of Essex's army, reinforced by thousands of Londoners, and forced to withdraw?

7. What was the name of the Archbishop of Canterbury who was executed in January 1645?

8. In which city did Charles establish his headquarters after being turned back from London in November 1642?

9. In January 1642, Charles tried to arrest five MPs in the Commons chamber. Pym, Hesilrige, Holles and Strode were four; who was the other?

10. After victory at the Battle of Langport, Cromwell reported, 'To see this, is it not to see the face of...' what?

11. The King's Secretary of State, Lord Falkland, was killed at which battle of September 1643?

12. Who was given command of the New Model Army after the Earls of Essex and Manchester had to comply with the Self-Denying Ordinance after Marston Moor?

13. In which city is the King Charles Tower from which, it is said, Charles watched the scattered remains of his forces retreating after the battle of Rowton Moor in September 1645?

14. In December 1648, which Colonel 'purged' the House of Commons of those MPs who wanted to negotiate with Charles?

15. At which town was a Scottish army under David Leslie heavily defeated by Cromwell, on 3 September 1650?

16. Which leading Leveller, known as 'Free Born John', was found not guilty of treason in 1649?

17. In which city in Kent did a riot take place after the Puritan mayor had ordered markets and shops to open on Christmas Day 1647?

18. On the eve of the Battle of Naseby, which future son-in-law of Oliver Cromwell captured a Royalist outpost while the Cavaliers were having supper and playing quoits?

19. The heavy armour worn by the men of Sir Arthur Hesilrige's mounted regiment of cuirassiers earned them what nickname?

20. Which famous architect was taken prisoner when Basing House was captured by the New Model Army in 1645?

21. After Naseby, Charles's private papers were captured. What title was given to these documents when they were published?

22. Which Parliamentary commander ended Scottish resistance by taking Stirling in August 1651 and Dundee the following month?

23. Charles was imprisoned in Carisbrooke Castle on which island in November 1647, in the custody of Robert Hammond?

24. The Second English Civil War effectively ended on 28 August 1648 with the Royalist surrender of which town to Sir Thomas Fairfax?

25. What nickname was given to remnant of the 'Long Parliament' that remained after Pride's Purge?

26. Who was the chief prosecutor at Charles's trial in January 1649, and read out the charges against him?

27. Seventeen days after Charles I's execution, on which island was his eldest son proclaimed King by Sir George Carteret with the words 'Vive le roy Charles second'?

28. Although he refused the crown, Oliver Cromwell became head of state in 1653 with what title?

29. Where did Charles II issue a Declaration on 4 April 1660, agreeing to an amnesty for most of those who had deposed and executed his father, and paving the way for the restoration of the monarchy?

30. When confronted with the corpse of Charles I, Oliver Cromwell is said to have described the King's execution as a 'cruel...' what?

General Knowledge 26.1

1. Which rodent with large defensive quills on its body and tail has a name that comes from the Latin for 'pig' and 'thorn'?

2. Which word for a person who sets too much value on social standing was originally a slang term for a cobbler?

3. Which English artist painted *Rain, Steam and Speed: The Great Western Railway*, which was first exhibited in 1844 and is now in the National Gallery?

4. Which Mediterranean island group came under the protection of the British Crown in 1802, and was finally annexed in 1814?

5. At the instigation of the Italian-American Civil Rights League, what term is never used in the dialogue of the film *The Godfather*?

6. A 'Carioca' is an inhabitant of which South American city?

7. Which crooner's last television appearance was with David Bowie on the *Merrie Olde Christmas Show*, recorded in September 1977?

8. What general term for blood poisoning is derived from the Greek for 'rotten blood'?

9. Which BBC television sports programme was first shown on 11 October 1958, and appeared for the last time on 28 January 2007?

10. In Greek mythology, which female monsters had live snakes for hair and were capable of turning people to stone?

11. The dish made from fillet steak topped with truffles, mushrooms or paté and enclosed in a puff pastry case is named after which soldier and statesman?

12. In which country is the city of Schaffhausen, which was mistakenly bombed by the Americans on April Fool's Day, 1944?

13. Which playwright, on being released from prison in 1897, went to live in France under the alias Sebastian Melmoth?

14. What is the name of the Stone Age village on Mainland in the Orkneys that was exposed by a storm in the 1850s after being covered for thousands of years by sand?

15. Who wrote the marches 'The Stars and Stripes Forever' and 'The Washington Post'?

16. What is the sinister common name of Amanita phalloides, the most poisonous of British mushrooms, which accounts for ninety per cent of fungus-related fatalities?

17. In *The Simpsons*, what is the name of Homer's tyrannical employer, who owns the Springfield Nuclear Power Plant?

18. Which crime of buying and selling ecclesiastical benefits is named after the biblical sorcerer who, according to the Acts of the Apostles, tried to buy spiritual powers from Peter and John?

19. One of six sisters, who, as co-editor of the volume of essays *Noblesse Oblige*, popularised the terms 'u' and 'non-u' for types of speech and behaviour?

20. Which document was introduced in its modern form, after

the passing of the British Nationality and Status Aliens Act of 1914?

21. Which Football League team are known as 'the Chairboys' because of the local furniture-making tradition?

22. In grammar, what name is given to a word used to connect words, clauses and sentences?

23. Patsy Cline, Aerosmith, Seal and Gnarls Barkley all had UK hits with different songs that had which title?

24. Which Middle Eastern city was rebuilt on the orders of the Emperor Hadrian in about AD 130, and renamed Aeila Capitolina in his honour?

25. Which modern French designer's works include the furniture for President Mitterrand's private suite in the Elysée Palace, the interior of the Café Costes in Paris and the 'Juicy Salif' lemon squeezer?

26. What is the common name for the three species of flightless birds of the genus Apteryx found in New Zealand?

27. Which cult comedy series starred Craig Charles as Dave Lister, the last human alive?

28. Krk, Cres and Pag are the largest of the Adriatic islands of which country?

29. The drink 'Dark and Stormy' consists of a mixture of ginger beer and which spirit?

30. What was C.P. Scott, the former editor of the *Manchester Guardian*, referring to when he reportedly said 'no good will come of this device. The word is half Greek and half Latin'?

International Rugby Union since 1987

1. Who captained England to victory at the 2003 World Cup? They are the only European team to win the tournament.

2. In 1997, the Lions toured which country for the first time in seventeen years?

3. Whose try helped Wales to a famous win over England in 1993 by 10 points to 9, ending their opponents nine-match winning run in the Five Nations?

4. In 2011, which team finally collected their second Rugby World Cup, twenty-four years after winning the inaugural tournament?

5. Who scored Scotland's try when they beat England 13-7 to win the Grand Slam in 1990?

6. Ahead of their 2005 tour of New Zealand, the Lions were held to a 25-25 draw by which country at the Millennium Stadium?

7. Where did Ireland play their home Six Nations matches between 2007 and 2010 while Lansdowne Road was being redeveloped?

8. At which club was Clive Woodward working as an assistant coach, when he was appointed England manager in 1997?

9. Whose late drop goal for the Lions won the second Test and the series against the Springboks in 1997?

10. What name is given to the imaginary 'trophy' that is 'won' by the country finishing last in the Six Nations?

11. Who made his World Cup debut in 1995, against Ireland, and

scored the first two of his record fifteen World Cup tries in a 43-19 New Zealand victory?

12. In 1998, Paul Grayson became the first England player to achieve what rare scoring feat in the same Five Nations game?

13. Who coached the Lions for the first time on their successful 1989 tour of Australia?

14. A number of Rugby League players have switched to Union since the introduction of professionalism, but before that era, which sport had Nigel Walker already competed in at the highest level before making his rugby debut for Wales in 1993?

15. In 2011, Italy beat which team in a Six Nations match for the first time with a 22-21 victory at the Stadio Flaminio?

16. Two Scottish players announced their international retirements after the third-place play-off at the 1991 World Cup. Finlay Calder was one; who was the other?

17. Which country handed England their heaviest ever defeat in 1998, by 76 points to nil?

18. Who scored 28 points for France when they scored a shock victory over the All Blacks in the 1999 World Cup semi-final, thought by many to be the best game in World Cup history?

19. In 2005, which team defeated the Lions for the first time, with a 19-13 victory?

20. In 1999, which Welsh player scored the final try in the Five Nations Championship before the tournament was enlarged to Six Nations with the addition of Italy? Neil Jenkins converted to give Wales a 32-31 victory over England.

21. At which stadium was that match played? The Welsh had to

play their 'home' games 'away' from Wales in that season's Five Nations, while the Millennium Stadium was being built.

22. Which South African Rugby board president caused a walk-out at the closing dinner of the 1995 World Cup, by claiming his country would have won the first two tournaments had they been allowed to take part?

23. What do the three handles on the Six Nations trophy represent?

24. In 2009, whose try for France against England in 1991 was chosen as the finest try ever scored at Twickenham?

25. Which country lost 145-17 to the All Blacks at the 1995 World Cup? Simon Culhane scored 45 points and Marc Ellis scored six tries in the match.

26. In 2009, whose drop goal against Wales clinched Ireland's first Grand Slam for 61 years?

27. The Samoan centre Brian Lima, who in 2007 became the first man to appear in five World Cups, is known by what nickname because of his ferocious tackling?

28. What non-rugby related reason meant that the final match of the 2001 Six Nations between England and Ireland wasn't played until October of that year?

29. Which winger scored two tries against Italy in the first-ever World Cup match, and later became the coach of the Italian team?

30. What was the number on the Springbok shirt that Nelson Mandela wore at the 1995 World Cup final?

General Knowledge 26.2

1. Which 1962 Oscar-winning film, starring Peter O'Toole, had no female speaking parts?

2. Which country fought the 'Great Patriotic War' from June 1941 until 1945?

3. Which author's first novel *Burmese Days*, published in 1934, was based on the time he spent serving with the Indian Imperial Police?

4. What is the name of the headland at the northwest extremity of Scotland, one of the few British place names with the prefix 'Cape'?

5. What name is given to a picture or relief carving on three panels, typically hinged vertically and often used as an altarpiece?

6. Which Florentine family provided the Roman Catholic church with four Popes, and the French monarchy with two Queens – Catherine and Marie?

7. In music, what is the general term for a song by a solo performer with instrumental accompaniment, such as one in an opera or oratorio?

8. Which monkey gets its name because its cap of hair resembles the cowl of an order of monks?

9. Who played a successful but world-weary stand-up comedian called Rick Spleen in the television comedy series *Lead Balloon*?

10. In India, which general term, from a Sanskrit word meaning 'accomplish', is given to any religious ascetic, swami or saintly holy man?

11. Who set up a whiskey distillery in Lynchburg, Tennessee in 1866, which is now the oldest registered distillery in America?

12. What is the singular of the word graffiti?

13. What was the surname of the mother and son who were, respectively, trainer and jockey of the 1991 Cheltenham Gold Cup winner Garrison Savannah?

14. Which material, similar in composition to bone, but perforated by tiny canals for nerve fibres and blood capillaries, forms the bulk of a tooth?

15. Who played the title role in the original London production of the musical *Barnum*?

16. Chittagong is the largest seaport and second largest city of which Asian country?

17. *The Last Battle*, first published in 1956, is the seventh and last in which series of children's books?

18. On first entering the House of Commons, newly elected MPs are assigned a coathanger with a piece of pink ribbon attached; what is the traditional purpose of the ribbon?

19. Who co-presented the television series *The Tube* with Paula Yates from 1982?

20. In Norse mythology, what name is given to the hall where warriors killed in battle spend eternity in joyful feasting, presided over by the god Odin?

21. Which aspect of filmmaking earned Edith Head eight Academy Awards and twenty-seven further nominations between 1948 and 1977?

22. Which bay incorporates two National Parks as part of its

shoreline, Snowdonia in the north and the Pembrokeshire Coast in the south?

23. What name is given to the representations, also known as 'smileys', used in emails and other electronic communications to indicate the writer's feelings or intended tone?

24. In which century did the dodo become extinct?

25. The album *OK Computer* topped the UK charts for which band in June 1997?

26. In 1314, the English army was on its way to relieve the garrison besieged at which castle, when it was defeated at Bannockburn?

27. Rodin's statue *The Thinker* was originally conceived as a portrait of which Italian poet?

28. In DIY, what term is used for the enlargement of the rim of a drilled hole so that a screw or bolt can be inserted flush with the surface?

29. According to accepted wisdom, it is best to eat oysters if the name of the month includes which letter?

30. What type of written work did Quentin Crisp describe as 'An obituary in serial form with the last instalment missing'?

Tips for would-be *Mastermind* contenders from former champions

Can you 'revise' general knowledge?

According to Nancy Dickmann, 'Quizzers are divided into two camps: those who revise general knowledge, and those (like me) who don't. In the long run, a reviser will nearly always beat someone who doesn't, but revising general knowledge is a life's pursuit rather than something you can do in a meaningful way in the couple of months you get to prepare for *Mastermind*.'

For anyone who is inspired to enter *Mastermind* and wants to prepare accordingly, Jesse Honey's advice is to try and join a local quiz league. He says that, in his experience, 'Quizzers are friendly, welcoming people and new members are always made to feel at home.' There are also the regular events organised by the British Quiz Association, where you might even get the chance to pits your wits against an 'Egghead' or a *Mastermind* champion... like Jesse, in fact.

Show 27

Specialist Subject 27.1
The Life and Works of J.R.R. Tolkien

1. In which South African city was Tolkien born on 3 January 1892?

2. In *The Lord of the Rings*, what is the full name of the gardener who overhears Gandalf tell Frodo the story of the Ring?

3. What name was given to the three brilliant jewels made by Féanor, which contained the light of the Two Trees and were stolen by the Valar Melkor?

4. Which birthday does Bilbo Baggins celebrate at the beginning of *The Lord of the Rings*?

5. In which village, often cited as one of the inspirations for the Shire, did Tolkien live for four years from 1896?

6. Tolkien and his friends C.S. Lewis and Charles Williams were members of an informal literary discussion group that met regularly at a public house in Oxford. What was the group called?

7. Which short story published in 1949 tells of the title character's encounters with a giant and the dragon Chrysophylax Dives?

8. In *The Lord of the Rings*, what does Frodo confess to having stolen from Farmer Maggot when he was a boy?

9. *The Road Goes Ever On* is a song cycle featuring Tolkien's words set to music by which composer and entertainer?

10. In *The Lord of the Rings*, which awful place with mysterious lights, near the hills of Emyn Muil, does Gollum guide Frodo and Sam through?

11. In *The Hobbit*, what was the maiden name of Bilbo Baggins' mother?

12. What disease, transmitted by body lice, did Tolkien catch while serving on the Western Front in 1916, resulting in his return to England on sick leave?

13. In *The Lord of the Rings*, what grows in the Party Field from the seed like a small nut given to Sam by Galadriel?

14. In the *Return of the King*, which battle takes place between the Hobbits and Sharkey's thugs who have invaded the Shire?

15. Tolkien often referred to himself and his wife by the names of which two Middle Earth characters? The names also appear on their gravestones.

16. Which chapter of *The Hobbit* did Tolkien largely rewrite between 1937 and 1951, making Gollum's character fit better with the portrayal of him in *The Lord of the Rings*?

17. According to the opening of *The Silmarillion*, who was known in the Elvish tongue as Ilúvatar, 'The One', and made the Ainur, the first race, of his own thought?

18. In *The Lord of the Rings*, Goldberry, who lives with Tom Bombadil, says she is the daughter of what when she introduces herself to Frodo?

19. On which letter of the alphabet did Tolkien specifically work during his time as an assistant lexicographer at the *Oxford English Dictionary*?

20. In *The Lord of the Rings*, which great spider lives in the cave at the top of the stairs of Cirith Ungol?

21. When they first meet in *The Hobbit*, with which question does Bilbo Baggins finally defeat Gollum in the riddle competition?

22. To which College did Tolkien receive an Open Classical Exhibition to study in 1911?

23. The Three Rings of the Elves are, after the One Ring, the most powerful of the Rings of Power. Which smith of Eregion forged them?

24. Which story in *Unfinished Tales* tells of the chance meeting of Gandalf and Thorin Oakenshield that is the starting point of the expedition detailed in *The Hobbit*?

25. In *The Hobbit*, what is the name of the dragon who had seized the lonely mountain and its treasure from the Dwarves' forefathers?

26. In 1925, Tolkien succeeded Sir William Craigie as Professor of which subject, at Oxford?

27. In *The Lord of the Rings*, which commander lost fifteen men and twelve horses in the battle against the Orcs near to the borders of the Entwood?

28. What name does Bilbo give the sword he discovered in the Trolls' cave, after he kills the great spider in the forest in *The Hobbit*?

29. In *The Lord of the Rings*, who shoots down the flying Nazgûl's steed in the dark above the rapids of Sarn Gebir?

30. Which great white jewel, which Thorin says is worth more than a river of gold, does Bilbo seize from the Dwarves and give to the Elvenking?

General Knowledge 27.1

1. The title of which novel by Joseph Heller has entered everyday language to describe a no-win situation?

2. In the Old Testament, how is the 'Decalogue' more usually known?

3. What was the name of the character played by Bernard Hill in the television drama series *The Boys from the Blackstuff*?

4. Which British general and Governor of the Sudan was killed by the troops of the Mahdi, at Khartoum in 1885?

5. Which number one 1979 hit by Buggles was, appropriately, the first video ever played on MTV on 1 August 1981?

6. What is the common term for the visual defect that is the subject of the Ishihara test?

7. Which famous British sculptor was born the son of a miner in Castleford, Yorkshire, in 1898?

8. Which word of medieval Latin origin means 'in exactly the same words as were used originally'?

9. Which wine is whisked to a froth with egg-yolks and sugar in the Italian dessert zabaglione?

10. Upon which West Midlands spa town did Queen Victoria confer the title 'Royal' in 1838?

11. Which actress won awards at the Golden Globes in 2007 for playing both Elizabeth I and Elizabeth II?

12. Named after a Yorkshire valley, which is the largest breed of terrier?

13. In 1400, which poet was buried in Westminster Abbey's St Benedict's Chapel, which later became known as 'Poet's Corner?

14. In which year did the General Strike take place in Great Britain?

15. Which distinctively named football club featured in a famous advert for milk in the 1980s?

16. Against which city state did Rome fight the three Punic wars between 264 and 146 BC?

17. By what name is the third movement of Debussy's Suite bergamasque for piano usually known?

18. Which country is surrounded by China to the north, Vietnam to the east, Cambodia to the south, with Thailand and Burma to the west?

19. Which part of a leaf is known as the 'petiole'?

20. Which pastry, made from very thin dough and most commonly filled with apple, takes its name from the German for 'whirlpool' because of the way it is rolled?

21. What is the longest river in Northern Ireland, with a total length of around eighty miles?

22. Which term was coined by Newton in the seventeenth century to describe the band of colour formed when a beam of visible white light is split into its constituent wavelengths, and literally means 'appearance' in Latin?

23. Which insect is commonly referred to in Britain as the Daddy Longlegs?

24. What name is given to the forced relocation of the Cherokee Native Americans to the Western United States during the winter of 1838–1839?

25. How is the Venetian artist, born Tiziano Vecellio, generally known in English?

26. In Scottish folklore, a Selkie is a human on land but takes the form of which marine mammal in the sea?

27. What surname links soul and blues performers Ben E., B.B. and Albert?

28. Haematite is the principal ore of which metal?

29. Under what penname did Harry Patterson write *The Eagle Has Landed* and many other thrillers?

30. What did John Steed usually carry in *The Avengers*?

Specialist Subject 27.2
The *Titanic*

1. *Titanic* was designated as which class of ship, named after her sister ship launched earlier in the year?

2. From which ship did the *Titanic* first receive warnings of ice on their route, during its voyage?

3. Who was appointed as Captain Smith's Chief Officer for the voyage at very short notice, after transferring from the *Olympic*?

4. At which port did the *Titanic* arrive from Belfast on 3 April 1912?

5. Which firm supplied Harland and Wolff with a 228-foot high gantry to hold the *Titanic*, the largest ever built at that time?

6. At which Irish port did the *Titanic* make her last call on 11 April 1912, allowing seven passengers to disembark?

7. There were two Marconi wireless operators on board the *Titanic*. Jack Phillips was the senior man; what was the name of the junior?

8. What was the name of the newspaper issued aboard the *Titanic* every morning to first-class passengers?

9. Who was the ship's First Officer, although he was originally intended to have been the Chief Officer before Henry Tingle Wilde's late arrival?

10. The passenger who was later referred to as the 'Unsinkable' Molly Brown boarded the ship at which port?

11. Who was the Managing Director of Harland and Wolff, and Head of the Draughting Department who designed the *Titanic*, and went on the maiden voyage to see what improvements could be made?

12. When the *Titanic* was leaving Southampton bound for Cherbourg, which other ship's mooring lines broke, causing a near-collision?

13. What was the name of the President of the White Star Line who was later vilified for entering a lifeboat while hundreds of female passengers still remained aboard the sinking ship?

14. To the nearest thousand, what was the gross registered tonnage of the *Titanic*?

15. What was the name of the lookout, who is credited with the first sighting of the iceberg with which the *Titanic* collided?

16. How many lifeboats in total was the *Titanic* equipped with, including all collapsible and emergency lifeboats?

17. Who was the captain of the principal rescue ship, the *Carpathia*?

18. Which Newfoundland wireless station received and monitored the *Titanic*'s wireless traffic, and later its distress signals?

19. As the ship was sinking, which wealthy passenger appeared on deck in full evening dress, with his valet, and declared, 'We've dressed in our best and are prepared to go down like gentlemen'?

20. What position on board was held by Charles Lightoller, the highest-ranking crewmember to survive the sinking?

21. Which passenger on the sinking *Titanic* declined the offer of a place in a lifeboat, saying to her husband, 'We have been together for many years. Where you go, I go'?

22. The *Titanic*'s distress signals, apparently ignored by the nearby *Californian*, were picked up by the *Carpathia* and which German vessel?

23. Which US senator chaired the Senate Sub-committee that investigated the *Titanic* disaster?

24. Those members of the *Titanic*'s crew who were not required for the inquiry into her sinking, returned to Britain on which Red Star liner?

25. At only nine weeks old, who was the youngest survivor of the sinking?

26. What was instituted in April 1913 as a result of the *Titanic*'s loss, in order to locate and give information about icebergs and the danger of ice in the North Atlantic?

27. Which bandleader on the ship, whose orchestra continued playing until the very last, was later buried in his home town of Colne?

28. In which city is the Women's *Titanic* Memorial, which was dedicated by the widow of President William Taft in 1931?

29. Which *Titanic* survivor, born in Switzerland, went on to win the US National tennis championship twice, as well as the men's doubles at Wimbledon and an Olympic gold medal?

30. In which year did Robert Ballard's expedition discover the wreck of the *Titanic*?

General Knowledge 27.2

1. In mathematics, what is represented by a symbol resembling a figure of eight, lying on its side?

2. Which method of preparing food so that it may be eaten by Muslims means 'lawful' in Arabic?

3. Which architect died after being run over by a tram in his native Barcelona in June 1926?

4. Which gas, that has the chemical formula HCHO, is used in a solution of water for preserving biological specimens?

5. Which German film actress and singer's adoption of trousers and other mannish clothes helped launch an American fashion craze in the 1930s?

6. The Roman province of Lusitania corresponds approximately to which modern-day country?

7. Which Italian word is used for the text of an opera?

8. Khan Younis and Rafah are towns in which territory in the Middle East?

9. In Indian cuisine, what name, derived from a Persian word meaning 'fried', is given to a dish of basmati rice mixed with meat, often topped with a thin omelette and served with a separate vegetable curry?

10. Which Kentish town gives its name to a species of warbler?

11. Which famous racehorse made his debut over fences in the Junior Novices Hurdle at Cheltenham on 18 September 1968, after a short career on the flat?

12. What name was given by westerners to members of the Mawlawi sect founded in Anatolia, because they chanted their ritual prayers with musical accompaniment, while spinning on their right foot?

13. Which television comedy series had the catchphrase 'And now for something completely different'?

14. Who resigned from his post of Leader of the House of Commons in March 2003, in protest over the decision to take military action against Iraq?

15. Which island was the home of the ancient Greek poet Sappho?

16. Whose first military success came as the commander of the artillery at the siege of Toulon in December 1793?

17. Who composed the songs 'Begin The Beguine' and 'Anything Goes' for popular musicals of the 1930s?

18. Which disease, one of whose main symptoms is jaundice, is principally transmitted to humans by the bite of the Aedes aegypti mosquito?

19. Which canal connects the west and east coasts of Scotland by linking the lochs in the Great Glen?

20. What word is used for the attribution of human characteristics to any non-human object, especially animals?

21. Which plant, formerly used as a treatment for breast tumours and herpes, was also used as a method of execution, its most noted victim being Socrates?

22. In Greek legend, whom did Theseus abandon on the island of Dia, after she had helped him kill the Minotaur?

23. Which writer was played by Toby Jones in the film *Infamous*, and in an Oscar-winning performance by Philip Seymour Hoffman?

24. Which port in south-western Norway is the country's second largest city?

25. Which type of dark coloured China tea has a name which is the Chinese for 'black dragon' or 'black snake'?

26. To what status was Pluto 'demoted' after a meeting of the International Astronomical Union in August 2006?

27. Which Scottish painter's work *The Singing Butler*, bought at auction for over £700,000 in 2004, had been rejected twelve years earlier by the Scottish Arts Council?

28. Which animals found in the tropical forests of the New World and Malaysia, are characterised by a short trunk that hangs down over their upper lip?

29. Whose 1969 novel *Portnoy's Complaint* is the story of a young Jewish male at odds with his domineering mother?

30. In 1965, who had a top twenty hit with a comedy version of 'A Hard Day's Night', in which he recited the lyrics in the style of Laurence Olivier's Richard III?

Tips for would-be *Mastermind* contenders from former champions

Should you pass or not?

Nancy Dickmann's strategy was not to pass at all, although she admits that on a few questions she blanked and had to, as she couldn't come up with a sensible guess. However, her strategy still paid off as she won her first-round heat because she had given fewer passes than one of her opponents.

Pat Gibson's advice to potential contenders is: 'Do not pass – it's as simple as that.' He certainly practised what he preaches in all ten of his visits to the Black Chair, and his strategy paid off as well as he won his heat and final of 'Champion of Champions' on passes.

Other *Mastermind* champions, including David Beamish and Mary-Elizabeth Raw, also went through the heats, semis and final without passing once.

Show 28

Specialist Subject 28.1
Kings and Queens of England and Britain since 1066

1. Which King of England was killed in battle on 22 August 1485, and was succeeded on the throne by the man who defeated him?

2. What derisive nickname is given to the Parliament that met briefly in 1614 during the reign of James I and VI? He dissolved it despite it having passed no legislation.

3. Which King erected monumental crosses along the route taken by the body of his wife, Queen Eleanor, when it was carried ceremonially from Lincoln to London after her death in 1290?

4. One of the first signs of George III's madness was allegedly addressing an oak tree as if it were the king of which country?

5. Edward II is one of two Plantagenet kings born in Wales; who is the other?

6. Edward VII's State Visit to France in 1903 is said to have paved the way for an agreement between Britain and France the following year. What name is given to this agreement?

7. Mary Tudor appointed Stephen Gardiner, the Bishop of Winchester, to which position in August 1553, despite his role in her parents' divorce?

8. Who led a revolt against Queen Mary in January 1554, marching from Kent to London where he was forced to surrender?

9. In 1604, James I and VI wrote a 'Counterblaste' to what substance, describing it as 'loathsome to the eye and hateful to the nose'?

10. Whom did the Prince of Wales, later George IV, secretly and illegally marry at her home in Park Street, Mayfair, on 15 December 1785?

11. Which animal was Richard II's personal badge, and was prominently displayed on his livery as well as being depicted on the Wilton Diptych?

12. Supervised by Edward III from a windmill, at which battle of 1346 did the King's 16-year-old son the Black Prince 'win his spurs'?

13. Who was Queen Victoria's first Prime Minister? He was a strong influence in the early years of her reign.

14. When James II's wife, Mary of Modena, gave birth to a son in 1688, it was rumoured that the child was not really hers and had been smuggled into her bedroom inside what object?

15. What title did Disraeli persuade Parliament to grant to Victoria in 1876?

16. Whom did Charles II appoint as Surveyor-General of the King's Works, in 1669?

17. The so-called 'anarchy' of King Stephen's reign was described by the Anglo-Saxon Chronicle as a period when 'Christ and his saints were...' what?

18. Who served Henry VII as Lord Chancellor from 1487, and gave his name to an alleged theory of taxation that was known as his 'fork'?

19. How is Richard II generally agreed to have died, either on the orders of Henry IV or by his own actions?

20. What was the name of William the Conqueror's half-brother, who fought with him at the Battle of Hastings but was later arrested for allegedly aspiring to the Papacy?

21. In which country was Princess Elizabeth on holiday, staying on a game reserve, when she received the news of her father's death and that she had become Queen Elizabeth II?

22. Lambert Simnel was one of the two main pretenders to the throne during the reign of Henry VII. What was the name of the other, who claimed to be Richard, Duke of York?

23. Which order of chivalry was remodelled and had its ordinances rewritten by Edward VI?

24. At which battle of May 1471 did the forces of Edward IV defeat those of Queen Margaret of Anjou?

25. George IV was finally persuaded to give his assent to which bill in April 1829, a year after reluctantly agreeing to the repeal of the Test and Corporation Acts?

26. In October 1936, Edward VIII personally asked which newspaper owner to limit the coverage of Wallis Simpson's divorce case in the British press?

27. What name was given to the five ministers who were Charles II's principal advisers from around 1667 to 1672? It was an anagram of the first letters of their names.

28. What was the full name of John of Gaunt's third wife, through whom Henry Tudor claimed direct descent from King Edward III?

29. What was the name of the house in Yorkshire, where the future Edward VII was staying when he became embroiled in a card-cheating scandal?

30. What is George II said to have replied to Queen Caroline when, on her deathbed, she urged him to marry again?

General Knowledge 28.1

1. What name is generally used in Britain for a drink of fresh orange juice mixed with champagne?

2. In 1867, the English physician Thomas Allbutt invented a short version of which basic clinical instrument? Earlier models had been a foot long and took 20 minutes to work.

3. What is the title of Thomas Hardy's last novel, about a young man with intellectual ambitions, who dies miserably after a series of misfortunes?

4. What is the name of the Roman road that followed a remarkably straight route for most the way between Exeter and Lincoln?

5. In his book *Towards a New Architecture*, what did the architect Le Corbusier describe as a 'machine for living in'?

6. What is the county town and administrative centre of Kent?

7. Which Francis Ford Coppola film is based on Joseph Conrad's *Heart of Darkness*?

8. The male of which fish gives birth to its young by expelling them from a single hole in its pouch?

9. What name is given to a loaf made from two rounds of dough; a smaller one placed on top of a larger one?

10. In Celtic folklore, which fairy's wailing outside a house was supposed to foretell of the approaching death of one of its inhabitants?

11. Which composer wrote *The Young Person's Guide to the Orchestra*?

12. Which spring flower is named after the Greek youth who was accidentally killed while Apollo was teaching him to throw the discus?

13. What name, from the luggage that northern political adventurers carried to the South after the American Civil War, is given to someone who comes to start a political career in a place where they have no roots?

14. In which flagship, formerly called the *Pelican*, did Sir Francis Drake circumnavigate the globe between 1577 and 1580?

15. The card game known as Solitaire in America is also known by which other name in Britain?

16. In which country is Mount Kilimanjaro, Africa's highest mountain?

17. In the television series *Life on Mars*, in which year does DI Sam Tyler find himself living and working after a car crash?

18. Which element has the lowest normal boiling point?

19. The song 'Another Suitcase In Another Hall' comes from which musical by Tim Rice and Andrew Lloyd Webber?

20. Which Israeli Prime Minister shared the 1978 Nobel Peace Prize with the Egyptian President Anwar el-Sadat?

21. In swimming, what term is used for an individual race or relay using all four recognised strokes?

22. In Hinduism, a leaf of which herb, closely related to a plant used in Italian cooking, is laid on a dead body to ensure its safe arrival in Paradise?

23. Which regular plane figure has internal angles of 108 degrees?

24. Which mammal has the longest gestation period; between 18 and 22 months?

25. Which Dutch-born artist's twentieth-century masterpiece, 'Broadway Boogie-Woogie', uses a series of small colour blocks, reflecting his interest in jazz and dancing?

26. On which Hebridean island is Fingal's Cave?

27. Which bestselling novel by Marina Lewycka, published in 2005, opens, 'Two years after my mother died, my father fell in love with a glamorous blonde Ukrainian divorcée'?

28. Who was the first King of the united Picts and Scots? His rule extended over the part of Scotland north of the Forth and the Clyde.

29. Which group topped the UK album charts for the fourth time in 2003 with *Hail to the Thief*?

30. Which actress allegedly said, 'The best time I had with Joan

Crawford was when I pushed her down the stairs in *Whatever Happened To Baby Jane*'?

Specialist Subject 28.2
Cinema 1910–2010

1. The sequel to which film was released with the tagline 'Just when you thought it was safe to go back in the water'?

2. Who composed the musical score for Westerns such as *The Good, the Bad and the Ugly* and *A Fistful of Dollars*?

3. Which animation studios, taken over by Disney in 2006, made films including *Toy Story* and its sequels?

4. Who directed and co-wrote the 1960 film *La Dolce Vita*?

5. Bert Lahr played which character in the 1939 film *The Wizard Of Oz*?

6. Which Oscar-winning 2010 film charts the rise of the Facebook website?

7. With which Spanish director did Salvador Dali make the Surrealist films *Un Chien Andalou* in 1928 and *L'Âge d'Or* in 1930?

8. Which 1995 film ends with a confrontation between Robert De Niro and Al Pacino near the main landing strip of Los Angeles airport?

9. Which of the Marx brothers never spoke in their films?

10. Which 2001 cult film stars Jake Gyllenhaal as an introverted student who has visions of a tall rabbit called Frank who tells him the end of the world is nigh?

11. In the film *Sex and Drugs and Rock 'n' Roll*, Andy Serkis plays which singer?

12. In which 1999 film does Keanu Reeves play a computer programmer who leads a secret life as a hacker under the alias 'Neo'?

13. Created by the writer Keith Waterhouse and played on screen by Tom Courtenay, how is the character William Terrence Fisher better known?

14. Steve McQueen had his first starring role in which 1958 cult horror film about an amorphous creature from outer space?

15. In *Four Weddings and a Funeral*, which actor plays Gareth, whose funeral takes place between the third and fourth weddings?

16. Which 1971 British crime film was set in Newcastle-on-Tyne, and starred Michael Caine as a London gangster seeking revenge for his brother's death?

17. Who does Michael Sheen play in Stephen Frears' 2006 film *The Queen*?

18. Which 1976 spoof gangster film, starring Jodie Foster, had a cast composed entirely of children?

19. In the 1930 film *Anna Christie*, which celebrated actress's first spoken words on screen were 'Give me a whiskey'?

20. What is the title of Michael Moore's Academy award-winning documentary film about a school shooting in America?

21. In 1971, Clint Eastwood took which role that had been rejected by John Wayne, Paul Newman and others including Frank Sinatra, who turned it down because he had an injured hand?

22. Starring Edward Woodward as a devoutly Christian policeman, which classic horror film of 1973 is set on the Scottish island of Summerisle?

23. Which Formula One racing driver was the subject of a 2010 biopic made by the British filmmaker Asif Kapadia?

24. Which 1956 film starring Grace Kelly was a musical remake of *The Philadelphia Story*?

25. Which actor won the Oscar for Best Supporting Actor in 1996, for his role as Roger 'Verbal' Kint in *The Usual Suspects*?

26. The film version of which novel by D.H. Lawrence includes a nude wrestling scene with Alan Bates and Oliver Reed?

27. Whose first Hollywood screen test allegedly resulted in this verdict: 'Can't act. Can't sing. Slightly bald. Can dance a little'?

28. In 1972, Isaac Hayes won the Oscar for Best Original Song for the theme tune of which detective film?

29. Who is the only person to speak in Mel Brooks' film *Silent Movie*?

30. The 'Golden Lion' is the highest prize given at which annual film festival?

General Knowledge 28.2

1. What Russian word is used to describe the Soviet government's policy of openness and transparency, introduced by Mikhail Gorbachov in the 1980s?

2. In the Bible, who was succeeded by Joshua as the leader of the Israelites?

3. Which 1973 cult musical was written by Richard O'Brien?

4. Which word of Russian origin is used for the flat, generally treeless grassland that extends eastwards from Hungary, through Siberia, and into north-eastern China?

5. Which television character had the catch-phrases 'lovely jubbly' and 'cushty'?

6. Spotted is the largest of three species of which scavenging animal, native to Africa and Asia?

7. What name is used for the sidepiece or post of a door or window frame?

8. Which Commonwealth country's National Day is 1 July, commemorating the date in 1867 when its federal government was established and its first Prime Minister took office?

9. Which champagne was first produced in 1876 in its characteristic clear bottle for the Tsar Alexander II?

10. What name is given to the protective, outermost layer of the skin?

11. The attempted assassination of Charles de Gaulle forms the plot of which novel by Frederick Forsyth?

12. Which thoroughfare, that forms the eastern boundary of Hyde Park, became synonymous with great wealth in the nineteenth century when it was one of London's most fashionable addresses?

13. Which rap artist won the 2002 Best Song Oscar for 'Lose Yourself' from his debut film *8 Mile*?

14. Memphis was established by Menes as the first capital of which ancient country?

15. Who won the Wimbledon Ladies' Singles title a record nine times between 1978 and 1990?

16. Which British tree, often planted on river banks to help prevent erosion, is suitable for charcoal-making and was once used for making clogs?

17. What name is traditionally used for seats in the uppermost gallery of a theatre, because the blue sky painted on many theatre ceilings was thought to represent heaven?

18. Which planet's existence was the first to be predicted by mathematical calculation?

19. Which band's only chart-topping UK single was 'Another Brick In The Wall Part 2'?

20. In Norse mythology, how many legs did Odin's magical horse Sleipnir have?

21. Bernard Leach established a pottery at which Cornish resort in 1920?

22. In science, which quantity is defined as 'mass per unit volume'?

23. Which smoked fish is one of the main ingredients in an Omelette Arnold Bennett?

24. The Canadian Provinces of Nunavut, Manitoba, Ontario, and Quebec all have a shoreline on which stretch of water?

25. In *M*A*S*H*, what was the nickname of Corporal Walter O'Reilly, played by Gary Burghoff?

26. Pancho Villa, who was assassinated on his ranch in 1923, was one of the revolutionary figures in which country?

27. Which playwright, who was born in Dublin in 1751, wrote the comedies *The Rivals* and *The School for Scandal*?

28. What type of creature is a bandy-bandy, which is found in Australia?

29. Whose only opera, *Duke Bluebeard's Castle*, was based on a fairy story by Charles Perrault?

30. Oscar Wilde reputedly said that what 'is the curse of the drinking classes'?

Tips for would-be *Mastermind* contenders from former champions

How winning *Mastermind* changed my life... or not

As the first female champion in 12 years, Nancy Dickmann faced the typical celebrity hazard of being recognised in the supermarket. She was also invited to join the quiz league team at a local pub – which caused a bit of a stir at their first competition as you can imagine – but best of all, she says, was appearing as a crossword clue in a well-known tabloid newspaper!

In typical British style, Jesse Honey's *Mastermind* victory earned him fewer column inches than an unfortunate contender on the same series who succumbed to an attack of nerves and set a new 'record' for the lowest score in the show's history – just five points. However, Jesse was able to put feats of *high* scoring on *Mastermind* back in the newspapers with his awesome display on 'Champion of Champions' (see High Scores).

Pat Gibson is now a member of the elite quiz team on the BBC programme *Eggheads*; he won his place – naturally – on 'Are You an Egghead?' He has also won *Brain of Britain*, the World Quizzing Championships and joined Sir David Hunt in the most exclusive club of all: *Mastermind* 'Champion of Champions', thanks to his knowledge of 'Great Mathematicians' and an awesome display of general knowledge. (If you want to test yourself against Pat – and David – see 'Champion of Champions' questions.)

Show 29

Three Great Composers:
Mozart, Beethoven and Tchaikovsky

1. According to E.M. Forster's *Howards End*, 'It will be generally admitted that...' what 'is the most sublime noise that has ever penetrated into the ear of man'?

2. What was the name of Wolfgang Amadeus Mozart's father, who was a violinist-composer in the service of the Prince of Salzburg and helped nurture his son's talents?

3. When Pyotr Ilyich Tchaikovsky left school in 1859, he took up a clerical post as a civil servant in which government office?

4. In which city was Ludwig van Beethoven born in 1770?

5. The young Mozart is said to have told which future Queen that he would marry her one day?

6. Which work by Tchaikovsky was performed for the first time in August 1882, at the Cathedral of Christ the Redeemer in Moscow?

7. With whom did Beethoven study shortly after his arrival in Vienna in 1792?

8. Which Mozart opera, from a libretto by Lorenzo da Ponte, was first performed in Vienna in 1786?

9. After the outbreak of the Franco-Prussian War in 1870, Tchaikovsky fled from Prussia to which country?

10. The unnamed woman to whom Beethoven wrote the famous love letters of 6 and 7 July, giving neither address nor year, has become known by what two-word term?

11. In Leporello's famous catalogue aria from Mozart's *Don Giovanni*, how many lovers does he say that his master has had in Spain alone?

12. Which opera did Tchaikovsky complete in early 1878, after separating from his wife Antonina Milyukova just months into their ill-fated marriage?

13. In which village, near Vienna, did Beethoven write a Testament to his brothers in 1802, revealing his despair at his increasing deafness?

14. Which of Mozart's operas features the character Despina, who claims falsely to speak Greek, Arabic, Turkish, Vandal, Swabian, and Tartar?

15. Which recently invented instrument features prominently in the 'Dance of the Sugar Plum Fairy' by Tchaikovsky?

16. What event of 1814 to 1815 led Beethoven to compose the cantata 'The Glorious Moment'?

17. Which of Mozart's operas, based on a play by C.F. Bretzner, was first performed at the Burgtheater in Vienna on 16 July 1782?

18. Which of Tchaikovsky's symphonies has the dedication 'To My

Best Friend', a reference to his benefactor Nadezhda von Meck?

19. Who described Beethoven in 1812 as 'an utterly untamed personality, who is not altogether wrong in holding the world to be detestable but surely does not make it any the more enjoyable for himself or others by his attitude'?

20. Which of Mozart's operas contains the aria 'Zum leiden bin ich auserkoren'?

21. In January 1892, which fellow composer conducted the German premiere of Tchaikovsky's opera *Eugene Onegin* in Hamburg?

22. Mozart's works are often referred to by 'K numbers', after the surname of which Austrian musicologist who published a catalogue of his complete works in 1862?

23. What popular name is shared by Beethoven's Piano Sonata Number 8 in C Minor and Tchaikovsky's Symphony Number 6 in B Minor?

24. What was the name of the Austrian composer who became a student of Mozart's, and produced the standard completion of the Requiem Mass in D Minor after his death, at the request of Constanze?

25. Which ballet did Tchaikovsky complete in 1892, the year before his death?

26. Whose ode 'An die Freude' was used by Beethoven in the finale of his Ninth Symphony?

27. In Mozart's second version of the Wind Serenade in E Flat Major, he enlarged the work from a sextet to an octet by adding a pair of which instrument?

28. Tchaikovsky and his mother both died of which disease, although it has been rumoured that he committed suicide over revelations about his private life?

29. What was the name of the Russian ambassador to the Viennese court who commissioned Beethoven to write the three string quartets, Opus 59, that included Russian folk tunes?

30. Which dramatist wrote the 1979 play *Amadeus*, which he adapted into an Oscar-winning film?

General Knowledge 29.1

1. How many years of marriage are celebrated at a ruby wedding anniversary?

2. The scientific study of birds is known by what specific name?

3. Which artist's painting *Going to the Match*, showing fans outside Bolton Wanderers' former ground Burnden Park, was bought by the Professional Footballers' Association for £1.9 million in 1999?

4. The flag of which Southeast Asian country is red with a five-pointed yellow star in its centre?

5. 'Dirty old river, must you keep rolling' is the opening line of which 1967 hit for The Kinks?

6. What alternative name for the Plantagenet Kings of England comes from the French countship held by Henry II at his accession in 1154?

7. Who plays Mr Brown in the film *Reservoir Dogs*?

8. The two species of New World vulture, the Andean and the rarer California, are better known by what name?

9. Which Greek dish is made from cucumber, garlic, yoghurt and often mint?

10. In Norse mythology, what name is given to the land of the giants?

11. Whose work *The History of the Decline and Fall of the Roman Empire* was published in six volumes between 1776 and 1788?

12. Which Ukrainian-born aviation pioneer designed the first serviceable helicopter, the VS-300, which he successfully flew in September 1939?

13. Which Scottish golfer played in eight Ryder Cups between 1991 and 2006 and never lost a singles match in any of them?

14. Which animals travel in mobs under the leadership of an 'old man' or 'boomer'?

15. In an essay of 1756, which French writer described the Holy Roman Empire as 'neither Holy, nor Roman, nor an Empire'?

16. Perth in Scotland stands on which river?

17. In which 1960s television series was an international spy organisation run from behind Del Floria's tailor shop in Manhattan?

18. Which prominent Labour politician was the MP for Ebbw Vale from 1929 to his death in 1960?

19. What French term is used in ballet for a dance for two people?

20. In Greek legend, the hundred eyes of which figure were set into a peacock's tail by the goddess Hera after he had been slain by Hermes?

21. In radio broadcasting, what does AM stand for?

22. Which desert in Western Australia is named after a member of an expedition who died during an attempt to cross it in 1874?

23. Who wrote the autobiographical play *A Voyage Round My Father*, about his relationship with his blind barrister father?

24. Which island group in the Indian Ocean was ceded to Britain from France in 1814, governed as a dependency of Mauritius until 1903, and became an independent republic in 1976?

25. Who wrote the song 'This Land Is Your Land', which became an anthem of the civil rights movement in the 1960s?

26. By what original trade name is the drug sildenafil citrate most commonly known? It began life as a medication for increasing blood flow to the heart.

27. Who was the Chief Designer at the French fashion house Chloé from 1997 until 2001, when she set up her own label in partnership with the Gucci group?

28. What type of fruit is a costard, from which we get the word 'costermonger'?

29. Which country, following their 1979 revolution, began producing 'ZamZam Cola' when its contract with a well-known American firm was cancelled?

30. In the film *Batman Returns*, which villain discovers that his real name is Oswald Cobblepot?

Rivers, Mountains and Volcanoes of the World

1. The capital cities of Budapest, Bratislava and Vienna all stand on which river?

2. Which mountain range extends in an almost north-south direction for around 2,500 kilometres through Russia and Kazakhstan, between the Arctic Ocean and the Caspian Sea?

3. Which Swiss city stands on the River Rhine where the French, German and Swiss borders meet?

4. In which country is Africa's highest mountain, Mount Kilimanjaro, mainly situated?

5. Which Australian river was explored in 1697 by a Dutch expedition, and named after its most distinctive bird by the ship's artist Victor Victorszoon?

6. In which country is the summit of Mount Aconcagua, the highest peak in South America?

7. Which tributary of the Mississippi is known as the 'Big Muddy' because of the amount of silt it carries?

8. Which Icelandic volcano that has erupted over twenty times since the eleventh century, is according to myth, the 'Gateway to Purgatory'?

9. Which river forms a vast delta as it reaches its mouth on the Adriatic coast of Italy between Venice and Ravenna?

10. In 1851, the New Zealand mountain Aoraki was given which name in honour of an English Sea Captain and explorer?

11. The five rivers that give the province of Punjab its name are tributaries of which river?

12. Which peak in Yukon Territory is the highest mountain in Canada?

13. Which city on the north bank of the River Plate estuary is the southernmost capital city in mainland South America?

14. Which mountain is the highest in Australia, rising to a height of 2,228 metres?

15. Near which city do both the Blue and White Nile merge to form one river?

16. The Serra da Estrela, that rise to a height of nearly 2,000 metres, are the highest mountains on the mainland of which European country?

17. What is the principal river of Burma? Its name is thought to come from the Sanskrit for 'elephant river'.

18. Which 700-mile-long mountain range runs parallel with the south-eastern coast of South Africa, and extends into Lesotho?

19. Which Canadian city at the confluence of the Yukon and Klondike rivers was the service and supply centre of the late nineteenth-century Gold Rush?

20. Monte Cinto, which reaches a height of 2,710 metres, is the highest point of which Mediterranean island?

21. Rising north-west of Moscow, and flowing about 3,700 kilometres before emptying into the Caspian Sea, which is Europe's longest river?

22. The Aberdare mountains are situated just south of the equator, in which country?

23. Which major German river empties into the North Sea near the port of Bremerhaven?

24. Which active volcano has the local name Mongibello, meaning 'beautiful mountain'?

25. In which country do the rivers Tigris and Euphrates both rise?

26. In which American State is Mount St Helens, which erupted with devastating effect in May 1980?

27. What is the longest river in the Iberian peninsula?

28. In which African country are the Simien Mountains, which are noted for their unique wildlife such as the Gelada Baboon and the Walia Ibex, a goat found nowhere else in the world?

29. What is the English name for the longest river in Asia, with a length of over 6,000 kilometres?

30. The name of which Mexican volcano means 'smoking mountain' in the local Indian language?

General Knowledge 29.2

1. On maps of the London Underground, which line is coloured red?

2. Which British city became known as 'Cottonopolis' in the nineteenth century?

3. Whose law states that, within the proportional limit, the extension produced in a spring or wire is proportional to the force producing it?

4. The crushed leaves of which plant yield a blue dye used by the ancient Britons as body paint?

5. The four main characters of which BAFTA award-winning comedy series were teenage boys called Will, Simon, Jay and Neil?

6. In Islam, what name is given to the official who summons the faithful to prayer five times a day?

7. Which art museum in Florence has a name meaning 'offices' because that was the building's original purpose, when constructed for Grand Duke Cosimo the First de' Medici?

8. The 16th Earl of Warwick, also known as the 'Kingmaker', was killed at which battle in 1471?

9. Literally meaning 'self-boiling', what is the usual Russian term for a tea urn?

10. In anatomy, which organs of the body are coated with a membrane known as the visceral pleura?

11. In Shakespeare's *Othello*, what is the name of Iago's wife?

12. Who both won and lost French Presidential elections against François Mitterand?

13. Which term, from the Italian 'to play the harp', is used for a chord in which the notes are played in rapid succession rather than simultaneously?

14. Chicago stands on the South Western shores of which of the Great Lakes?

15. In the 1925 film *The Gold Rush*, which actor tucks into a Thanksgiving day meal of a boiled shoe?

16. What name is given to a young hare, strictly speaking one in its first year?

17. In which sport have the Euroleague champions included Real Madrid, Panathinaikos and Maccabi Tel Aviv?

18. What was the codename for the Allied landings in North-West Africa in November 1942?

19. Whose first solo hit was 'Suedehead', which reached number five in the UK charts in February 1988?

20. The name of what instrument for measuring high temperatures comes from the Greek words meaning 'fire' and 'measure'?

21. Which fashion designer opened her first boutique, in Chelsea's King's Road in 1955, with her future husband Alexander Plunket Greene?

22. Which ferry port lies on Holy Island on the north-west tip of Wales?

23. The name of which thick, reddish-brown Chinese sauce means 'seafood' although there is no fish in it?

24. Which leader, of Kurdish origin, had united all of Syria, Mesopotamia, Palestine and Egypt under his rule by 1186?

25. *Stalin Ate My Homework* is the title of which comedian's childhood memoirs?

26. In Greek and Roman mythology, who was the muse of erotic and love poetry?

27. Which American comedian was famous for his parodies of pop songs of the mid 1950s such as 'The Great Pretender' and 'The Banana Boat Song'?

28. Which insects belong to the order Coleoptera?

29. What does a cruciverbalist like to set or solve?

30. In which cartoon series did the lawyer Perry Masonry appear?

Tips for would-be *Mastermind* contenders from former champions

What is it like to sit in the Black Chair and undergo 'the toughest test on television'?

According to Pat Gibson, 'Both the *Who Wants To Be A Millionaire?* and *Mastermind* studios are very theatrical, with atmospheric lighting and wraparound audiences. It is quite a thrill to take the seat.'

Nancy Dickmann found that 'the spotlight effectively blocks out everything else once you're sitting in the chair. You can't see the other contestants, or the studio audience, just John Humphrys.'

Jesse Honey says the same, and that, 'As John is all you can see, it's actually relatively easy to concentrate on him asking the questions and to forget that this will be on TV.'

As for the mindset required to succeed – rather than just survive – the ordeal in the Black Chair, Pat's advice is 'trust that you have prepared properly, concentrate on giving a fluent answering performance, listening to every word John Humphrys says and answer promptly...' Oh and, of course, 'Never pass!'

Show 30

Specialist Subject 30.1
Flowers, Trees and Plants

1. Which carnivorous plant has a botanical name that loosely translates as 'Aphrodite's mousetrap'?

2. What is the usual colour of the flower of the saffron crocus?

3. What is the common name of the family of flowering plants most of which belong to the genus 'Papaver'?

4. The linden is an alternative poetic name for which tree?

5. What is the common name of the fast-growing, twining plant 'Ipomoea'?

6. Which large nut that grows in the Seychelles gets its name because it was found floating in the Indian Ocean before the palm producing it was known?

7. The name of which flower comes directly from the Middle English name for the asphodel?

8. Which plant of the genus 'Pogostemon' produces a strongly scented essential oil used in perfumes and aromatherapy?

9. Which shrubs with pendulous flowers are named after a

sixteenth-century German botanist, and also give their name to a deep reddish-purple colour seen in the blooms of some species?

10. Which vegetable has varieties including Ailsa Craig, Bedfordshire Champion and Express Yellow?

11. Which common early flowering wild plant, whose stems each carry a single yellow flower, has the scientific name 'primula vulgaris'?

12. The name of which fungal disease of trees of the species 'Ulmus' comes from the country where it was first researched in 1919?

13. Alba, gallica and damask are all types of which flowering shrub?

14. According to legend, which yucca plant, found in the Mojave desert, got its name because its branches reminded Mormon settlers of the upraised arms of a Biblical leader?

15. What colour are the berries on the common mistletoe that grows in Britain?

16. Which valuable hardwood tree with the scientific name 'Tectona grandis' has been used for timber in India for more than 2,000 years, and is common in shipbuilding because of its durability?

17. 'Blue Jacket' and 'Delft Blue' are varieties of which scented flower?

18. Which tree has sweet-smelling white flowers that can be used to make a cordial, and black berries that can be used to make wine?

19. Which Alpine flower, famed in song, has a name meaning 'noble white' in German?

20. The Jerusalem artichoke, also known as the Girasole, is related to which tall, yellow-flowered plant?

21. Black piano keys are traditionally made from the wood of which group of trees?

22. The name of which shrub, related to the rhododendron and cultivated for its spectacular blooms, comes from the Greek for 'dry' because of the soil some species prefer?

23. What North American vine, mainly grown for its red autumnal foliage, is also known as American ivy or, in the USA, as woodbine?

24. What name is given to the bright red petal-like leaves surrounding a cluster of yellow flowers on the poinsettia plant?

25. Belonging to the genus 'Fagus', which common deciduous tree has sweet nuts traditionally used for fattening pigs?

26. Which ancient group of plants, most of which have large leaves known as fronds, grow mainly in damp areas, have no flowers and reproduce using spores?

27. Which plant takes its name from a port in Mexico, and is a source of fibre used especially for making ropes and matting?

28. What is the popular name of the tree, also known as the Chile Pine, which has spiny leaves arranged on stiff branches that discourage animals from climbing it?

29. What common name is used for the seed pods of the Ash tree, which flutter down to earth in little bunches?

30. In Afghanistan, which nut is known as 'charmarghz', meaning 'four brains'?

General Knowledge 30.1

1. What phonetic form of the French for 'help me' is an internationally recognised distress signal?

2. Which Indian city, whose economy is based primarily upon tea, was developed as a sanatorium and hill station for British troops during the period of the Raj?

3. In 1966, who became the first footballer to be voted BBC Sports Personality of the Year?

4. Before decimalisation, what name was given to the British two shilling coin that had been minted originally in 1849?

5. What name is given to a sweet pancake served in a flaming orange sauce?

6. Which halogen has the lowest atomic number and is represented by the letter F?

7. In music, what word is generally used for a counter melody either composed or improvised above a familiar melody?

8. Traditionally, devotees of which religion leave their dead on 'Towers of Silence' to be devoured by vultures?

9. Which early Florentine artist is supposed to have drawn a perfect circle when the then Pope asked to see a sample of his work?

10. The Silverback is the mature male form of which ape?

11. Which novel about public school life, published in 1857, was originally credited to 'An Old Boy'?

12. In printing and word processing, what term is used for the arrangement of text so that it is aligned with the left or right

margins, or both?

13. On board ship, how long does a dog watch last?

14. In 1892, who first entered Parliament as an Independent Labour MP for West Ham South?

15. In which Verdi opera do the gypsies sing the 'Anvil Chorus' while sitting round their camp fire?

16. In Greek mythology, who was married first to Tantalus and then to Agamemnon?

17. Who won the 2001 Whitbread Book of the Year award with *The Amber Spyglass*, which was the first children's novel to win the prize?

18. What name, derived from the Greek for 'gland', is given to the mass of lymphatic tissue between the back of the nose and the throat that can inhibit breathing and speaking, particularly in children?

19. In which television series did Ricky Gervais play the struggling actor Andy Millman?

20. By what ancient name were the two outcrops Calpe and Abyla, which mark the eastern entrance of the strait of Gibraltar, collectively known?

21. How is Count Laszlo de Almasy better known, in the novel by Michael Ondaatje that was made into a film starring Ralph Fiennes?

22. Which 'Latin' name for Wales was coined in the Middle Ages?

23. What name is given to the style in which hair of shoulder length or longer is rolled under on either side, from the tops of the ears to the nape of the neck?

24. Who was the first signatory of the American Declaration of Independence? His name has become a colloquial term for a signature.

25. Kumiss, a traditional drink of Central Asian nomads, is normally made from the fermented milk of which animal?

26. The god Dagon, who was worshipped extensively throughout the ancient Middle East, is traditionally said to be the inventor of which agricultural implement?

27. The singer, born as Mary O'Brien in 1939, achieved fame in the 1960s under what name?

28. Which planet takes longer to complete one rotation on its own axis, relative to the stars, than it does to orbit the Sun?

29. What name is given to both a young tree that is larger than a seedling, and also to a greyhound before it is a year old?

30. What was presented to Walt Disney along with the full-size Oscar he received in 1938 for *Snow White and the Seven Dwarfs*?

Specialist Subject 30.2
The Novels of Evelyn Waugh

1. In *Brideshead Revisited*, what event brings Charles Ryder back to England in 1926?

2. By what nickname are both Guy Crouchback and Apthorpe known by the younger officers, due to the age at which they joined the Halberdiers?

3. At the beginning of *Vile Bodies*, what is the name of 'last week's Prime Minister', who has taken more than twice the prescribed amount of chloral and moves 'in an uneasy trance'?

4. Off which country's coast does Azania lie according to the map in *Black Mischief*?

5. In *Scoop*, who was foreign editor at *The Beast*, though he would have preferred to be in charge of the Competitions?

6. According to Dr Fagan in *Decline and Fall*, to what can almost all the disasters of English history be traced?

7. Which of Evelyn Waugh's characters owns a Gothic style house called Hetton Abbey?

8. Which notoriously bungled wartime operation of May 1941 forms the backdrop for the later stages of *Officers and Gentlemen*?

9. In *Vile Bodies*, which author particularly excites the attentions of a customs officer, who thinks he is French and therefore likely to write 'pretty dirty books'?

10. Which of Waugh's friends dismissed 'The Temple at Thatch' as 'too English for my exotic taste', prompting Waugh to destroy the novel?

11. In 'Happy Warriors', what is Guy Crouchback's one-word description of the novel *No Orchids for Miss Blandish*?

12. Which of Waugh's heroines has the misfortune of being eaten at a feast, by the hero amongst others?

13. In *A Handful of Dust*, which Dickens novel does Mr Todd suggest that Tony Last should read to him after his two days of drugged sleep?

14. On which journalist, politician, and associate of Churchill did Waugh model the character of Rex Mottram in *Brideshead Revisited*?

15. According to Anthony Blanche, what is 'the great English blight' that kills art, love, and finally, Charles Ryder as an artist?

16. To whom did Waugh dedicate *The Loved One*?

17. What present does Guy give to Apthorpe, when he visits him in hospital, which unexpectedly leads to Apthorpe's death?

18. Who is discovered taking shelter under the billiard table at Bellamy's, despite being the most senior officer there, on the night that Turtle's Club is destroyed during an air raid?

19. Originally conceived as the hero of *Black Mischief*, Basil Seal reappears in which 1942 novel?

20. The character of Julia Stitch in Scoop was modelled on which of Waugh's friends?

21. How does Ivor Claire get D troop into position so quickly, when on manoeuvres on Mugg?

22. Which character in *Decline and Fall* has doubts, because he cannot understand why God created the world?

23. In addition to Emperor of Azania, Chief of the Chiefs of Sakuyu, Lord of Wanda and Tyrant of the Seas, what other title does Seth hold in *Black Mischief*?

24. What does Gilbert Pinfold agree to 'in an idle moment', that he instantly regrets?

25. What name did Guy's grandfather give to his house in Italy, although the locals called it 'Castello Crouchback?'

26. In *Unconditional Surrender*, what does Arthur Box-Bender decide to do that distresses his father?

27. From which work of children's literature did Waugh take the epigraph for *Vile Bodies*?

28. In *The Loved One*, who is revealed to actually be 'two gloomy men and a bright young secretary'?

29. In *Put out More Flags*, which of the poet Parsnip's works is praised for its 'wonderfully dramatic old chestnuts'?

30. What does Charles Ryder describe as 'Great bosh' in conversation with Cordelia in *Brideshead Revisited*?

General Knowledge 30.2

1. Which Oxford college, founded in 1438 by Henry VI and Henry Chichele, traditionally has no undergraduates?

2. Which rocky promontory is known in Cornish as Penn an Wlas?

3. Which record label, that played an important role in the birth of rock and roll, was founded in Memphis in the early 1950s by Sam Phillips?

4. Which Jamaican-born nurse went to Crimea at her own expense to tend the wounded, later becoming a popular figure after the publication of her memoirs?

5. In a famous scene from the 1923 film *Safety Last*, which actor is seen hanging from the hands of a clock over the side of a skyscraper?

6. Which order of monks was founded by St Bruno in 1084?

7. What name, derived from an Italian word for 'trouser leg',

is given to a pizza which is folded in half before cooking to contain the filling?

8. Vexillology is the term for the study of what?

9. Mrs Boyle is the murder victim in which famous stage play, which has a title taken from *Hamlet*?

10. Extremely hard and widely used as an abrasive, what is the more common name for the solid compound silicon carbide?

11. In which region of France is the white wine known as Chablis produced?

12. Which cephalopod is the world's largest invertebrate?

13. Which novel of 1914 tells of a year in the lives of a group of painters and decorators in the town of Mugsborough?

14. The Strait of Otranto separates Italy from the Greek island of Kerkira, and which other neighbouring country?

15. Who played the Mafia boss Tony Soprano in the television series *The Sopranos*?

16. What was the name of the mother of Tiberius and Gaius Gracchus, who was considered the model Roman matron?

17. Who wrote the orchestral work, first performed in 1841, that is known as the 'Spring Symphony'?

18. An increment of five degrees on the Celsius scale corresponds to an increment of how many degrees on the Fahrenheit scale?

19. Which metaphysical poet wrote 'And therefore never send to know for whom the bell tolls; it tolls for thee'?

20. In ancient Greek religion, who was the goddess of victory?

21. Salvador Dali, Joan Miro and Rene Magritte are among the principal exponents of which art movement that began in the 1920s?

22. Found mainly in the Fens, what is the largest species of butterfly native to Britain?

23. Which term has been taken from the game of bridge to indicate a player or team winning all the major matches or tournaments in the same year?

24. Which southern African country became an independent nation on 4 October 1966 under the rule of King Moshoeshoe II?

25. In which 1969 film does Michael Caine say 'Just remember this – in this country they drive on the wrong side of the road'?

26. Which virulent lung disease was known as the 'white death' or the 'white plague' because sufferers from it appear very pale?

27. Which musical, featuring the songs 'Let The Sunshine In' and 'Aquarius', opened on Broadway in April 1968?

28. Which island off the coast of Dorset is the source of the nearest stone to true marble quarried in England?

29. Which type of engraving, in which a metal plate was roughened and then polished to produce areas of light and shade, takes its name from the Italian for 'half tone'?

30. Which candidate for the American presidency used the made-up chemical formula $AuH2O$ as an election slogan during his campaign?

'Champion of Champions': Sir David Hunt

In 1982, to celebrate the 10th anniversary of *Mastermind*, a special 'Champion of Champions' mini-series was held and the eventual winner was an Oxford don, who had served under Field Marshal Alexander during the Second World War and as a private secretary to Attlee and Churchill in peacetime; he was a published author, and had been High Commissioner in Uganda, Cyprus and Nigeria, and Ambassador to Brazil. Knighted in 1963, Sir David Hunt won *Mastermind* in 1977 before, five years later, defeating the nine other previous champions to become the 'Mastermind of Masterminds' – as he listed it in his lengthy entry in *Who's Who*.

These are Sir David's general knowledge questions. He scored 15 in two minutes (the ones he didn't get are asterisked) to win by five points – and it is fascinating to compare these with the questions from the 2010 series (see 'Champion of Champions' – Pat Gibson). Clearly, the definition of what is and is not considered to be 'general knowledge' has changed considerably over the years, and even 'the toughest test on television' has had to adapt. Ironically, one subject notably lacking from Sir David's questions is... television.

1. Saint Paul told the chief captain who arrested him that he was a citizen of no mean city. Which city?

2. Wat Tyler was leader of the Peasants' Revolt in 1381. From which county did he lead his followers to London?

3. What's the capital of the Canadian province of Alberta?

4. In the Muslim religion, what's the name for the crier who proclaims the hours of prayer from a minaret?

5. In yacht racing, why is the America's Cup so called?

6. Who was the former attorney general who organised the Ulster Volunteers opposed to Home Rule for Ireland, just before the First World War?

7. Which of Rossini's operas was originally subtitled 'The Useless Precaution'?

8. In the ancient Roman calendar, what were the kalends?

9. Who was the English statesman and historian, Lord Chancellor under Charles II, whose name was given to a printing house for the Oxford University Press?

10. What kind of creature is a cottonmouth or water moccasin?

11. Name one of the two West African states which formed a confederation in February 1982?

12. A series of etchings, *The Disasters of War*, are a record of the horrors of the French invasion of Spain in the early 19th century. By which artist?

13. In one of Scott's *Waverley* novels, what was *The Heart of Midlothian*?

14. What is the name for an ancient manuscript in which the writing has been effaced to make room for new writing?

15. Colonel Gaddafi of Libya gained power after a military coup overthrew the King in 1969. Who was the former King?

16. Which English philosopher and statesman wrote in an essay, 'Money is like muck; not good except it be spread'?

17. Jacopo Peri is believed to have composed the earliest operas. In which Italian city were they first performed?

18. What is the style of boat-building called in which the external planks or strakes overlap downwards?

19. What was the name of the Russian Marshal who achieved victory over Finland in 1939–1940?

20. In the human body, what is the more common name for the scapula?

Answers

1. Tarsus

2. Kent

3. Edmonton *

4. Muezzin

5. It is named after the schooner America or after the first winner of the contest

6. (Edward) Carson

7. *Barber Of Seville* Or *Almaviva* *

8. First of the month

9. Clarendon

10. Snake

11. Gambia or Senegal

12. Goya

13. A prison (in Edinburgh) – accept Tolbooth (prison)

14. Palimpsest

15. Idris

16. Francis Bacon *

17. Florence *

18. Clinker

19. (Semyon) Timoshenko *

20. Shoulder blade

Show 31

Specialist Subject 31.1
UK History since 1700

1. At Dettingen in 1743, who became the last British monarch to lead his troops personally into battle?

2. In his speech of March 1946, Winston Churchill said that two cities were linked by an 'Iron Curtain' that had descended across Europe; Stettin was one, what was the other?

3. What did Robert Peel reintroduce as a 'temporary measure' in 1842 to rectify the Budget deficit left by the Whigs?

4. Disraeli, on his return from which conference, told the gathered crowd that he had brought back 'peace ... with honour'?

5. Which pioneer of steam power went into partnership with Matthew Boulton of the Soho Works in Birmingham in 1775, to develop and build the engines he had invented?

6. In January 1879, British troops suffered a disastrous defeat to the Zulus under King Cetshwayo in the shadow of which rocky outcrop?

7. What was abolished in Britain initially for a trial period of five years following Sidney Silverman's Private Members bill of 1965?

8. In 1909, Lloyd George described the House of Lords as 'five hundred men, ordinary men, chosen accidentally from among...' whom?

9. The so-called madness of King George III is now generally regarded as being what rare inherited disease which causes an imbalance in the pigment of the blood?

10. Sometimes described as 'the best prime minister we never had', which Minister of Education introduced the groundbreaking 1944 Education Act?

11. On 23 and 24 January 1900, during the Boer War, British troops briefly captured which hilltop, although they were forced to retreat the following day having suffered huge numbers of killed and wounded?

12. Between 20 and 30,000 people died as a result of the first epidemic of which disease in Britain, in 1832?

13. In which village near Rotherham was the British Steel Corporation coking plant that was the scene of a violent confrontation between police and striking miners in June 1984?

14. Which inventor was born in 1847, at South Charlotte Street in Edinburgh?

15. Which new class of all-big-gun battleship, firing eight 12-inch guns on a broadside, was introduced by the Royal Navy in 1906?

16. What was the name of the political party that Sir Oswald Mosley formed after breaking from Labour in 1931, and before launching the British Union of Fascists the following year?

17. On 6 May 1840, the Post Office issued two adhesive postage stamps for general use, the Penny Black and which other?

18. Whose work *The Economic Consequences of the Peace* was published in 1919, and criticised the reparations burden on Germany?

19. What was the name of the triple defence line that was constructed, at Wellington's command, north of Lisbon from October 1809?

20. When he created the World Wide Web in 1989, Tim Berners-Lee was working for which organisation in Geneva?

21. Prompting the passage of the Clean Air Act four years later, in December of which year did the infamous 'Killer Smog' claim the lives of an estimated 4,000 people in London?

22. In 1856, which engineer patented the process for decarbonising molten pig iron with a blast of cold air to produce low-cost steel?

23. The practices of which company and its chief executive were described by Edward Heath in May 1973 as being 'the unpleasant and unacceptable face of capitalism'?

24. Which architect, who went on to design the traditional red telephone box, was the designer and originally joint architect of Liverpool's Anglican Cathedral?

25. During the Boer War, which besieged town was relieved by a cavalry charge, led by Major-General John French in February 1900?

26. At Vimiero during the Peninsular Wars, which British officer tested his own design of hollowed-out shell, which burst in the air scattering grapeshot downwards?

27. What was the name of the MP for Jarrow who led the hunger march to London in 1936, in protest against high unemployment?

28. On 1 January 1801, George III relinquished which title that had been claimed by English kings since 1340, in the reign of Edward III?

29. Who designed the interiors of the new Palace of Westminster, after the old building had been destroyed by fire in 1834?

30. In September 1978, Bulgarian defector Georgi Markov was killed in London after being stabbed with a poisoned... what?

General Knowledge 31.1

1. Who stars as the Private Eye Philip Marlowe in the original 1946 film version of *The Big Sleep*?

2. Where in the body are the intercostal muscles situated?

3. Since 1928, athletes from which country have led the parade at the opening of the Olympic Games?

4. Which river, for part of its length, forms the boundary between the cities of Salford and Manchester?

5. The Pipes and Drums and Military Band of the Royal Scots Dragoon Guards took an instrumental version of which hymn to number one in the UK singles charts in 1972?

6. What Latin legal term means 'under judicial consideration'?

7. According to William Blake's poem, which bird in a cage, 'Puts all heaven in a rage'?

8. What is the French for 'false step', which is in common use in English as a term for a blunder?

9. Which British artist created the video of a sleeping David Beckham, and the crying photos of Jude Law and Robert Downey Jr?

10. Which animal has double the blood pressure of other large mammals, and a tight sheath of thick skin over its lower limbs to maintain high extravascular pressure?

11. The name of which ancient religious philosophy is derived from the Chinese for 'way'?

12. What is the name of Queen Victoria's home near Cowes on the Isle of Wight where she died in 1901?

13. Who resigned his seat as Labour MP for Knowsley North in 1986 to become a daytime television presenter?

14. Which prefix used in the SI system of units denotes a multiplying factor of 10-to-the-minus-12?

15. In Japanese cuisine, which name indicates a dish of meat or shellfish marinated in a soy sauce and grilled or broiled?

16. On which island does the Owen Stanley mountain range rise to over 4,000 metres?

17. In music, what is the usual name for the male voice which comes roughly midway between tenor and bass?

18. Count Mède de Sivrac is generally considered to have invented which means of transport in about 1790, his invention being variously known as a 'célèrifère' or 'wooden horse'?

19. What is the name of the Kazakhstan TV presenter created by the comedian Sacha Baron Cohen?

20. Which British finch gets its name from its unusually shaped beak, which it uses for extracting seeds from conifer cones?

21. Which popular board game is thought to have its origins in an ancient game, called Moksha-patamu, played in India to teach children the difference between good and evil?

22. In Norse mythology, what name, from the Old Norse for 'doom of the gods', is given to the final battle between the gods and the powers of evil?

23. Which liqueur is added to gin and lemon juice to make a White Lady cocktail?

24. Which beautiful ornamental tree that is widely grown in warm parts of the world, has blue or purple foxglove-like flowers and attractive, oppositely paired, compound leaves?

25. What is the name of Don Quixote's horse in Cervantes' novel?

26. Which pungent gas is a compound whose molecules contain three atoms of hydrogen and one of nitrogen?

27. *Signing Off* was the aptly titled first album of which group, most of whose members had previously been unemployed?

28. Which range of hills form the so-called backbone of Italy?

29. The works of which Berlin-born British artist, noted for his nude paintings, include *Girl with a White Dog* and *Naked Man with a Rat*?

30. What was Mahatma Gandhi's alleged reply when asked by a British journalist in 1931 what he thought of western civilisation?

The 'Carry On' films

1. What was the name of the 1958 film about a group of National Service recruits that launched the series?

2. Which actor, who appeared in 19 'Carry On' films, was born in Johannesburg in 1913 (and had the original surname Cohen)?

3. Because of translation problems, which of the films was renamed 'Carry On Round the Bend' for the majority of its foreign export releases?

4. Which regiment guards the North-West Frontier in *Carry On Up the Khyber*?

5. What method of transport does the inept Secret Agent Charlie Bind use to travel from London to Vienna in *Carry On Spying*?

6. In which of the films does Kenneth Williams play Dr Soaper, the headmaster of St Chayste Ladies Seminary?

7. Which of the Carry On regulars cross-dresses to become Lady Puddleton in *Carry On Again Doctor*?

8. Which of the Carry On films was filmed partly on location at Camber Sands in Sussex?

9. Which German actress was given top billing and paid £30,000 for her part as Professor Anna Vooshka in *Carry On Behind*?

10. In *Carry On Up the Jungle*, Mr Chumley finds the tail feather of which bird thought to be extinct?

11. In which of the films did EastEnders star Wendy Richard play Miss Willing, a mother who is being discharged from hospital with her new baby?

12. Which of the regulars first got to use his catchphrase 'I only asked' in *Carry On Camping*?

13. In *Carry On Up the Khyber*, Captain Keene admits to wearing knickers made of what fabric under his kilt?

14. Which 1971 'historical' film, set in sixteenth-century England, was subtitled 'Mind My Chopper'?

15. Which character, played by Kenneth Williams in *Carry On Cleo*, exclaims 'Infamy! Infamy! They've all got it in for me!'?

16. Two of the regulars made their last appearances in the series in *Carry On Dick*. One was Sid James; who was the other?

17. Which famous event from British history is depicted in the opening scene of *Carry On Jack*?

18. Which actor, who appeared in eleven of the films, wrote the words for the 1966 Oscar nominated song 'Georgy Girl'?

19. In *Carry On At Your Convenience*, the strike at the W C Boggs factory is called off for one day to allow the workers to go on their annual outing to which resort?

20. Which American comedian starred as Sergeant Nocker in *Carry On, Follow That Camel*?

21. Which of the films featured Jim Dale as a sanitary engineer called Marshall P. Knutt who is mistaken for a US marshal and sent to clean up Stodge City?

22. In *Carry On Screaming*, what two-word phrase does Kenneth Williams' character shout as he is immersed in a vat of boiling liquid?

23. Which actor made his fourth appearance in a 'Carry On' film when he played King Ferdinand in *Carry On Columbus*?

24. What does Matron find the nurses have used to take the temperature of the unsuspecting Colonel in the closing scene of *Carry On Nurse*?

25. Which singer, who appeared as a bus conductor in *Carry On Loving*, wrote the song 'Love Crazy' for *Carry On Emmanuelle*?

26. What are the names of the two brothers who run a slave-trading business in *Carry On Cleo*?

27. What was Charles Hawtrey's final 'Carry On' film; he claimed the scripts had become too vulgar?

28. Which character, played by Bill Maynard, appears in *Carry On Henry*, even though this is historically inaccurate?

29. What is the name of Hengist Pod's wife, played by Sheila Hancock, in *Carry On Cleo*?

30. What happens to the top button of Private Easy's tunic during Captain Melly's first company inspection in *Carry On England*?

General Knowledge 31.2

1. In which American television comedy series do the six main characters meet at the Central Perk coffee shop?

2. In physics, which lower-case letter is conventionally used to denote the speed of light in a vacuum?

3. Who played Harry Lime, a racketeer dealing in watered-down penicillin, in the film *The Third Man*?

4. At which battle of 1620 were the Bohemian Protestant

reformers decisively defeated by combined Catholic forces, marking the end of the Bohemian period of the Thirty Years' War?

5. The police chief Baron Scarpia is the villain of which Puccini opera?

6. Which river, after rising high in the Cairngorms, flows past the village of Braemar and Balmoral Castle on its way to the sea?

7. In painting, what name is given to a colour that cannot be created by mixing other colours?

8. 'Pongo pygmaeus' is the Latin name for which primate, which is found in the wild in Malaysia predominantly?

9. Which playwright's works include *Mother Courage and Her Children* and *The Caucasian Chalk Circle*?

10. Which British officer commanded the Arab force that captured the Red Sea port of Aqaba on 6 July 1917?

11. Which frozen dessert, usually consisting of two or more kinds of ice cream, is named after the spherical mould in which it was traditionally made?

12. In the NATO phonetic alphabet, the name of which city represents the letter 'L'?

13. Which colourful, tender plant often with reddish-purple papery bracts, and popular in the Mediterranean, is named after a French navigator?

14. Sodium and which other metallic element were first isolated in 1807 by Sir Humphry Davy using electrolysis?

15. Which French Rugby League team joined the British Superleague in 2006?

16. Which former priest, who was excommunicated in about 1366 for sermonising about a classless society, was one of the leaders of the Peasants' Revolt?

17. Which song from the musical *Cats* is based mainly on T.S. Eliot's poem 'Rhapsody on a Windy Night'?

18. Which sea, the northernmost part of the Pacific Ocean, is named after a Danish navigator?

19. What name is commonly used in the UK to refer to 'Paraguay tea', which is brewed from the dried leaves of a shrub related to holly?

20. What middle name is shared by Bill Clinton and William Hague?

21. For which 1988 film did Dustin Hoffman win an Academy Award as Best Actor for his role as the autistic Raymond Babbitt, who inherits his father's 3 million dollar estate?

22. In ornithology, which word derived from the Latin for 'sparrow', is used for the huge order of perching birds?

23. Who painted *Flood at Port Marly* in 1876, in which the houses are reflected in the floodwater?

24. What name is given to inflammation of the thin, double-layered membrane separating the lungs from the chest cavity caused by a virus, which led to the death of the ballerina Anna Pavlova in 1931?

25. Which Latin poet, in his *Odes*, first wrote the line 'Dulce et decorum est pro patria mori'?

26. What was traditionally measured in ells?

27. What is the highest point in the Peak District National Park?

28. Which heavy metal band, formed in 1976 with bassist Steve Harris as a founder member, was named after a medieval instrument of torture?

29. In Greek mythology, Odysseus was king of which island?

30. What title was won by Gervaise Brook-Hampster in a classic Monty Python sketch?

'Champion of Champions': Pat Gibson

In the final of the 2010 series of 'Champion of Champions', Pat got through 23 general knowledge questions and correctly answered all but the three that are asterisked. (If you get near to his score in the 2½ minutes that the finalists were allowed, please do consider applying for *Mastermind* yourself!)

1. Which former Prime Minister wrote a history of cricket entitled *More Than a Game: The Story of Cricket's Early Years*?

2. Which building in Whitehall was designed by Inigo Jones and completed in 1622?

3. What Spanish name, meaning 'the child', is given to the periodic warming of the Eastern Pacific that disrupts weather patterns?

4. Which red dwarf, the second closest star to our sun after the Alpha Centauri system, is named after an American scientist who studied its motion?

5. Which writer, together with Dick Clement, has created several classic television shows including *The Likely Lads*, *Porridge* and *Auf Wiedersehen, Pet*?

6. Which English Field Marshal's defeat of Turkish forces at Megiddo in 1918 was quickly followed by Turkey's surrender?

7. What word is used in synagogues for a male singer who chants the liturgy and leads the congregation in prayer, and in Christian churches for the leader of the choir?

8. Which Scottish chemist is credited with inventing the vacuum flask?

9. Which 13-year-old British swimmer became a double gold medal winner at the 2008 Beijing Paralympics?

10. Who wrote the poems 'The Dong With a Luminous Nose' and 'The Courtship of the Yonghy-Bonghy-Bò'?

11. Which species of moth shares its name with a legendary prophetess who lived in Knaresborough, Yorkshire?

12. Which American director's films include *Klute*, *All the President's Men* and *Sophie's Choice*?

13. What is the Latin word for 'liquid'; it can describe an emulsion of resins, proteins and other organic substances extracted from certain plants?

14. Which granddaughter of Edmund Ironside fled to Scotland after the Norman Conquest, where she became Queen; she was later canonised for her devotion to the Church?

15. Which kind of soft felt hat, popularised by King Edward VII, takes its name from the town in Germany where it was first worn?

16. In June 2010, 17-year-old Arjun Rajyagor from Essex became the first winner of which reality TV show?

17. Which present-day Welsh county incorporates the area once known as the county of Radnorshire?

18. Who is typically pictured with the risen Christ in an artwork titled *Noli-me-tangere*, which translates as 'do not touch me'?

19. Which German-born composer wrote the popular harpsichord piece commonly called 'The Harmonious Blacksmith'? It comes from his 1720 suite in E Major.

20. Which nineteenth-century American social reformer's name was given to an outfit consisting of a skirt worn over loose trousers gathered at the ankle?

21. What was the penname of the Chilean poet and diplomat Neftali Ricardo Reyes Basoalto, who won the 1971 Nobel Prize for Literature?

22. Which small dog, first bred in Belgium to guard canal barges, is known by a Dutch name meaning 'little boatman'?

23. In which 1841 short story by Edgar Allen Poe does the character Auguste Dupin display his skills as a detective?

Answers

1. (Sir John) Major

2. The Banqueting House (or Hall)

3. El Niño

4. Barnard's Star – accept Edward Barnard

5. (Ian) La Frenais

6. (Viscount Edmund Hynman) Allenby *

7. Cantor

8. (James) Dewar

9. (Ellie or Eleanor) Simmonds

10. (Edward) Lear

11. Mother Shipton

12. (Alan J.) Pakula

13. Latex *

14. Saint Margaret or Margaret of Scotland

15. Homburg

16. *Junior Apprentice* (do not accept *The Apprentice*) *

17. Powys

18. Mary Magdelene

19. (Georg Frideric) Handel

20. (Amelia Jenks) Bloomer – accept Bloomers

21. (Pablo) Neruda

22. Schipperke

23. 'The Murders in the Rue Morgue'

The Answers

SHOW 1

Specialist Subject 1.1 – Academy Awards

1. Bob Hope
2. *As Good as It Gets*
3. (Charlie) Chaplin
4. Ten
5. *A Streetcar Named Desire*
6. (Cedric) Gibbons
7. (Wallace and Gromit) *The Curse of the Were-Rabbit*
8. Liza Minnelli
9. *Crouching Tiger, Hidden Dragon*
10. (Dame Judi) Dench
11. He streaked
12. (Jake) La Motta
13. *Who's Afraid of Virginia Woolf?*
14. (Jacques) Cousteau
15. 'Let It Be'
16. (Jackson) Pollock
17. *Mask*
18. George C. Scott
19. *Life Is Beautiful* or *La Vita È Bella*
20. John Williams
21. Western

22. (Cate) Blanchett
23. *Oliver!*
24. (Colin) Welland
25. *Beauty and the Beast*
26. Henry Fonda
27. *The Killing Fields*
28. (George) Bernard Shaw
29. *Pinocchio*
30. (Jack) Palance

General Knowledge 1.1

1. Victoria Cross or VC
2. Shropshire
3. *Carmina Burana*
4. Ed (not David) Miliband
5. Potato
6. *L'Absinthe* or *The Absinthe Drinker* – accept *Absinthe*
7. Sans Souci
8. Jehovah's Witnesses
9. Bishop
10. (Sir) Robin Day
11. Monkey
12. *The Comedy of Errors*
13. Pavilion
14. Steady-State (Theory)
15. *True Grit*
16. Tattenham Corner
17. Cyberspace
18. Seychelles
19. Duran Duran
20. Catalytic converter
21. Mouse
22. *A Taste of Honey*

23. Mozambique
24. Et al.
25. Clove
26. Ares
27. (New) Half-Penny
28. 'God Save The Queen' – accept National Anthem
29. Marsupials
30. Kettling

Specialist Subject 1.2 – The French Revolution
1. Jacobins
2. (Jacques) Necker
3. Versailles
4. 'Montagnards' or '(Men of the) Mountain'
5. (Georges) Danton
6. (The names of the days and months in the) Revolutionary Calendar
7. (Cult of the) Supreme Being
8. (Thomas) Paine
9. Phrygian Cap (of Liberty) – accept Bonnet Rouge or Red Cap Of Liberty
10. Girondins
11. (Charlotte) Corday
12. Varennes
13. Committee of Public Safety
14. (Jacques-Louis) David
15. Civil Constitution of the Clergy
16. Abbé Edgeworth – in full, Abbé Henry Essex Edgeworth De Firmont
17. Duke of Orleans
18. Enragés
19. (Claude Joseph) Rouget de Lisle
20. First Consul
21. Gracchus

22. Sans-Culottides – accept Jours Epagomenes
23. Le Père Duchesne
24. Champs de Mars
25. Lyon
26. Augustin (Robespierre)
27. Council of Elders (or Ancients)
28. 22 September
29. Valmy
30. (Marie-Jean Herault de) Sechelles

General Knowledge 1.2
1. Hay fever
2. (Gianni) Versace
3. Brent
4. Martin (not Charlie) Sheen
5. Okapi
6. Cosmopolitan (or Cosmo)
7. Karakoram
8. (Paddy) Ashdown or Lord Ashdown (of Norton-Sub-Hamdon)
9. Virgil
10. York
11. (Sir Ernest) Shackleton
12. Athena (or Pallas Athene)
13. (Hydro-) Cortisone – accept Cortisol or Glucocorticoid
14. (Fred) Trueman
15. Oboe
16. Porcelain
17. (Seamus) Heaney
18. South Sea Bubble
19. (David) Lynch
20. (Cambridge) Footlights
21. Gecko
22. (White) Grapes

23. Caribbean (Sea)
24. Massachusetts
25. Wimbledon – in full, Wimbledon Tennis Championships Men's Singles
26. (Leonardo) Fibonacci
27. Poisons (and their antidotes)
28. Christine
29. Longleat (House)
30. Carbon dioxide emissions (in grams per kilometre) – accept Carbon footprint

SHOW 2

Specialist Subject 2.1 – The Apollo Space Program
1. 21 July (NB in the USA it was still 20 July)
2. Saturn 5
3. Apollo 7
4. (Jim) Lovell
5. Grumman (Aircraft Engineering Corporation)
6. (Virgil 'Gus') Grissom
7. A feather
8. (German) Measles or Rubella
9. Sleep or Rest
10. Lightning (strikes)
11. Oxygen
12. *Charlie Brown* and *Snoopy*
13. Air purifier, or Carbon dioxide scrubber / filter
14. (Pete) Conrad – accept Charles Conrad
15. The Genesis Rock
16. Steak and eggs
17. Aquarius
18. (Alan) Shepard
19. Lunar Rover – in full, Lunar Roving Vehicle or L.R.V.

20. (Gene) Kranz

21. 'Magnificent desolation'

22. Loss of radio signal or contact with Earth

23. (Harrison 'Jack') Schmitt

24. 6 iron

25. Orange

26. (Rusty) Schweickart

27. (He celebrated) Communion

28. (Frank) Borman

29. Apollo 20 (NB 18 and 19 were later cancelled as well)

30. Gene Cernan

General Knowledge 2.1

1. Dick Whittington – in full, Sir Richard Whittington

2. La Scala – in full, Teatro Alla Scala

3. Lizard

4. Thomas (not Oliver) Cromwell

5. Cannelloni

6. Bath

7. *Girl with a Pearl Earring*

8. Liver

9. Augusta (National)

10. Atlas

11. 1922 (Committee)

12. (Isaac) Asimov

13. Caldera – accept the English translation, Cauldron

14. 'Born To Run'

15. (Mustafa Kemal) Ataturk – accept Mustafa Kemal

16. *The Goon Show* or *The Goons*

17. Bootlegger

18. (Tiger) Shark

19. Burkina Faso

20. D

21. *Much Ado About Nothing*
22. Neighbourhood Watch (scheme)
23. Sea horses
24. Beef
25. Ted Hughes
26. (Gottfried Wilhelm) Leibniz
27. Rowing – accept Sculling
28. 'Fifth Column'
29. Chasuble
30. Norway (not Iceland – their flag is a red cross outlined in white on a blue background)

Specialist Subject 2.2 – Summer Olympics
1. Canada
2. Tug of war
3. 'Jesse' Owens – in full, James Cleveland Owens
4. Amsterdam or 1928
5. (Rebecca) Romero
6. Handball
7. (People's Republic of) China
8. (2000 Metres) Tandem
9. Boxing
10. (George) Patton
11. Uneven bars – accept Asymmetric(al) bars
12. Six
13. Rowing
14. Moscow or 1980
15. (David) Wilkie
16. Table Tennis or Ping Pong
17. Sir Matt Busby
18. (10 Metre Platform) Diving
19. Zimbabwe
20. (Men's 3000 Metres) Steeplechase (NB they actually ran 3460 metres!)

21. Swim the (English) Channel
22. Dressage – accept Equestrianism
23. (Asafa) Powell – not Usain Bolt
24. Archery
25. Oddjob
26. Judo
27. (Suzanne) Lenglen
28. Polo
29. (Ben) Ainslie
30. Halswelle was the only competitor (one was disqualified after the original race, and the two others withdrew in protest)

General Knowledge 2.2
1. SAS – in full, Special Air Service (Regiment)
2. ('Frankie' or Lanfranco) Dettori
3. 360 (degrees)
4. (Lieutenant) Uhura
5. Ontario
6. (John) Grisham
7. Administration
8. (Benjamin) Disraeli
9. Kumquat
10. Sonata
11. Jaguar
12. (Paul) Cézanne
13. Juggernaut
14. *The Truman Show*
15. Blue blood
16. Sudoku
17. (London) Stock Exchange
18. *Cats*
19. Bavaria
20. (*The Vision of*) *Piers Plowman*

21. Hydrochloric (acid)
22. Bangladesh
23. (Oil of) Wormwood
24. Buoy
25. Borsetshire
26. (Vidkun) Quisling
27. 'Property is theft'
28. Tristan da Cunha
29. Aretha (Franklin)
30. (Sir John) Gielgud

SHOW 3

Specialist Subject 3.1 – The Plays of Shakespeare
1. *As You Like It*
2. Cassius
3. 'Mercy'
4. *Titus Andronicus*
5. 'Made glorious summer by this sun of York'
6. Falstaff
7. *A Midsummer Night's Dream*
8. (*The Tragedy of King*) *Richard II*
9. Mantua
10. *Henry VIII*
11. Cordelia
12. (*King*) *Lear*
13. *The Two Gentlemen of Verona*
14. 'Lechery'
15. Elbow
16. *Cymbeline*
17. (Contact with) Women
18. *Much Ado* (*about Nothing*)
19. Figs

20. Henry Percy or 'Hotspur'
21. *The Comedy of Errors*
22. Harfleur
23. Weaver
24. *Pericles* (*Prince Of Tyre*)
25. Rosaline
26. Strawberries
27. Donalbain
28. Ship's boy
29. Autolycus
30. Hedgehog

General Knowledge 3.1

1. Venus
2. Baring's
3. Tony Robinson
4. (Giant) Panda
5. Pollyanna
6. Vermont
7. Miles Davis
8. (Mount) Zion
9. Minced or Ground
10. 'A nation of shopkeepers'
11. (Upper) Arm
12. (J.M.W.) Turner
13. Saltire
14. Aspirin
15. Notts County
16. Venezuela
17. (Powdery) Mildew
18. Palme d'Or – accept Golden Palm
19. 'Milk Snatcher'
20. *Swan Lake*

21. Equinox(es)
22. Simone de Beauvoir
23. Margarita
24. Bull
25. *Beggars Banquet*
26. *The Surrender of Breda*
27. Smell
28. Mornington Crescent (in the show they play a game called Mornington Crescent)
29. Ronald (or Ronnie) Biggs
30. Alastair Cook

Specialist Subject 3.2 – World Geography
1. Ararat – accept Agridagi
2. Honshu
3. Pampas
4. Australia
5. Baffin (Island)
6. Sahel
7. Wenceslas (Square)
8. Silver
9. Dead Sea
10. Sunda (Strait)
11. (Lake) Superior
12. Abuja
13. Peru
14. Bratislava (capital of Slovakia)
15. Alaska
16. (Lake) Baikal
17. South Africa
18. Indonesia
19. Helsinki
20. New Zealand

21. Fray Bentos
22. Nunavut
23. Eritrea
24. Atomium
25. Guayaquil
26. Queensland
27. Laos
28. Nile
29. Aconcagua
30. Checkpoint Charlie

General Knowledge 3.2

1. *Treasure Island*
2. (Sir Robert) Peel
3. 'Waterloo Sunset'
4. Suriname
5. (European) Eels
6. Tour de France
7. Defenestration
8. Sir Michael Caine (his real name is Maurice Micklewhite)
9. Random-Access Memory
10. (Pierre-Auguste) Renoir
11. Sphinx
12. *E.R.*
13. Mulligatawny
14. Liver
15. *Nineteen Eighty-Four* (by George Orwell)
16. Preston
17. Violin
18. (Dr Richard or Lord) Beeching
19. Strategy – accept Stratagem
20. Sheep
21. *Till Death Us Do Part*

22. Supercilious

23. (Fencing) Sword

24. Hydrogen

25. Abbey Road

26. Hegira or Hijrah

27. Forties

28. Foot

29. *From Here to Eternity*

30. Egypt

SHOW 4

Specialist Subject 4.1 – British Political History since 1900

1. (Harold) Wilson

2. Good Friday Agreement

3. Barbara Castle

4. (Herbert) Asquith

5. Tribune (Group)

6. (Sir Samuel) Hoare

7. Jeremy Thorpe

8. 'Labour Isn't Working'

9. (James) Callaghan

10. 'Flipping'

11. (Sir Winston) Churchill

12. (John) Stonehouse

13. Natural Law Party

14. (Michael) Portillo

15. (Hugh) Gaitskell

16. The Limehouse Declaration

17. David Laws

18. (Anthony Wedgwood) 'Tony' Benn – previously 2nd Viscount Stansgate

19. The House of Lords

20. (William) Hague
21. (Donald) Dewar
22. 'Business as usual'
23. (Jeffrey) Archer – later Lord Archer
24. Jack Straw
25. 'Safety First'
26. (Bernard) Ingham
27. (Denis) Healey
28. Communist (Party of Great Britain)
29. (Jonathan) Aitken
30. 'Selsdon Man'

General Knowledge 4.1
1. Germany
2. (Gavrilo) Princip
3. Andante
4. Gobi Desert
5. Hamlet
6. (War of the) Spanish Succession
7. (Leonard) Nimoy
8. Glasgow
9. Jeanette Winterson
10. Pancetta
11. Sparta – accept Lacedaemon
12. *The Rake's Progress*
13. (Søren) Kierkegaard
14. Cruciate ligaments
15. *The Winslow Boy*
16. The Philippines
17. *Madam Butterfly*
18. Quinine
19. James Cameron
20. St Austell

21. Flora Macdonald
22. Tottenham (Hotspur) – accept Spurs
23. Holt
24. (Friedrich von) Schiller
25. St Stephen
26. 'Hammer of the Scots'
27. (Konstantin) Chernenko
28. Chukka
29. Musée d'Orsay
30. Apache or Chiricahua (Apache)

Specialist Subject 4.2 – Pop Music of the 1970s
1. Led Zeppelin
2. 'New Rose'
3. Art Garfunkel
4. Bay City Rollers
5. 'Ashes To Ashes'
6. Jilted John
7. Chas Chandler
8. (Moog) Synthesizer
9. 'Smoke On The Water'
10. Ultravox
11. Stevie Wonder
12. *A Night at the Opera*
13. Whitesnake
14. Mike Batt
15. 'Money Money Money'
16. Mick Taylor
17. The Undertones
18. Bob Marley
19. 'Yesterday'
20. Joe Strummer (of the Clash)
21. 'What A Waste'

22. Tina Charles
23. Human League
24. Bryan Ferry
25. 'Baker Street' (by Gerry Rafferty)
26. Alvin Stardust (born Bernard Jewry)
27. 'We Don't Talk Anymore'
28. Tom Robinson
29. 'Roxanne'
30. Elvis Costello

General Knowledge 4.2
1. *To Kill a Mockingbird*
2. Dr Christiaan Barnard
3. Woodwind
4. Lundy
5. Friar Tuck
6. (Frida) Kahlo
7. Ash Wednesday
8. Ghana
9. Crêpe Suzette
10. Galileo (Galilei)
11. Nicolas Cage
12. Finial
13. 'Peter and the Wolf'
14. Lampreys
15. (Philip) Glenister
16. Albania
17. (Émile) Zola
18. Italy
19. Elstree
20. Armadillo
21. Scoundrel
22. Copper

23. (John L.) Sullivan
24. Epicentre
25. Green
26. *HMS Pinafore*
27. Green Park
28. (Edouard) Manet
29. Arizona
30. The Eiffel Tower

SHOW 5

Specialist Subject 5.1 – British TV Comedy and Sitcoms
1.   Nelson Mandela House
2.   Carla Lane
3.   Jane Austen
4.   (Private James) Frazer (played by John Laurie)
5.   Waldorf (Salad)
6.   'Loadsamoney'
7.   *Just Good Friends*
8.   Alan Partridge (played by Steve Coogan)
9.   The Royle Family (he's the son of Denise Best, née Royle, played by Caroline Aherne)
10. (Reginald Iolanthe) Perrin (played by Leonard Rossiter)
11. Tooting
12. Dorien (Green)
13. *The Liver Birds*
14. Jane Horrocks
15. *Never the Twain*
16. (John) Cleese
17. Maplin's
18. Leadbetter
19. Slough
20. Norman Stanley Fletcher

21. 'Acorn Antiques'
22. Alexei Sayle
23. *The Fast Show*
24. *Chef!*
25. Alan B'stard (played by Rick Mayall in *The New Statesman*)
26. (British) Sausage
27. Brabinger
28. John Thaw (in between playing Jack Regan in *The Sweeney* and Inspector Morse)
29. (Dawn) French and (Jennifer) Saunders
30. Cupid Stunt

General Knowledge 5.1
1. *Encyclopaedia Britannica*
2. Stornoway
3. Lady Caroline Lamb
4. Danzig or Gdansk
5. *'Enigma' Variations*
6. Lemon grass
7. Sikh
8. Spinks
9. Spectacled bear
10. (Georges) Seurat
11. Chromosomes
12. Joe Orton
13. Hoplite
14. Portico
15. Greenland
16. The Killers
17. Neutral Wire
18. Aethelred the Unready – accept Athelred II
19. *Punch*
20. Marble Arch

21. (Ivor) Novello
22. Mimosa
23. *The Sopranos*
24. Hectare
25. Glass
26. Interregnum
27. *A Shropshire Lad*
28. Quakers
29. *The World Is Not Enough*
30. Pole Star or Polaris

Specialist Subject 5.2 – The Human Body
1. Liver
2. Metatarsals
3. Quadriceps (Femoris) or Quads
4. Middle ear
5. Duodenum
6. Melanin
7. Tricuspid – accept Right atrioventricular valve
8. Gluteus maximus
9. Capillaries
10. Anaemia
11. Twenty-seven
12. The mandible
13. Lymphocytes
14. Humerus (not the funny bone – a term used for a point at the lower end of the humerus)
15. Islets of Langerhans – accept Islands of Langerhans or Pancreatic Islets
16. Mumps
17. Pericardium
18. Adenoids – accept Naso-pharyngeal tonsil
19. (Adrenal) Medulla

20. Hydrochloric (acid) – accept Hydrogen chloride
21. Vitreous humour – accept Vitreous body
22. Leukocytes
23. Thymus
24. Fontanelle
25. Polio (-Myelitis)
26. Peristalsis
27. Nephrons
28. Coccyx
29. Cruciate (Ligaments)
30. Pituitary gland – accept Hypophysis

General Knowledge 5.2
1. Red
2. Sean Connery
3. Herodotus
4. Semibreve
5. (General Leopoldo) Galtieri
6. Tennessee Williams
7. Baltic Sea
8. (Jacopo Robusti) Tintoretto
9. Andromeda
10. The Beach Boys
11. Potato
12. *Wuthering Heights*
13. Shrub
14. Camera obscura
15. Architecture
16. Ullswater
17. RKO (Radio Pictures Incorporated)
18. (Gian or Giovanni Domenico) Cassini
19. Challenge Cup
20. Malawi

21. Garrick Club
22. Passover or Pesach
23. *James and the Giant Peach*
24. Morphine
25. *The Thieving Magpie*
26. Tail Fin
27. Blinis
28. Corsica
29. *I, Claudius*
30. Red Lion

SHOW 6

Specialist Subject 6.1 – English and Scottish History, 1066–1707

1. Stamford Bridge
2. Theatres
3. Robert the Bruce
4. Defender of the Faith or Fidei Defensor (often abbreviated to Fid. Def.)
5. Bloody Assizes
6. Catherine of Aragon (Arthur died before his father and so Catherine was betrothed to his younger brother Henry)
7. Henry I
8. Darien
9. Robert Aske
10. Charing Cross
11. 1314
12. Lambert Simnel
13. Nottingham
14. Field of the Cloth of Gold
15. Piccadilly
16. William Wallace
17. 'The Ironsides'

18. Baronet – accept Hereditary knighthood
19. The Junto – accept Junta
20. The Western Isles or Hebrides
21. Inigo Jones
22. (Royal) Mint
23. Titus Oates
24. Flodden
25. Pudding (Lane)
26. Act of Settlement
27. (George Villiers, the First) Duke of Buckingham
28. Rye House plot
29. (Thomas) Pride (it's known as 'Pride's Purge')
30. (Act of) Supremacy

General Knowledge 6.1
1. Green belt
2. Martin Luther
3. Aspic
4. (Dame Barbara) Hepworth
5. Autumn
6. Jurisprudence
7. Holy Island
8. (Franz) Schubert
9. (Common) Wombat
10. Division lobby
11. Alice Springs
12. Vulcanisation
13. (Martin) Scorsese
14. Kazakhstan
15. Hector
16. Harrow
17. Oleander
18. Prisons or Gaols

19. 'I Don't Like Mondays'
20. Hypotenuse
21. Andy Flower
22. Virginia Woolf
23. Silicon Valley
24. Piano (not Organ)
25. Palatine Hill
26. 'On the rocks'
27. Kraken
28. Katharine Hepburn
29. Thigh bone or Upper leg
30. Manneken-Pis

Specialist Subject 6.2 – James Bond Novels and Films
1. *Casino Royale*
2. Jaws
3. *You Only Live Twice*
4. Felix Leiter
5. *Live and Let Die*
6. Beretta (.25)
7. San Francisco
8. Robbie Coltrane
9. *On Her Majesty's Secret Service*
10. Auric
11. Timothy Dalton
12. Le Chiffre
13. *Thunderball*
14. (Ernst Stavro) Blofeld
15. Atlantis
16. *Diamonds Are Forever*
17. (Admiral Sir) Miles Messervy
18. Duran Duran
19. '(No, Mr Bond.) I expect you to die!'

20. *From Russia with Love*
21. 'Tomorrow' (from *Tomorrow Never Dies*)
22. 'Q' – accept Major Boothroyd
23. *Octopussy*
24. He (or they) played an ally of Bond in one and the villain in the other – accept he (or they) played a different character in each film (just to confuse matters further, Gray played three different versions of Blofeld in *Diamonds Are Forever*!)
25. *Licence to Kill*
26. Solitaire
27. Brussels
28. Madonna (who also supplied the theme tune)
29. Knife-throwers – accept Wheel of Death
30. Nipples

General Knowledge 6.2
1. Calligraphy
2. Bath
3. (Daniel) Defoe
4. Simultaneous (equations)
5. *Nabucco*
6. Calliope
7. West Lothian Question
8. (Sir) Ridley Scott
9. Jutland
10. (Levi) Strauss
11. Mites
12. Garam Masala
13. Hannibal
14. Kaiser Chiefs
15. Magellan Strait
16. Laurie Lee
17. Italy

18. Mary Magdalene or Mary of Magdala
19. Aphorism
20. (Aaron) Copland
21. Broom
22. (William) Hogarth
23. (First Battle of the) Marne
24. Gaffer
25. Angel Falls
26. Angelica
27. Rickets or Rachitis
28. *Tom Jones*
29. San Diego
30. Beach hut

SHOW 7

Specialist Subject 7.1 – Impressionist Art and Artists
1. (Claude) Monet
2. *Salon des Refuses*
3. (Alfred) Sisley
4. (En) Plein Air
5. (Louis) Leroy
6. Japan
7. (Edouard) Manet
8. American
9. (Camille) Pissarro
10. *Olympia*
11. (Berthe) Morisot
12. Argenteuil (not Giverny)
13. (Pierre-Auguste) Renoir
14. (Paul) Cezanne
15. (Boulevard) Montmarte
16. *Moulin de la Galette*

17. (Georges) Seurat
18. Black
19. (Edgar) Degas
20. Law or Lawyer
21. (Henri De) Toulouse-Lautrec
22. (Paul) Signac
23. (Gare) St-Lazare
24. (Suzanne) Valadon
25. *Déjeuner sur l'herbe* or *Luncheon on the Grass*
26. Pastel
27. Theo van Gogh (brother of Vincent)
28. (The Houses of) Parliament – accept Palace of Westminster or Big Ben
29. (Paul) Gauguin
30. Fauve or Fauvism

General Knowledge 7.1
1. Bill Gates
2. Liechtenstein
3. *Romeo and Juliet*
4. Tarantula
5. Guitar
6. (Good King or Saint) Wenceslas
7. Pesto
8. Collar Bone
9. William Morris
10. (Great Proletarian) Cultural Revolution
11. Break
12. Oxygen
13. *Cabaret*
14. Anti-Social Behaviour Order
15. *The Cruel Sea*
16. Cheviot Hills

17. Woodstock
18. Delta
19. Castanets
20. Insects
21. Madness
22. Khaki
23. Narcissus
24. River Shannon
25. *It's a Knockout*
26. Enzyme
27. *Vanity Fair*
28. Tolpuddle Martyrs
29. Robin Knox-Johnston
30. Sheep

Specialist Subject 7.2 – The Bible

1. (Gospel of St) John
2. Mercy Seat
3. Seth
4. Judas (Iscariot)
5. 120
6. (Gospel of St) Matthew
7. (Queen) Jezebel
8. Mount of Olives – accept Olivet
9. Purim
10. Kingdom of God
11. (Tribe of) Dan
12. Six Hundred, Three Score And Six or 666
13. Aramaic
14. Isaiah – in full, First Isaiah of Jerusalem
15. 'Hosanna'
16. (A line of) Scarlet thread
17. Matthias

18. The raising of Lazarus
19. (Archangel) Gabriel
20. '(My God, My God,) Why have you forsaken me'
21. Fishing
22. Deborah
23. The Peacemakers
24. (Book of the Prophet) Malachi
25. Bethany
26. (Prophet) Job
27. 'Jesus Wept'
28. Zadok
29. Deacon
30. 'By the rivers of Babylon (, there we sat down; yea, we wept, when we remembered Zion)'

General Knowledge 7.2
1. Rio de Janeiro
2. Triptych
3. *Lady Chatterley's Lover*
4. Algebra
5. Mace
6. Curare
7. Hat
8. Ionian Islands
9. Felix Mendelssohn
10. (Crossed) Swords
11. Danny Boyle
12. Cetacea or Cetacean
13. Soft Cell
14. Lord Mayor of London
15. Roy Plomley
16. Switzerland
17. Blackcurrant

18. Oedipus
19. Fire
20. Teal
21. Lady (Augusta) Bracknell
22. Horseradish
23. Libretto
24. Convection
25. Bosworth (Field)
26. Iron Gate
27. Snowplough
28. Nottingham
29. Helena Bonham Carter
30. (War of) Jenkins' Ear

SHOW 8

Specialist Subject 8.1 – The Solar System

1. Earth
2. (Nicolaus) Copernicus or Mikolaj Kopernik
3. Solar Wind
4. Venus
5. Chromosphere
6. Olympus Mons or Mount Olympus
7. Mercury
8. Jeremiah Horrocks
9. Sidereal period
10. Saturn
11. Japanese
12. Vulcan
13. The Moon
14. Uranus
15. Nitrogen
16. 'Shepherd' (moons or satellites)

17. Jupiter
18. Methane
19. Roche limit
20. Neptune
21. Io
22. Valles Marineris (also known as Coprates Canyon, the Grand Canyon of Mars or Agathodaemon)
23. Enceladus
24. Pioneer Four (also known as Artificial Planet 2)
25. Miranda
26. Its magnetosphere
27. The Leonids
28. (Öpik-) Oort Cloud
29. Rille
30. 7 miles per second or 11 kilometres per second (equivalent to around 25,000 mph or 40,000 kph)

General Knowledge 8.1
1. '1812 (Overture)'
2. Tithe
3. Sherry
4. Mountain Ash
5. Bob Dylan
6. Delaware
7. *The Graduate*
8. Devon
9. Malvolio
10. Ten Minute Rule Bill
11. Twelve
12. Seed Drill
13. (Brian) Lara
14. Palm Sunday
15. Cerebellum

16. Festival of Britain
17. Douglas Adams
18. Marquess
19. Manx
20. Mockingbird – accept Common or Northern mockingbird
21. (Giorgio) Vasari
22. Anglesey or Ynys Môn
23. *Lohengrin*
24. Jordan
25. (Auguste) Escoffier
26. Dionysus
27. (Ship's) Cook
28. Emeritus
29. Phoenix (Club)
30. Captain (James) Cook

Specialist Subject 8.2 – The Football World Cup
1. Carlos Alberto
2. Scotland
3. 1958
4. David O'Leary
5. (Juste) Fontaine
6. Jairzinho
7. Holland or the Netherlands
8. Argentina (in 1986)
9. (Davor) Suker
10. (Helmut) Schon
11. Maracana
12. 2002 – accept Japan / South Korea
13. USSR or Soviet Union
14. Pelé (in full, Edson Arantes Do Nascimento)
15. (Paul) Breitner
16. Cameroon

17. (Laurent) Blanc
18. Egypt
19. (Sandor) Kocsis
20. (They were for) different countries (Argentina in 1930 and Italy in 1934)
21. Van de Kerkhof
22. (Antonio) Carbajal
23. El Salvador
24. The King or King Carol
25. (Mario) Zagallo
26. Swiss (not Russian… though the 'Russian linesman' was actually from Azerbaijan!)
27. (George) Raynor
28. Forty-two
29. 'Battle of Berne'
30. (He had to take his final) University exams

General Knowledge 8.2
1. *The Haywain*
2. Carbon
3. 'Help!'
4. Marengo
5. *A Room with a View*
6. Brecon Beacons
7. Lime
8. (Bachelor of) Law
9. Finland
10. Mentor
11. (Christopher) Marlowe
12. 'Entente Cordiale'
13. (Pete) Sampras
14. Arctic tern
15. Lead

16. Dominican Order – accept Order of Friars Preachers
17. James Brown
18. Wadi
19. *The Likely Lads*
20. Barbara Castle
21. (Susan) Sarandon
22. Socrates
23. Laputa
24. Tacking
25. (Alexander) Borodin
26. River Severn
27. Courgette
28. Leg (below the knee)
29. Buttercup
30. *Sunday Express*

SHOW 9

Specialist Subject 9.1 – Gilbert and Sullivan
1. They say they are orphans
2. Eating sausage rolls
3. Assistant Tormentor
4. Man
5. Burglary – accept 'A rather serious crime, to marry two wives at one time'
6. (Private) Willis
7. Basingstoke
8. 'He found it less exciting'
9. 'Palace Peeper'
10. The Back Stairs
11. Helen of Troy
12. Mrs Cripps
13. Bunthorne

14. Pilot
15. *Troilus and Cressida*
16. 'Grumble at'
17. By marrying Angelina himself
18. Sloane Square and South Kensington
19. It was a Bank Holiday
20. Don Alhambra (de Bolero)
21. Public Exploder
22. (Her left) Shoulderblade
23. John Wellington Wells
24. HMS *Victory*
25. Raffle himself – accept By lottery
26. Salisbury Plain
27. A farmyard
28. 'Atomic Globule'
29. Tea-Cup Brindisi
30. W.H. Smith

General Knowledge 9.1
1. Michelangelo (Buonarroti)
2. River Wear
3. (*I*) *Pagliacci*
4. Palm of the hand
5. Forest Whitaker
6. Asgard (not Valhalla)
7. Passim
8. Rhea
9. Evelyn Waugh
10. 'Winter of Discontent'
11. Watercress
12. Phosphorus
13. *Frankenstein* (or *The Modern Prometheus*)
14. Norway

15. 'Mad Dogs and Englishmen'
16. Borgia
17. Sumo Wrestling
18. Cactus
19. Willy Loman
20. Wall Street
21. Yves Saint Laurent – accept Y.S.L.
22. Hogmanay
23. Brian Epstein
24. Peterloo (Massacre)
25. *The Ladykillers*
26. Tintern (Abbey)
27. (Dr Samuel) Johnson
28. Troy Weight
29. La Legion d'Honneur or Legion of Honour
30. Jerry Springer

Specialist Subject 9.2 – British Birds
1. Dabbling ducks or Dipping ducks
2. (Common) Swift
3. Red grouse
4. Syrinx
5. Peregrine falcon
6. Stonechat
7. Kestrel
8. Oak
9. Tawny or Brown owl
10. Osprey
11. St Kilda
12. Lapwing
13. Merlin
14. Mistle thrush
15. Baffles

16. Bittern
17. Buzzard
18. Shoveler
19. It was perceived to be a threat to carrier pigeons
20. Manx Shearwater
21. Pipit
22. Great Auk
23. Black
24. Barn owl
25. Oystercatcher
26. Martin Mere
27. Dabchick
28. Coniferous
29. Quail
30. Breaking its neck

General Knowledge 9.2

1. HMS *Bounty*
2. Fox
3. Laurence Sterne
4. Madagascar
5. Sir Thomas Beecham
6. Spectrum
7. *Have I Got News For You*
8. 'In the beginning'
9. John Nash
10. Thermopylae
11. Rugby Union
12. Beachy Head
13. Cary Grant
14. Lobe
15. Sir Tom Stoppard (born Tomas Straussler)
16. Stamen

17. Corkscrew
18. David Steel
19. The Hollies
20. Ravens
21. (Captain) Nemo
22. Ridings
23. Austin Powers
24. William Pitt
25. Vitruvian Man
26. Agra
27. Gabriel Garcia Marquez
28. Eurostar
29. Lionel Bart
30. Mortgage

SHOW 10

Specialist Subject 10.1 – US Presidents
1. (Abraham) Lincoln
2. First Lady
3. Hawaii
4. Theodore Roosevelt – not Franklin D. Roosevelt
5. The Vice-Presidency
6. (James) Buchanan
7. *Profiles in Courage*
8. (Calvin) Coolidge
9. Whig Party
10. Harrison
11. Director of the CIA
12. (Ronald) Reagan
13. 'Dewey Defeats Truman' (there is a famous photo of Truman with a copy!)
14. Johnson (Andrew and Lyndon succeeded Lincoln and JFK

respectively)

15. Fleetwood Mac
16. 'Lemonade Lucy'
17. Little Rock (Arkansas)
18. (Martin) Van Buren
19. Sherman (Anti-Trust Act)
20. 'Bull Moose' Party
21. (Federal) Income tax evasion – accept Not declaring bribes on his income tax return
22. (James) Monroe
23. Ambassador to Great Britain
24. Russo-Japanese War
25. (Geraldine) Ferraro
26. The Great Society
27. (Grover) Cleveland
28. The Peace Corps
29. Chief Justice (of the United States Supreme Court)
30. (Gerald) Ford (after succeeding Nixon, who resigned rather than face impeachment)

General Knowledge 10.1
1. Wikipedia
2. Isosceles
3. *Ulysses*
4. Alabama
5. 'Pastoral'
6. Claudius
7. (Charles) Addams
8. Tiger
9. Onions
10. German
11. Corinthian
12. Woburn Abbey

13. (Charlie) Chaplin
14. Rainbow
15. Compass
16. Assay
17. Ozymandias (King of Kings)
18. Forsythia
19. *Doctor Zhivago*
20. Iguaçu Falls
21. (René) Magritte
22. Tibia
23. Barcelona
24. Cuba
25. Walter Greenwood
26. (François) Mitterrand
27. 'The Times They Are A-Changin'"
28. The age of the monarch
29. Pinocchio
30. Sanskrit

Specialist Subject 10.2 – The *Star Wars* Films
1. Carrie Fisher
2. Tatooine
3. Anakin (Skywalker) – not his alter-ego Darth Vader
4. Lando (Calrissian)
5. Mos Eisley
6. Chewbacca or Chewie
7. (Over) Six million
8. Frank Oz
9. 'Apology accepted'
10. Peter Cushing
11. General Grievous
12. Ewoks
13. Count Dooku

14. Sarlacc
15. Terence Stamp
16. Spice freighter
17. An asteroid field
18. Qui-Gon (Jinn)
19. Red 5
20. Fett
21. Dagobah
22. A bounty hunter
23. Samuel L. Jackson
24. Proton torpedo
25. Carbonite
26. Ansion
27. Captain Antilles
28. Lawrence Kasdan
29. Rancor
30. They both supplied the voices only (Ray Park plays Darth Maul, while Dave Prowse is Darth Vader)

General Knowledge 10.2
1. Jolly Roger
2. Channel Islands
3. *The Crucible*
4. (Giant) Panda
5. *Easy Rider*
6. (Eponymous) Archon
7. Hieronymus Bosch
8. Amino Acid
9. (John) Profumo
10. Caesura
11. Lennox Lewis
12. Camargue
13. 'Fanfare For The Common Man'

14. Moon
15. Zabaglione
16. Pericardium
17. *La Fanciulla del West* or *The Girl of the Golden West*
18. Numbers
19. Disc (Brake)
20. (George) Gallup
21. Sobriquet
22. 'The Internationale' – not 'The Red Flag'
23. (Thomas) Cranmer
24. Anne Bancroft
25. Ghana
26. (William) Wordsworth
27. Conifer
28. Harlow
29. (The Theory of) Evolution (by Natural Selection) or Darwinism
30. Snail

SHOW 11

Specialist Subject 11.1 – Agatha Christie's Hercule Poirot Novels
1. Styles Court (in *The Mysterious Affair at Styles* and *Curtain*)
2. Achille
3. *Taken at the Flood*
4. (Mr Henry) Morley
5. Fifty pounds
6. In his sock drawer
7. Meadowbank (School for Girls)
8. *Cards on the Table*
9. 'The Little Dog Laughed'
10. Strychnine
11. Sir Joseph Higgin
12. Her own stepmother – accept Mary Restarick

13. Double (headed) axe
14. *Sad Cypress*
15. Sir Montague Corner
16. Messarro Gratz
17. Philip Blake
18. Prison warder or guard or officer
19. Mrs Pearson – accept Mrs Funnyface (Dr Ridgeway's name for her)
20. 'The Double Clue'
21. (Dr Eric) Leidner
22. Revivit
23. Rosemary
24. (Growing) Marrows
25. Bob
26. *Towards Zero*
27. Miss Livingstone
28. (The handle of her) Tennis racquet
29. Glengowrie Court (Hotel)
30. 'Cher ami'

General Knowledge 11.1
1. Canute or Cnut
2. 'Turnip' (Townshend)
3. Salman Rushdie
4. Scorpion
5. Phil Redmond
6. Louis XIV (the Sun King)
7. Bell (in full, Currer, Ellis and Acton Bell)
8. Montserrat
9. The Move
10. Dharma
11. *The English Patient*
12. Tuberculosis or TB
13. Peter Blake

14. G-Men (the G is believed to stand for 'Government')
15. Mustard
16. (Common, Natural or Napierian) Logarithms
17. Curling
18. River Tamar
19. *Anna Karenina*
20. Kiwi
21. Cocoa – accept (Drinking or Hot) Chocolate
22. Gordonstoun
23. India
24. *North by Northwest*
25. Brunhilde
26. Fez
27. Metropolis
28. *La Bohème*
29. Semaphore
30. Moat

Specialist Subject 11.2 – Ancient Rome
1. (Marcus Tullius) Cicero
2. Emperors
3. The Samnites
4. Claudius
5. York – accept Eboracum
6. Vercingetorix
7. Egypt
8. (Lucius Cornelius) Sulla (Felix)
9. Nicaea
10. Pontifex Maximus
11. Corinth
12. Incitatus
13. Antonine Wall
14. Pompey (the Great) or Gnaeus Pompeiius Magnus

15. Petra
16. Seneca
17. Cannae
18. Flavians
19. Philippics
20. (Gaius Sempronius) Gracchus
21. Jerusalem
22. (Gaius) Suetonius Paulinus
23. Tribune
24. God
25. Ravenna
26. 'Veni, vidi, vici' or 'I came, I saw, I conquered'
27. Marcus Aurelius
28. Arianism
29. (Lucius Licinius) Lucullus
30. 'What an artist dies with me' or 'Qualis artifex pereo'

General Knowledge 11.2
1. Encore
2. (Henry J.) Heimlich
3. Crab
4. Liberty
5. (Pablo) Picasso
6. Caspian Sea
7. Zither
8. Paris
9. Look (Butcher's hook … Look!)
10. Knowsley (Safari Park)
11. (George) Smiley
12. Algae or Alga
13. *Frasier*
14. Calais
15. Widget

16. Pressure
17. Albatross
18. Witchfinder (-General)
19. (Stan) Laurel and (Oliver) Hardy
20. Darwin
21. Joe DiMaggio
22. Fritillaries
23. (Doctor) Jekyll
24. Fingerprints
25. (Mr) Spock
26. Vishnu
27. Mickey Mouse
28. Red Ensign
29. St Moritz
30. Gigolo

SHOW 12

Specialist Subject 12.1 – World History since 1800
1. Trafalgar
2. (Leon) Trotsky
3. Albania
4. *La Pasionaria*
5. (Grand Duchy of) Luxembourg
6. Lateran (Treaty)
7. (Arthur) Balfour
8. Solidarity or Solidarność
9. (George C.) Marshall
10. (People's Republic of) China
11. (Baron Georges Eugene) Haussmann
12. Dien Bien Phu
13. (Coal) Miner (the word 'Stakhanovite' is derived from his name)
14. Meiji Restoration

15. (Boris) Yeltsin
16. Ems Telegram or Ems Dispatch
17. (H. 'Stormin' Norman) Schwarzkopf
18. Cuba
19. Ostpolitik
20. Michael Collins
21. Austerlitz
22. Mutual(ly) Assured Destruction – also known as MAD
23. Chrysler (Building)
24. Czechoslovakia (which later split up into the Czech Republic and Slovakia after the 'Velvet Divorce')
25. Chiang Kai- Shek
26. (Raymond) Poincare
27. Kulaks
28. Paraguay
29. 25 December or Christmas Day
30. Abbottabad

General Knowledge 12.1
1. Bayeux Tapestry
2. Mediterranean Sea
3. Mussel
4. (Secretary of State for) Education (and Science)
5. Leaning Tower of Pisa
6. Barabbas
7. Leviathan
8. Stewart
9. Relativity
10. Oryx
11. (Joe) Orton
12. Chimaera
13. *Barbarella*
14. Wye

15. Biathlon
16. Chlorophyll
17. *Top of the Pops*
18. Lumpenproletariat
19. Brighton
20. Quadrilateral
21. *Rebecca*
22. Ypres
23. Liza Minnelli
24. Swans
25. *The Well-Tempered Clavier*
26. Souvlaki
27. And
28. King's Road
29. Fumarole
30. (Erwin) Schrödinger

Specialist Subject 12.2 – English Test Cricket
1. (Ian) Botham
2. (Gordon) Greenidge
3. 766 (at an average of 127.66 as he was not out in one of his innings)
4. Nasser Hussain
5. (Dennis) Lillee
6. Bramall Lane – accept Sheffield
7. (Len) Hutton
8. India
9. (Mike) Brearley
10. Old Trafford – accept Manchester
11. (Kevin) Pietersen – not Paul Collingwood
12. South Africa
13. (Eddie) Hemmings
14. 45

15. Graeme Smith
16. He batted on all five days of the match
17. (Sydney F.) Barnes
18. New Zealand
19. (Mike) Gatting
20. Handled the ball
21. Nawab of Pataudi (Senior)
22. (Viv) Richards
23. Pakistan
24. (Bob) Willis
25. Three countries took part (England, Australia and South Africa)
26. (Fred) Trueman
27. Two runs
28. Tony Lewis
29. (Eric) Hollies
30. 'Dominion' (Jardine's team did indeed win the 1932–1933 Ashes, but his use of 'bodyline' made the series infamous)

General Knowledge 12.2
1. Pisces
2. The Fens or Fenlands
3. (Alexander) Pope
4. Sparta
5. Judo
6. Horse
7. Glenn Miller
8. Solstice
9. Michael Caine
10. Roc
11. Chardonnay
12. Appalachian Mountains
13. *Fahrenheit 451*
14. Hydrangea

15. Waterloo Bridge
16. Miles Coverdale
17. The Spanish Inquisition
18. Weekly
19. Witchcraft Act
20. Amalgam
21. Casca
22. (En) Pointe
23. Grenadier Guards
24. Marmalade
25. Police
26. The Joker
27. Waxing
28. Kenya
29. Onyx
30. Theresa May

SHOW 13

Specialist Subject 13.1 – The Beatles

1. The Quarry Men
2. Hamburg
3. Pete Best
4. Decca (Records) – apparently in the belief that guitar groups were on the way out!
5. 'Can't Buy Me Love'
6. (Eric) Clapton
7. *Rubber Soul*
8. Baker Street
9. 'From Me To You'
10. Ed Sullivan
11. 'Paperback Writer'
12. Royal Variety Show

13. 'Get Back'
14. The Philippines
15. 'Hare Krishna'
16. (Richard or Dick) Lester
17. Shea Stadium
18. 'Yellow Submarine'
19. Billy J. Kramer (and the Dakotas)
20. 'The Isle of Wight'
21. 'In His Own Write'
22. Kenny Everett
23. 'Do You Want To Know A Secret'
24. 26 December or Boxing Day
25. 'The Ballad of John And Yoko'
26. San Francisco
27. 'All You Need Is Love'
28. Marmalade
29. Seventeen
30. 'Mister Brian Epstein'

General Knowledge 13.1
1. Joseph
2. Grub Street
3. San Francisco
4. Oche
5. Calcium
6. Ukulele
7. Ottoman Empire – accept Turkish Empire
8. Fletcher
9. Ely
10. Axe or Halberd
11. Medicine or Physiology or Human Biology
12. Cawl
13. (David) Bowie

14. Atoll
15. Golden Globes
16. Net
17. Frederick Forsyth
18. Aqua Regia
19. Finnish
20. Stephanie Flanders
21. Ordnance Survey
22. 'Moon River'
23. The Balkans
24. *The Old Devils*
25. Italy
26. Duke Ellington
27. Crayfish
28. Eton Wall Game
29. Artemis
30. LSD

Specialist Subject 13.2 – British and European Geography
1. Mersey
2. The Urals
3. Bodmin (Moor)
4. Bratislava (Capital of Slovakia)
5. Salisbury
6. Danube
7. Birmingham
8. Calabria
9. (Kingston upon) Hull
10. Kerch Strait
11. Helvellyn
12. Bodensee or Lake Constance
13. Brecon Beacons
14. Galway

15. Tees
16. Ukraine
17. Quantock (Hills)
18. Istria
19. Wiltshire
20. Harz (Mountains)
21. Saltaire (founded by Titus Salt)
22. Maquis
23. Wells
24. Bulgaria
25. Les Minquiers or The Minkies
26. Shannon
27. Exeter
28. Kaliningrad
29. Tay
30. Marmolada

General Knowledge 13.2
1. A handbag
2. (Gustave) Eiffel
3. Borat
4. Ears
5. (Steve) Ovett – not Steve Cram
6. Yukon Territory
7. Backgammon
8. Hubris
9. Prime (numbers)
10. Cucumber
11. (House of) York
12. 'Ring of Fire'
13. Empiricism
14. Water Lilies
15. Amritsar

16. *Star Trek*
17. Welcome
18. Aluminium
19. Koala (Bear)
20. *Othello*
21. Battle of the Pyramids – accept Battle of Embabeh
22. Lumière
23. Jordan
24. Toccata
25. (A.P. 'Tony') McCoy
26. Corpuscle
27. Yiddish
28. Diffraction
29. Mandrake
30. Politics

SHOW 14

Specialist Subject 14.1 – Snakes
1. King Cobra or Hamadryad
2. Colubrids
3. (Common or European) Adder
4. Salt
5. Russell's Viper
6. (Birds') Eggs
7. Montpellier Snake
8. Guam
9. Sea-Kraits
10. Tail
11. Gabon Viper
12. (The inside of) Its mouth
13. Boomslang
14. Squamata

15. Puff Adder
16. Martinique
17. Coral Snake
18. Duvernoy's Gland
19. Pit Viper
20. Australia – accept Australasia or Oceania (but not Antarctica, which doesn't have a snake population!)
21. (Timber or Banded) Rattlesnake
22. It rolls or curls into a ball (hence is known as the Ball Python)
23. Spectacled (Cobra)
24. Vietnam
25. Sidewinder
26. Feigning Death
27. (Common) Garter (Snake)
28. Haemotoxic
29. (European) Grass Snake
30. Eel

General Knowledge 14.1
1. Lee Harvey Oswald
2. Timbuktu
3. Taramosalata
4. Carthage
5. *Look Back in Anger*
6. Sheep
7. Damien Hirst
8. Brain
9. Spandau Ballet
10. Cambridge
11. Rex Harrison
12. Orchid Family
13. 'O Mio Babbino Caro'
14. Hagar

15. St Leger
16. Binary (stars)
17. *Seinfeld*
18. Ivy League
19. Tintoretto
20. Canada
21. Columbia
22. Stephen
23. Brandy
24. (Common) Hermit (Crab)
25. San Quentin (not Folsom)
26. Mull
27. Henning Mankell
28. Tiberius
29. Poisoning
30. (Richard) Nixon

Specialist Subject 14.2 – *The Archers* since 1970
1. Dame Judi Dench
2. Hungary
3. Pat Archer
4. Blossom Hill Cottage
5. John Archer
6. Stephen
7. Clive Horrobin
8. Canadian
9. (John) Higgs
10. Hit by a falling branch (while felling a tree)
11. Caroline (Bone or Pemberton or Sterling)
12. Nightingale Farm
13. Joby
14. The Sealed Knot
15. Spearmint

16. Bridge Farm
17. Cameron Fraser
18. Hollerton Junction
19. Mary Weston
20. Police Cadet – accept Policewoman
21. Rodway and Watson
22. Cornet
23. Alf or Alfred
24. New Zealand
25. Lord Lichfield
26. Vet
27. Chris(topher) Carter
28. (In the library of) Kensington Palace
29. Sophie Barlow
30. A llama (named Wolfgang) … She got one for herself at the same time, named Constanza.

General Knowledge 14.2
1. *Slumdog Millionaire*
2. Squirrel
3. (J.M.W.) Turner
4. Swansea
5. *Hamlet (Prince of Denmark)*
6. Marie Stopes
7. Thyme
8. St Augustine (of Canterbury)
9. *Pictures at an Exhibition*
10. Drupe
11. Three Points
12. Rhodes
13. *Friends*
14. (Sir Richard) Stafford Cripps
15. Chortle

16. Ambrosia
17. Vincent Price
18. Sternum
19. Ridley Scott
20. Benedict Arnold
21. Cabbage
22. Hereford
23. Sylvia Plath
24. Ibis
25. (David) Hockney
26. Oahu
27. Nina Simone
28. Butterflies
29. Convection
30. 'A thin man'

SHOW 15

Specialist Subject 15.1 – Sherlock Holmes
1. *Beeton's (Christmas) Annual*
2. Afghanistan
3. A jellyfish or 'Cyanea Capillata'
4. Mrs (Martha) Hudson
5. '(The Adventure of) Silver Blaze'
6. Wiggins
7. 'The Mazarin Stone' (in the story of that title)
8. Mycroft (Holmes)
9. Yellow Fever
10. Agra treasure
11. Submarine
12. Monkey – accept Langur or Ape
13. Park Lane
14. He hypnotises her – accept Post-hypnotic suggestion

15. Sidney Paget
16. Begging
17. Diogenes Club
18. (Steel) Harpoon
19. Reichenbach Falls
20. Bookselling or He (says he) owns a bookshop
21. His thumb
22. Thucydides
23. Bohemia (in 'A Scandal In Bohemia')
24. He wants her money
25. 'His Last Bow'
26. Swamp Adder
27. Eduardo Lucas (in 'The Adventure of the Second Stain')
28. (Pages of the) *Encyclopaedia Britannica*
29. Sherman (who refers to him as 'Mr Sherlock')
30. '(The Adventure of) Shoscombe Old Place'

General Knowledge 15.1
1. (Commander James) Bond or 007
2. Potomac
3. Photography
4. Amphibians
5. Singapore Sling
6. The universities
7. Mars
8. Cadmium
9. Best Boy (also known as Second Electrician)
10. Tea
11. Henry Cooper
12. Site of A Roman camp – or Army / Military camp
13. Michael Bond
14. Dandelion
15. Alf Garnett

16. Zealot
17. 'As Time Goes By'
18. Orion
19. (Salvador) Dali
20. Sybarite or Sybaritic
21. (Three) Brass balls
22. Krakatoa
23. Brill Building
24. Their hair
25. 'The cuckoo clock'
26. Comrade
27. Medium Density Fibreboard
28. Prometheus
29. Penne
30. (Royal) Tunbridge Wells

Specialist Subject 15.2 – The Life and Reign of Queen Elizabeth I
1.   Tilbury
2.   Hatfield
3.   Treaty of Edinburgh
4.   (Francis) Walsingham (known as Elizabeth's 'Spy Master')
5.   Jesus (College)
6.   Smallpox
7.   Archbishop of Canterbury
8.   Robert Dudley or Earl of Leicester
9.   Governor
10. (Roberto Di) Ridolfi
11. Calais
12. Pius V
13. The (Queen's) Horse
14. Ark Royal (previously Ark Raleigh)
15. William Cecil
16. Lord Chancellor

17. Cadiz
18. Thomas Cranmer
19. (Nicholas) Hilliard
20. Doubt
21. Francis Throckmorton
22. (Earl of) Essex
23. His wife (Amy Robsart)
24. *Richard II*
25. (Duke of) Parma
26. Tower of London
27. 'My little Frog'
28. The Battle of Yellow Ford
29. Sir Henry Bedingfield
30. Richmond (Palace)

General Knowledge 15.2

1. Hastings (also known as Senlac Hill)
2. Evelyn Waugh
3. Vole
4. Thames
5. *On the Waterfront*
6. Etruscans
7. Bricks
8. Diet of Worms
9. (John Philip) Sousa – it's known as the Sousaphone
10. Insulin
11. Heston Blumenthal
12. Non-violence
13. (Kevin) Pietersen
14. Victoria
15. Angus Deayton – in full, Gordon Angus Deayton
16. Tap (root)
17. (Jimi) Hendrix – real name Johnny Allen Hendrix

18. Fuzzy logic
19. (Martin) Scorsese
20. Rosa Parks – born Rosa Louise McCauley
21. Lapis Lazuli
22. Skylab
23. David Hume
24. (Sir Robert) Peel
25. Chambré
26. Stadium
27. *Aspects of Love* – accept 'Aspects'
28. Jerusalem
29. Seventy
30. Thief

SHOW 16

Specialist Subject 16.1 – Mammals
1. (Of the) Breast
2. Orca or Killer Whale (also known as Grampus)
3. (Earth)Worms
4. Sumatra
5. Jaguar
6. Narwhal
7. Szechwan – accept Sihuan
8. Hazel nuts (it's also known as the Hazel Mouse)
9. Rhinoceros
10. Sloths
11. Gir (Forest National Park)
12. Tamworth
13. (Japanese) Macaque
14. Baikal
15. Otter
16. Pangolin

17. (It has) No pouch
18. Bonobo
19. Capybara
20. Cairngorms
21. Dugong
22. Fennec (fox)
23. Horseshoe
24. Minke
25. Aardwolf
26. Red
27. Lemurs
28. Pronghorn or Prongbuck
29. Velvet
30. Spectacled Bear

General Knowledge 16.1
1. Sir David Attenborough (not Richard Attenborough)
2. Fife
3. *Lohengrin*
4. Dandruff – accept Scurf
5. Fresco
6. (Ernest) Shackleton
7. Sherry (not Port)
8. Nemesis
9. Ian McEwan
10. Tree rings or (Annual) Growth rings (in timber and tree trunks)
11. Turin
12. (Sir Edward or 'Ted') Heath
13. Netball
14. Rabbi
15. *My Fair Lady*
16. Ombudsman
17. Turmeric – accept Curcuma longa

18. Tewkesbury
19. *The Great Gatsby*
20. Aphids – accept Plant lice
21. Staircase
22. Fisher
23. A mermaid
24. Galvanising
25. Sam Cooke (not Louis Armstrong – that's 'What A Wonderful World')
26. Euclid
27. (Bobby and Jack) Charlton
28. Stop (or similar)
29. Euston
30. *The Two Ronnies*

Specialist Subject 16.2 – Pop Music of the 1980s and 1990s
1. The Pretenders
2. 'Billie Jean'
3. Nirvana
4. *Smash Hits*
5. 'Into The Groove'
6. Japanese
7. Johnny Marr
8. 'Common People'
9. Diana Dors
10. 'Need You Tonight'
11. Musical Youth
12. Annie Lennox
13. The Style Council
14. 'The Power Of Love'
15. Shakin' Stevens
16. D:Ream
17. Neil Diamond

18. Madness
19. Christie Brinkley
20. *Parklife*
21. ZZ Top
22. 'Wake Me Up Before You Go-Go'
23. Bono (real name Paul Hewson)
24. Bonehead
25. Fine Young Cannibals
26. George Michael
27. Trainspotting
28. Kate Bush
29. Blondie
30. Trevor Horn

General Knowledge 16.2

1. Blue
2. The Gherkin
3. Finn Mac Cool or Fingal
4. Nano
5. Richard Griffiths
6. Newport
7. (William) Somerset Maugham
8. Henna
9. Adele (Adkins)
10. Switzerland – accept Swiss Confederation (its name at the time)
11. Jovial
12. Vanessa Redgrave
13. Tea
14. (Tomas De) Torquemada
15. (Colin) Montgomerie (often known as Monty)
16. Morocco
17. *Countdown*
18. Tarpeian (Rock)

19. 'White Christmas'
20. Tinnitus (Aurium)
21. (George) Stubbs
22. Martinet
23. Zinc
24. Black Pudding – accept Blood pudding or Blood sausage
25. Tern
26. (Leonard) Bernstein
27. Atlanta
28. Billie Jean King (originally Billie Jean Moffit)
29. Termites
30. *Catch-22*

SHOW 17

Specialist Subject 17.1 – Formula One Motor Racing
1.   Silverstone
2.   (Sebastian) Vettel
3.   Lotus
4.   (Keke) Rosberg (not Nico Rosberg)
5.   USA or Indianapolis
6.   Jacques Villeneuve (not Gilles Villeneuve)
7.   Italy or Monza
8.   (Ross) Brawn
9.   McLaren
10. (Mika) Hakkinen
11. Nurburgring
12. (Riccardo) Patrese
13. Hungary or Hungaroring
14. (Juan Manuel) Fangio
15. Brabham
16. (Gerhard) Berger
17. Valencia

18. (Jean) Alesi
19. Williams (-BMW)
20. (Emerson) Fittipaldi
21. Donington (Park)
22. (Alberto) Ascari
23. Jordan (-Honda)
24. (Fernando) Alonso
25. Swiss (a 'Swiss Grand Prix' was held in 1982 ... at Dijon in France!)
26. (Olivier) Panis
27. Force India
28. (John) Surtees – the only man to win world titles in motor cycling and Formula One
29. (Ligne Droit Du) Mistral
30. It had six wheels!

General Knowledge 17.1
1. Edward VIII
2. Sheffield
3. *The Laughing Cavalier*
4. Yemen
5. Biltong
6. Nimby – it stands for Not In My Back Yard
7. *Some Like It Hot*
8. (Garden) Peas
9. *On the Road*
10. Toronto
11. Jason Robinson
12. Peccary – accept Javelina
13. Isaac Hayes
14. Socrates
15. (Aram) Khachaturian
16. Scurvy

17. Aramaic
18. Plums
19. Pluperfect
20. Sound
21. Brenner Pass
22. *The Color of Money*
23. Jerusalem
24. Sancho Panza
25. Karma
26. (Tim) Henman
27. Binary (number system)
28. Boeing
29. Codpiece
30. Village People

Specialist Subject 17.2 – The Great War and the Second World War
1. (Battle of the) Somme
2. (General Douglas) MacArthur
3. Ultra
4. (Battle of) Tannenberg
5. (Georgy) Zhukov
6. Sea Lion
7. (T.E.) Lawrence (of Arabia)
8. Field Marshal
9. (Hawker) Hurricane
10. Scapa flow
11. (Erwin) Rommel
12. Iwo Jima
13. Versailles
14. Bouncing bomb – accept Dambuster bomb
15. (Charles) Orde Wingate
16. Passchendaele
17. Desert Rats

18. Tehran
19. (Nurse) Edith Cavell
20. Okinawa
21. Hugh Dowding (in full, Air Chief Marshal Lord Dowding or 1st Baron Dowding of Bentley Priory)
22. Brest-Litovsk
23. (Wing Commander) Douglas Bader – he was later promoted to Group Captain
24. Omaha
25. (David) Lloyd George
26. Baedeker (raids)
27. Arnhem
28. (Sir Edwin) Lutyens
29. Dresden
30. (General Alfred) Jodl

General Knowledge 17.2
1. (J.R.R.) Tolkien
2. Lepidoptera
3. *Rigoletto*
4. Montenegro
5. Egg (Yolk)
6. (Christopher) Columbus (whose real name was Cristobal Colon)
7. *The Goodies*
8. (Papal) Bull
9. (Ebenezer) Scrooge
10. (Edwin) Hubble
11. Siena
12. Odysseus (or Ulysses)
13. Calvados
14. Greenham Common
15. (Scott) Joplin
16. Raffia

17. Wildfell Hall
18. Aviemore
19. (J.M.W.) Turner
20. Hadith
21. Tartare (sauce)
22. Paranoia
23. Judi Dench
24. Birmingham
25. Accidents
26. Alexandria
27. Ray Davies
28. (Duck-billed) Platypus
29. Time flies or Time is flying
30. (*Monty Python's*) *Life of Brian*

SHOW 18

Specialist Subject 18.1 – Great Scientists: Galileo, Newton, Darwin and Einstein

1.   (Jean-Baptiste, Chevalier de) Lamarck
2.   (*Philosophiae Naturalis*) *Principia* (*Mathematica*)
3.   Patent Office (in Berne)
4.   (Nicholas) Copernicus
5.   *Beagle*
6.   The Plague
7.   Speed of Light
8.   Pisa (though it is almost certainly apocryphal that he did so by dropping weights off the Leaning Tower!)
9.   (Sir Charles) Lyell
10. Third (Law of Motion)
11. Brownian Motion
12. Jupiter
13. Eating it (for dinner)

14. Lucasian (Professor of Mathematics)
15. Malicious
16. Sunspots
17. (Alfred) Russell Wallace
18. Alchemy
19. Photoelectric (effect)
20. Urban (VIII)
21. (Samuel) Wilberforce – accept Bishop of Oxford
22. Royal Mint
23. (Institute of) Advanced Study (in Princeton) – not Princeton University
24. Thermometer
25. *The Descent of Man*
26. (Gottfried Wilhem von) Leibniz
27. President of Israel
28. The Netherlands or Holland
29. Down House
30. (Robert) Hooke

General Knowledge 18.1
1. *The Wizard of Oz*
2. Kalahari
3. 'Moonlight Serenade' (not 'In The Mood')
4. Gerardus Mercator – born Gerhard de Kremer
5. Pastis
6. (Neil) Kinnock – now Lord Kinnock (of Bedwelty)
7. Norman Foster or Lord / Baron Foster (of Thames Bank)
8. Withers
9. *Martin Chuzzlewit*
10. Loki
11. Meteor shower
12. St Peter Port
13. (Archery) Bow

14. Fir (not pine)
15. Rihanna
16. Rogation (Sunday)
17. *Dallas*
18. Pain
19. Raphael
20. Greece
21. Oratorio
22. Khyber Pass
23. (Joseph Rudyard) Kipling
24. Crustacean
25. Joe Calzaghe
26. Marathon
27. Fish or Bummalo
28. Hemlock
29. Derry or Londonderry
30. *The Music Lovers* (it's a biopic of Tchaikovsky)

Specialist Subject 18.2 – The Films of Alfred Hitchcock

1. *Psycho*
2. Mount Rushmore
3. Kim Novak
4. *Rope*
5. (Daphne du) Maurier
6. *Miss Torso*
7. *To Catch a Thief*
8. Shirley MacLaine
9. *Spellbound*
10. (Bernard) Herrmann
11. *Lifeboat*
12. Mrs Danvers – also known as 'Danny'
13. *The Wrong Man*
14. A dead body

15. Grace Kelly or Princess Grace (of Monaco)
16. *The Man Who Knew Too Much*
17. Marion Crane
18. *The 39 Steps*
19. (David O.) Selznick
20. Bird trainer
21. MacGuffin
22. *Stage Fright*
23. Reflected in her (dropped) glasses
24. Bruce Dern
25. *Family Plot*
26. Joan Fontaine
27. *The Lady Vanishes*
28. Winston Graham
29. (A pair of) scissors
30. A baby

General Knowledge 18.2
1. Photosynthesis
2. Hay (-on-Wye)
3. Pi (or approximately 3.14 or 22/7)
4. Rorke's Drift
5. Potatoes
6. Rodents or Rodentia
7. Coppola (he is the nephew of Francis Ford Coppola)
8. Lisbon
9. *Peer Gynt*
10. Ariadne
11. Sesame seeds
12. House of Keys (not Tynwald)
13. *The Rivals*
14. Krishna
15. Reginald Perrin

16. Carbolic (acid) or Phenol
17. Mobo (Awards) – in full, Music Of Black Origin Awards
18. (William Augustus, the Duke of) Cumberland – accept 'Butcher' Cumberland
19. Lintel
20. Aberdeen
21. Beatrice or Bice Portinari (not Gemma Donati)
22. Banyan
23. Ice Hockey
24. Constantine (I or the Great)
25. *Grease*
26. Colombia
27. Gerry and the Pacemakers (not The Beatles)
28. Prehensile
29. Daleks
30. 'Freedom Fries'

SHOW 19

Specialist Subject 19.1 – The TV Series *Blackadder*
1. (General Sir Anthony Cecil Hogmanay) Melchett
2. Turnip – Baldrick found it 'particularly ironic' as he has 'a thingy that's shaped like a turnip'…
3. Percy (Duke of Northumberland)
4. 'Edmund, A Butler's Tale'
5. Dandruff
6. Richard Curtis
7. (A new, and extremely wide) Ruff
8. Knighthood
9. 'Bob' – accept 'Bobby Parkhurst'
10. A dog
11. 'A small sausage factory in Tanganyika'
12. 'So has syphilis'

13. Mrs Miggins
14. The King or Richard III
15. Shooting (and eating) Melchett's (pet carrier) pigeon (Speckled Jim)
    – accept 'Deliberately, callously and with beastliness aforethought
    murder(ing) a lovely innocent pigeon'
16. (The 'Baby-Eating') Bishop of Bath and Wells
17. (The Royal) Privies
18. John Lloyd
19. (Charlie) Chaplin
20. Archbishop (of Canterbury)
21. Dunny-on-the-Wold
22. Martin Luther
23. (Nurse) Mary (Fletcher-Brown)
24. He cut off his head (and fried it in garlic)
25. Frank Finlay
26. A turbot – accept Fish
27. 'King And Country'
28. Don Speekingleesh
29. (Adrian) Edmondson
30. 'It takes more than a maniac trying to cut off my goolies to
    'inconweenience' me'

General Knowledge 19.1
1. Newcastle (upon Tyne)
2. Bats
3. Béchamel
4. Venezuela
5. (Edward) Hopper
6. Plebeians or Plebs
7. John Stuart Mill
8. Photosphere
9. (Martin) Scorsese
10. Apostrophe

11. *La Bohème*
12. Milk and Honey
13. Polo
14. South Carolina
15. Apse
16. Willow
17. Pizzicato
18. Cork
19. Alan Bennett
20. Mulberry Harbours
21. Miss World
22. Vedas
23. Pete Doherty
24. (John) Poulson
25. Spritzer
26. Grebe
27. Bell-Bottoms
28. Vladivostok
29. Lactic Acid
30. *Jabberwocky*

Specialist Subject 19.2 – The Nobel Prize

1. (Albert Arnold 'Al') Gore
2. 10 December
3. Dorothy Hodgkin
4. Literature
5. (Non Co-operative) Games – accept Game Theory
6. (Pierre and Marie) Curie – their daughter Iréne and her husband Frédéric Joliot were also Nobel laureates
7. (Vitamin) K
8. Astronomy – accept Radio Astronomy or Astrophysics
9. (Tomas) Tranströmer
10. Oslo City Hall

11. Tinbergen
12. Monetarism
13. (Enrico) Fermi
14. Digestion
15. Winston Churchill
16. Posthumous winners
17. (Ernest) Rutherford, later Lord Rutherford (of Nelson)
18. Prion (Proteinaceous Infectious Particle)
19. (Joseph) Stalin
20. Wireless Telegraph(y)
21. Toni Morrison
22. Central Bank of Sweden – accept Sveriges Riksbank
23. Positron
24. (Francis) Crick – for their discoveries in the field of DNA
25. (Buckminster) Fullerene
26. (UN) International Atomic Energy Agency or IAEA
27. (Count Leo) Tolstoy
28. Fifty
29. In-Vitro Fertilisation or IVF – accept (Human) Fertility or 'Test Tube Baby'
30. They were all under arrest – accept in jail or similar

General Knowledge 19.2
1. Loch
2. (John) Major
3. Campanile – not Belfry
4. Avignon
5. Aniseed
6. Atrium
7. *Anna Karenina*
8. Curlew
9. 'Bow Bells' – in full, the Bells of St Mary-Le-Bow, Cheapside
10. Pundit

11. Harold Abrahams
12. Azores
13. (Igor) Stravinsky
14. Shinto(-ism)
15. *Ashes to Ashes*
16. First day
17. Oasis
18. Rhododendron – also known as the Rosebay
19. (Sir Jacob) Epstein
20. (Earl of) Orrery
21. Agatha Christie
22. Jibril or Gabriel
23. (Anthony James) 'Lonnie' Donegan
24. Somerset
25. (Bradley) Wiggins
26. Frog
27. Paco Rabanne
28. Norse or Scandinavian, though we will accept Viking
29. Delbert Wilkins
30. Brawn ... or Head cheese as it's apparently known in America!

SHOW 20

Specialist Subject 20.1 – Winston Churchill
1. Blenheim Palace
2. 'Victory' – in full, 'Victory. Victory at all costs, victory in spite of all terror, victory, however long and hard the road may be.'
3. *Morning Post*
4. Dundee
5. (His predecessor, Neville) Chamberlain
6. Sidney Street – known as 'the Siege of Sidney Street'
7. Evacuation of Dunkirk
8. Pretoria

9. Clementine or 'Clemmie' (Hozier)
10. *Savrola*
11. Singapore
12. (Sir John) Jellicoe – though he later commented that Jellicoe was 'the only man on either side who could lose the War in an afternoon'
13. Chartwell (Manor) – he was allegedly offered, and accepted, membership of the Amalgamated Union of Building Trade Workers, only for the union's executive to rule he was ineligible!
14. Harvard
15. Chancellor (of the Exchequer)
16. (Arthur) Greenwood
17. India
18. (Restoration of) the Gold Standard (at the pre-war level)
19. (Sir Stafford) Cripps
20. *Life*
21. The Poles
22. (Professor Frederick) Lindemann – Later 1st Viscount Cherwell
23. The King's Party
24. Eighty
25. Bessie Braddock
26. Woodford (previously Epping)
27. Reconciliation of France and Germany and/or the Establishment of a United (States of) Europe – accept A Council of Europe
28. Omdurman
29. Honorary citizenship (of the USA)
30. 'Re-rat'

General Knowledge 20.1
1. Bantam
2. Saliva
3. Custard
4. Mulberry

5. (Sir Henry) Moore
6. Chartism
7. Philip K. Dick
8. Firth
9. Traveling Wilburys
10. Chipmunk
11. (Static) Electricity
12. Bow (Group)
13. Chicago Bulls
14. Nero
15. Counterpoint
16. Cana (of Galilee)
17. Javier Bardem
18. Embryo
19. *Only Fools and Horses*
20. American Samoa
21. 'Franglais'
22. Newt
23. Dormer
24. Leinster
25. Sangiovese
26. Babylon
27. Dr. Seuss
28. Lollards
29. (Laurens) Hammond
30. Basil Fawlty

Specialist Subject 20.2 – The Novels of Charles Dickens
1. *David Copperfield*
2. 'The Aged P' – accept 'The Aged Parent'
3. *Martin Chuzzlewit*
4. Half-brothers
5. *Pickwick Papers*

6. Wackford Squeers
7. 'A Tale of the Riots of 'Eighty'
8. 'Recalled to Life'
9. *Bleak House*
10. 'The Infant Phenomenon'
11. Cloisterham
12. *The Old Curiosity Shop*
13. Sam Weller
14. *Little Dorrit*
15. The Maypole (Inn)
16. *Our Mutual Friend*
17. Wilkins
18. *Hard Times*
19. (Doctor) Blimber
20. Gamp
21. Bentley Drummle
22. Marshalsea
23. (Mr Seth) Pecksniff
24. Eatanswill
25. Kit Nubbles
26. Salem House (School)
27. Bradley Headstone
28. Circus Proprietor
29. Satis – accept Enough
30. Spontaneous combustion

General Knowledge 20.2
1. Unicorn
2. Consul
3. Figaro – accept The Barber of Seville
4. Formosa
5. Veuve Clicquot(-Ponsardin) – her late husband was François Clicquot, so she was La Veuve (the Widow) Clicquot

6. Crane
7. Lord's (Cricket Ground)
8. Pioneer
9. (Jean-Paul) Sartre
10. Cranium
11. (Republic of) Ireland
12. Lily of the Valley
13. *Giant*
14. The pale – hence the term 'beyond the pale'
15. David Gray
16. Waterfall
17. Citric
18. Islam
19. 'Summer Holiday'
20. (Scaly) Anteater
21. *Blazing Saddles*
22. Keratin
23. (Nick) Faldo
24. Hex
25. Pottery or Ceramics
26. Kon-Tiki
27. *The Comedy of Errors*
28. (Grizzly) Bear
29. Nicaea – hence Nicene Creed
30. Sir Geoffrey Howe

SHOW 21

Specialist Subject 21.1 – Frank Sinatra
1. Hoboken
2. Tommy Dorsey
3. *Songs for Swingin' Lovers*
4. Ava Gardner

5. Reprise
6. 'Who Wants To Be A Millionaire?'
7. Lana Turner
8. 'Somethin' Stupid'
9. (President John F.) Kennedy or JFK
10. 'Strangers In The Night'
11. Zeppo
12. Perforated eardrum
13. (Private Angelo) Maggio – accept *From Here to Eternity*
14. 'My Way'
15. Lauren Bacall
16. *Robin and the Seven Hoods*
17. Nelson Riddle
18. *Marriage on the Rocks*
19. (Nikita) Khrushchev
20. *Ol' Blue Eyes Is Back*
21. Bono – born Paul Hewson
22. *The Man with the Golden Arm*
23. Don Costa
24. Sun City
25. Charlie Brown
26. 'Three Coins In The Fountain'
27. Peter Lawford
28. MCA (Music Corporation of America)
29. Count Basie (and His Orchestra)
30. *(Who Framed) Roger Rabbit?*

General Knowledge 21.1
1. Rock
2. Bletchley Park
3. Pineapple
4. (Northern) Gannet
5. Brutus

6. Iraq
7. Hammer (Films)
8. Jericho
9. Faust
10. Hustings
11. Camden Town (Group)
12. Chain reaction
13. Erasure
14. Black Sea
15. (Mr) Spock
16. Fallopian tubes
17. Tottenham (Hotspur) or Spurs
18. Royal
19. *Quadrophenia*
20. Salisbury
21. Preposition
22. Sita
23. Neptune
24. Indigo or Indigofera
25. Brobdingnag
26. (James) Wolfe
27. Drambuie
28. Trinidad – accept Trinidad and Tobago
29. Nat 'King' Cole
30. *Manneken Pis*

Specialist Subject 21.2 – Leonardo da Vinci
1. *Mona Lisa*
2. Caterina
3. *The Last Supper*
4. (Andrea del) Verrocchio – born Andrea di Cione
5. Pisa
6. Michelangelo (Buonarroti)

7. Santa Maria delle Grazie
8. Sforza
9. *Lady with an Ermine*
10. *Adoration of the Magi*
11. Cesare Borgia (Duke of Valentinois)
12. Mantua
13. (Giovanni Francesco) Melzi or Da Melzo
14. *On Divine Proportion*
15. A flower
16. (Niccolo) Machiavelli (author of *The Prince*)
17. Ornithopter
18. Bill Gates
19. A Bridge (over the Bosporus or Golden Horn)
20. A cross
21. (St) John the Baptist
22. Romorantin
23. Anatomy or Dissection
24. Francis I (of France)
25. *Vitruvian Man*
26. (Leoni Battista) Alberti – his first name is sometimes given as Leon or Leona
27. Cloux – now called the Chateau du Clos Lucé
28. (Jacopo) Saltarelli
29. Mechanical lion
30. (Giorgio) Vasari

General Knowledge 21.2
1. GCSE – or General Certificate of Secondary Education
2. Enoch Powell
3. Tommy Steele (born Thomas Hicks)
4. New Lanark
5. (White) Bread
6. Picts

7. *Of Mice and Men*
8. Maple or Acer
9. Dennis Potter
10. (Cardinal de) Richelieu
11. Malta
12. Guru
13. Primal Scream
14. Thyroid (gland)
15. Emu
16. Zambezi
17. Delia Smith
18. Organic chemistry
19. Bodega
20. Pore
21. Byzantine
22. (Cleaner) Wrasse
23. Cellos
24. Isle of Wight
25. *The Importance of Being Earnest*
26. Hadrian
27. Tour de France – hence the yellow jersey awarded to the winner
28. (St) Luke (the Evangelist)
29. Ceilidh
30. *Samson and Delilah*

SHOW 22

Specialist Subject 22.1 – The Life and Reign of Henry VIII
1. Arthur – Henry married Catherine eight years later
2. (Cardinal Thomas) Wolsey
3. Your or His Majesty
4. Hampton Court
5. Flodden

6. Anne Boleyn
7. New Year's Day or 1 January
8. Leviticus
9. (Sir Thomas) More
10. An empire
11. Mary, Queen of Scots
12. Martin Luther – the Pope Conferred the title 'Defender of the Faith' on Henry as a result
13. 'Mary Rose'
14. Anne of Cleves
15. Joust(ing)
16. Thomas Cromwell
17. Falcon
18. (Hans) Holbein (the Younger)
19. Holy Roman Emperor
20. Howard – Henry Howard, Earl of Surrey was executed and his father Thomas Howard, Duke of Norfolk was sentenced to death but saved
21. Act of Succession
22. Erasmus
23. (Earl of) Essex
24. Valor Ecclesiasticus
25. The Five Wounds of Christ
26. Jane (Seymour)
27. Stephen Gardiner or Bishop of Winchester
28. Wolf Hall
29. Thomas or Lord Seymour (of Sudeley)
30. (Communal) Lavatory

General Knowledge 22.1

1. Chameleon
2. Rutland
3. Mickey Mouse

4. Quorum
5. *Bubbles*
6. Draco or Dracon – hence Draconian
7. (Madame or Emma) Bovary
8. Hydroponics
9. (Stephen) Sondheim
10. Pascal
11. Cointreau
12. The Koran
13. The Beautiful South – apparently the name reflected his dislike of southern England!
14. Vancouver
15. Anorak
16. Quadriceps or Quads
17. *Sleuth*
18. Air-raid shelters
19. Gum shield or Mouthguard
20. Comma
21. (Max) Bruch
22. Antimony
23. Dopiaza
24. Derbyshire
25. Impasto
26. Titus
27. *The Prisoner*
28. Jehu
29. (*The*) *Screwtape* (*Letters*) – accept 'Screwtape Proposes a Toast'
30. Monster Raving Loony Party

Specialist Subject 22.2 – The England Football Team since 1945
1. (David) Beckham
2. (United States of) America or USA
3. Stuart Pearce

4. Bobby Charlton – not Jack Charlton
5. Italy
6. Bryan Robson (not Bobby Robson, who managed the team in 1986 and 1990)
7. (Clint) Dempsey
8. Uruguay
9. (Peter) Bonetti
10. Clown
11. (Frank) Swift
12. Spain
13. (Peter) Beardsley
14. (Owen) Hargreaves
15. Chile
16. John Barnes
17. Neil Webb
18. Sardinia
19. (Jimmy) Greaves
20. Ray Wilkins (not David Beckham or Wayne Rooney)
21. Sapporo
22. Alan Smith (the Leicester and Arsenal striker, not the Leeds, Manchester United and Newcastle player)
23. (Tom) Finney
24. Eleven – accept The whole team
25. Ian Callaghan
26. (Wolfgang) Weber
27. Six goals to three
28. (David) Platt
29. (Alan) Mullery
30. Munich

General Knowledge 22.2
1. *Star Wars*
2. Proteins

3. Philip Marlowe
4. Crow
5. Bourbon
6. Baha'i
7. (Hieronymous) Bosch
8. Mountains of Mourne
9. *The Vicar of Dibley*
10. The Hundred Days or Cent Jours
11. (Benjamin) Disraeli – later (First) Earl of Beaconsfield
12. Googol
13. 'The Ballad of John and Yoko'
14. Scots Pine
15. (John) McEnroe
16. Bratislava
17. *The Beggar's Opera*
18. Delphi
19. Action painting
20. Kidney stones
21. Tommy Cooper
22. Naming
23. Fred Flintstone
24. The East India Company
25. Linguine
26. The Netherlands
27. (P.G.) Wodehouse
28. Feral
29. Glockenspiel
30. (Saint) Matthew – accept St Levi

SHOW 23

Specialist Subject 23.1 – Stanley Kubrick
1. *Full Metal Jacket* (he played Private Pyle)

2. Sydney Pollack
3. *The Shining*
4. (Jack D.) Ripper
5. (Henry) Purcell
6. *Paths of Glory*
7. R. Lee Ermey (Gunnery Sergeant Hartman)
8. The Overlook Hotel
9. *Barry Lyndon*
10. Warren Clarke (who later played Andrew Dalziel in *Dalziel and Pascoe*)
11. 'Hi There!'
12. Jack Nicholson
13. *The Dawn of Man*
14. Walter or Wendy Carlos
15. *Spartacus*
16. Sue Lyon
17. Warner Bros
18. Michael Hordern
19. Ludovico
20. (William) Randolph Hearst
21. *The Killing*
22. Arthur C. Clarke
23. The (US) President (Merkin Muffley)
24. Lois Maxwell
25. Hué
26. (The Voice of the Computer) Hal (9000)
27. Oregon
28. Leonard Rossiter
29. Peter Ustinov
30. '(Mein Fuhrer) I can walk'

General Knowledge 23.1
1. Balaclava (helmet)

2. (Saint Thomas) Becket
3. (William) Hogarth
4. Stomach chambers – accept Parts of the stomach
5. (Andrew, now Lord) Lloyd Webber
6. Durham
7. *Middlemarch*
8. Conclave
9. John Noakes
10. Tennis elbow (not Golfer's elbow)
11. Borscht
12. (Robert) Maxwell
13. 'For Valour'
14. Charybdis
15. *Shaft*
16. (White and Blue) Nile
17. (Franz) Schubert
18. Topiary
19. Rowing
20. Remote control
21. Caryatid
22. The Diggers
23. Günter Grass
24. Jurassic Coast
25. Vulcan
26. Plantigrade
27. Nebuchadnezzar
28. Esperanto
29. (Aimee) Duffy
30. Spam

Specialist Subject 23.2 – Aircraft and Aerial Warfare of the First and Second World Wars

1. (Boeing) B-29 or Superfortress

2. (British) Roundel
3. Coventry
4. Photo Reconnaissance
5. Sopwith Camel – accept Sopwith Biplane F.1
6. Taranto
7. Sky-train
8. (Assault transport) Glider
9. Eagle
10. (Adolf) Galland
11. (Boeing) B-17 or 'Flying Fortress'
12. 'Flying Porcupine'
13. (Flight Lieutenant John William) Alcock
14. Sixth Army (at Stalingrad)
15. (Gloster) Gladiator
16. Sir Arthur Tedder
17. (Supermarine) Seafire (Mk. I)
18. Boulton and Paul
19. (Hawker) Tempest (Mk. V)
20. Brest
21. (De Havilland) Mosquito (Mk. I)
22. Pusher
23. (Consolidated) B-24 or Liberator
24. Austin
25. (Hawker) Typhoons
26. Cleland Davis
27. 'Marianas Turkey Shoot'
28. Séguin
29. (Direct) Fuel-injection
30. (Paul W.) Tibbets

General Knowledge 23.2
1. Wombles
2. (Sir) Galahad

3. Requiem Mass (in D Minor)
4. Ecuador
5. Pomegranate
6. Chrysalis or Pupa
7. French
8. (Sir Alec Douglas-)Home (as he was known while he was PM; he had various titles both before and after)
9. Mullion
10. Wahhabi(sm)
11. *Cool Hand Luke*
12. Oxalic – accept Calcium oxalate
13. Netball
14. Valois
15. Larry Sanders
16. Inverness
17. Michael Jackson
18. Beryl
19. Panettone
20. Ishtar – accept Inanna
21. Crows
22. Riboflavine
23. Zero zero one
24. Pygmalion
25. (James Abbott McNeill) Whistler
26. Ionian Islands
27. Oliver Goldsmith
28. Gastropods or Gastropoda
29. Django Reinhardt – originally Jean-Baptiste Reinhardt
30. (Sam) Goldwyn

Specialist Subject 24.1 – Sharks and Whales, Dolphins and Porpoises

1. Cetaceans
2. Basking Shark
3. Yangtze
4. Ampullae of Lorenzini
5. Baleen (Whales) – accept Mysticeti
6. Stingray
7. Flukes
8. Liver
9. Spinner Dolphins
10. Tail or Caudal fin
11. Rorquals
12. (Shortfin) Mako or Bonito
13. Melon
14. Tiger Shark
15. Humpback Whale
16. Dermal denticles
17. Gulf of California or Sea of Cortez
18. Sulphur Bottomed Whale
19. Remora
20. Bowhead Whale
21. Lobtailing
22. Hawaii (the Island of Oahu to be exact)
23. Sperm Whale
24. Sea Canary
25. Dogfish
26. Pink Dolphin or Pink Porpoise
27. Shagreen
28. Gray Whale – accept Mussel-Digger or Scrag Whale
29. Hunting or similar
30. 'Cookiecutter' Shark

General Knowledge 24.1

1. Rabies
2. Adriatic
3. (Anton) Chekhov
4. Madrasa
5. (Antony) Gormley
6. Aardvark
7. Cello – in full, Violoncello
8. Charlemagne (or Charles the Great)
9. *A Passage to India*
10. Zombie
11. Rice
12. 'Cassandra'
13. Lance Todd Trophy
14. (Clement) Attlee
15. Stephen Hawking
16. Staffordshire
17. Vangelis (Papathanassiou)
18. Tulip
19. Greenwich (Observatory) – accept Flamsteed House
20. Sedgemoor
21. Rachel
22. Cheetah – accept Hunting Leopard
23. Pandora (Braithwaite)
24. Kilimanjaro
25. (Gian Lorenzo) Bernini
26. 'Homeward Bound'
27. Two point five four (2.54)
28. William Hartnell
29. Marzipan or Almond paste – accept Eleven marzipan balls
30. Grantham

Specialist Subject 24.2 – The Hitchhiker's Guide to the Galaxy by Douglas Adams

1. 'Don't Panic'
2. Innsbruck
3. A bypass (in the case of the Earth, a hyperspace bypass or hyperspatial express route)
4. Babel Fish
5. ZZ Nine Plural Z Alpha
6. 'So long and thanks for all the fish'
7. To insult everybody in the universe (in alphabetical order)
8. Norway
9. He talks to it (and explains his view of the universe)
10. A hyena
11. A towel
12. A second head and a third arm – accept either
13. Random
14. Blue
15. 'Tax reasons'
16. Oh-Well
17. (Aerosol) Deodorant
18. 'Mad About The Boy'
19. '(What do you get if you) Multiply six by nine'
20. It rains wherever he is, as he is a rain god – accept either
21. Oolon Colluphid
22. Bad news
23. The Big Bang Burger Bar – accept Big Bang Burger Chef
24. Nibbled to death by an okapi
25. Inflation (it costs 'three deciduous forests' to buy 'one ship's peanut')
26. 'Somebody Else's Problem'
27. Belgium
28. 'We apologise for the inconvenience'
29. 'Stick your finger down its throat'

30. The Ningi is (a triangular rubber coin) six thousand eight hundred miles along each side – accept 'The Galacticibanks refuse to deal in fiddling small change'

General Knowledge 24.2

1. Tom Jones
2. Nepal
3. Art Deco
4. (Second Battle of) El Alamein (not Stalingrad)
5. Tipperary
6. Jocasta
7. (Dame) Judi Dench
8. Horse
9. (Dame) Catherine Cookson
10. Usk or Wysg
11. Mince pie
12. Smallpox
13. Newmarket
14. Transistor
15. (Dmitri) Shostakovich
16. Tomato
17. Graeme Garden
18. William Rufus or William II
19. Yo-yo
20. Patriarch
21. Henry James
22. Nova Scotia
23. (Stone) Lithography
24. Grouse
25. Harvey Wallbanger
26. (Palace of) Holyroodhouse
27. Donald Duck
28. (Stanley) Baldwin

29. Jack
30. Fibre (not Food … or anything else!)

SHOW 25

Specialist Subject 25.1 – Pop Music of the 1950s and 1960s
1. *The Blackboard Jungle*
2. Drums
3. 'Green Green Grass Of Home'
4. 'Penny Lane' / 'Strawberry Fields Forever'
5. Wendy Richard
6. The Yardbirds
7. 'All Shook Up'
8. Tony Blackburn
9. 'I'm A Boy'
10. Terry Dene (born Terence Williams)
11. 'Cathy's Clown'
12. Stevie Winwood
13. Procol Harum
14. 'Great Balls of Fire' (by Jerry Lee Lewis)
15. Fontella Bass
16. Sonny and Cher
17. 'You'll Never Walk Alone'
18. Duane Eddy
19. 'Leader Of The Pack'
20. Engelbert Humperdinck
21. 'Hey Joe'
22. Graham Nash
23. 'It Doesn't Matter Anymore'
24. Joe Cocker
25. Two Is (pronounced 'Two Eyes')
26. 'Anyone Who Had A Heart' (it was Cilla's first number one)
27. King Crimson

28. '19th Nervous Breakdown'
29. Peter Green
30. Pink Floyd

General Knowledge 25.1
1. Dom (Pierre) Pérignon
2. Sparta
3. Architect (denoting a member of the Royal Institute of British Architects)
4. Forth
5. (Ensign Pavel) Chekov – played by Walter Koenig
6. SDP (Social Democratic Party)
7. (Jean-François) Millet
8. Penguin
9. Beowulf
10. Gethsemane
11. Liverpool
12. Willow or Salicacae
13. Cricket
14. Nitrogen
15. *The Departed*
16. Toledo
17. *Sleeping Beauty*
18. Hector
19. Asparagus
20. Tin
21. Oxymoron
22. Termites or White Ants
23. Lewis Carroll – real name Charles Lutwidge Dodgson
24. Devon / Devonshire
25. *Steptoe & Son*
26. Richard III
27. Atelier

28. Milton Friedman
29. Heaven 17
30. Sneezing

Specialist Subject 25.2 – Astronomy and Cosmology
1. Black hole
2. Pollux (the northernmost is Castor)
3. Binary (stars)
4. Andromeda galaxy – accept Great Spiral in Andromeda or M31
5. Dark matter (not Black holes)
6. Transit of Venus (across the Sun)
7. Magellanic clouds
8. Bellatrix
9. White dwarf
10. Redshift
11. (Edwin) Hubble
12. 'The Big Crunch'
13. Centaurus or The Centaur
14. Parallax
15. Pleiades
16. Gibbous
17. Microwave
18. Main sequence
19. Copernicus (the other is Kepler)
20. Hale-Bopp
21. Lepus or The Hare
22. (Norman) Pogson
23. Aldebaran
24. Palomar (Observatory)
25. Great Rift
26. Mars
27. Wormholes
28. Quadrantids

29. Ecliptic

30. Local Group

General Knowledge 25.2

1. Eureka – or Heureka, meaning 'I have found it'
2. Orang-utan
3. Rococo
4. Horsa
5. Gazpacho
6. Surtsey
7. Fred Astaire
8. (Gerald) Ford
9. Athens
10. Sulphuric acid
11. (Graf Joseph) Radetzky
12. Clio
13. Portuguese
14. Long-sightedness or Far-sightedness
15. Sheffield Wednesday
16. Bloomsbury
17. *Kind of Blue*
18. Raspberry
19. Nigel Havers
20. Jainism
21. Duran Duran
22. Great Britain or UK
23. (Mark) Rothko
24. Finland
25. Edgar Rice Burroughs
26. Storm Petrel
27. Pils or Pilsener
28. Ulster Unionist Party
29. Seven

30. Bamber Gascoigne

SHOW 26

Specialist Subject 26.1 – The Civil War and Interregnum
1. The Grand Remonstrance
2. Robert Devereux or Earl of Essex
3. 'The Ironsides'
4. (Dr William) Harvey (who discovered the circulation of the blood)
5. Theatres
6. Turnham Green
7. (William) Laud
8. Oxford
9. John Hampden
10. 'God'
11. (First Battle of) Newbury
12. (Sir Thomas) Fairfax
13. Chester
14. (Thomas) Pride – it became known as 'Pride's Purge'
15. Dunbar
16. John Lilburne
17. Canterbury
18. (Henry) Ireton
19. Lobsters
20. Inigo Jones
21. *The King's Cabinet Opened*
22. (George) Monck
23. Isle of Wight
24. Colchester
25. 'The Rump'
26. John Cook
27. Jersey
28. Lord Protector (of England, Scotland, and Ireland)

29. Breda
30. 'Necessity'

General Knowledge 26.1
1. Porcupine
2. Snob
3. (J.M.W.) Turner
4. Malta
5. Mafia (or Cosa Nostra)
6. Rio (de Janeiro)
7. Bing Crosby
8. Septicaemia
9. *Grandstand*
10. The Gorgons
11. Duke of Wellington
12. Switzerland
13. (Oscar) Wilde
14. Skara Brae
15. (John Philip) Sousa
16. Death's Cap
17. (Montgomery Charles or Mr) Burns
18. Simony
19. Nancy Mitford
20. Passport
21. Wycombe (Wanderers)
22. Conjunction
23. 'Crazy'
24. Jerusalem
25. (Philippe) Starck
26. Kiwis
27. *Red Dwarf*
28. Croatia
29. (Dark) Rum

30. Television

Specialist Subject 26.2 – International Rugby Union since 1987
1. Martin Johnson
2. South Africa
3. Ieuan Evans
4. New Zealand – accept All Blacks
5. (Tony) Stanger
6. Argentina
7. Croke Park
8. Bath
9. (Jeremy) Guscott
10. 'Wooden Spoon'
11. (Jonah) Lomu
12. A 'Full House' (of all four scoring methods) – accept He scored a try, conversion, penalty and drop goal
13. Ian McGeechan
14. Athletics – he ran in the 110 Metres Hurdles at the 1984 Olympics
15. France
16. (John) Jeffrey
17. Australia
18. (Christophe) Lamaison
19. (New Zealand) Maori
20. (Scott) Gibbs
21. Wembley
22. (Dr Louis) Luyt – according to his autobiography his real name is Oswald Louis Petrus Poley
23. The referee and touch judges – accept The officials
24. (Philippe) Saint-Andre
25. Japan
26. (Ronan) O'Gara
27. 'The Chiropractor'
28. (Outbreak of) Foot and Mouth (disease) – it caused the match,

originally scheduled for March, to be postponed

29. (John) Kirwan
30. Six (the number of the South African Captain, Francois Pienaar, to whom he presented the trophy after the match)

General Knowledge 26.2

1. *Lawrence of Arabia*
2. Soviet Union
3. (George) Orwell – born Eric Blair
4. Cape Wrath
5. Triptych (also known as a Polyptych)
6. Medici
7. Aria
8. Capuchin
9. Jack Dee
10. Sadhu
11. Jack Daniel(s)
12. Graffito
13. (Jenny and Mark) Pitman
14. Dentine
15. Michael Crawford
16. Bangladesh
17. *The Chronicles of Narnia*
18. To hang up their swords
19. Jools Holland
20. Valhalla
21. Costume (design)
22. Cardigan Bay
23. Emoticon
24. 17th century
25. Radiohead
26. Stirling
27. Dante (Alighieri)

28. Countersinking
29. R
30. Autobiography

SHOW 27

Specialist Subject 27.1 – The Life and Works of J.R.R. Tolkien
1. Bloemfontein
2. Samwise Gamgee
3. Silmarils
4. Eleventy-First (or 111th)
5. Sarehole
6. Inklings
7. 'Farmer Giles of Ham'
8. Mushrooms
9. Donald Swann
10. The Dead Marshes
11. Beladonna Took
12. Trench Fever
13. Mallorn Tree
14. Battle of Bywater
15. Beren and Luthien
16. 'Riddles in the Dark'
17. Eru
18. The River
19. W
20. Shelob (the Great)
21. 'What have I got in my pocket'
22. Exeter College
23. Celebrimbor
24. 'The Quest of Erebor'
25. Smaug (the Golden)
26. Anglo-Saxon

27. Eomer
28. Sting
29. Legolas (Greenleaf)
30. The Arkenstone (of Thrain) – accept The Heart of the Mountain

General Knowledge 27.1
1. *Catch-22*
2. Ten Commandments
3. Yosser (Hughes)
4. (General Charles) Gordon
5. 'Video Killed The Radio Star'
6. Colour blindness
7. Henry Moore
8. Verbatim
9. Marsala
10. Leamington Spa
11. Helen Mirren
12. Airedale
13. (Geoffrey) Chaucer
14. 1926
15. Accrington Stanley
16. Carthage
17. *Clair de Lune* or *Moonlight*
18. Laos
19. Stalk
20. Strudel
21. River Bann
22. Spectrum
23. Crane fly
24. Trail of Tears
25. Titian
26. Seal
27. King

28. Iron
29. Jack Higgins
30. Rolled umbrella

Specialist Subject 27.2 – The *Titanic*

1. Olympic Class
2. *Caronia*
3. (Henry Tingle) Wilde
4. Southampton
5. (Sir William) Arrol (and Company)
6. Queenstown or Cobh
7. Harold Bride
8. *The Atlantic Daily Bulletin*
9. William (McMaster) Murdoch
10. Cherbourg
11. Thomas Andrews
12. *New York*
13. (Joseph Bruce) Ismay
14. Forty-six (thousand)
15. Frederick Fleet
16. Twenty
17. (Captain Sir Arthur Henry) Rostron
18. Cape Race
19. (Benjamin) Guggenheim
20. Second Officer
21. Ida Straus
22. *Frankfort*
23. William Alden Smith
24. *Lapland*
25. (Elizabeth Gladys) Millvina Dean
26. International Ice Patrol
27. (Wallace) Hartley
28. Washington (DC)

29. Richard (Norris) Williams
30. 1985

General Knowledge 27.2

1. Infinity
2. Halal
3. (Antoni) Gaudí
4. Formaldehyde or Methanal
5. Marlene Dietrich
6. Portugal
7. Libretto
8. Gaza (Strip)
9. Biryani
10. Dartford
11. Red Rum
12. Dancing or Whirling Dervishes
13. *Monty Python's Flying Circus*
14. Robin Cook
15. Lesbos
16. Napoleon (Bonaparte) or Napoleon I
17. Cole Porter
18. Yellow Fever (not Malaria)
19. Caledonian Canal
20. Anthropomorphism
21. Hemlock
22. Ariadne
23. (Truman) Capote
24. Bergen
25. Oolong (or Wulong)
26. Dwarf planet
27. (Jack) Vettriano
28. Tapirs
29. Philip Roth

30. Peter Sellers

SHOW 28

Specialist Subject 28.1 – Kings and Queens of England and Britain since 1066

1. Richard III – he was defeated and killed at Bosworth Field and succeeded by Henry VII
2. 'Addled Parliament'
3. Edward I
4. Prussia
5. Henry V
6. L'Entente Cordiale
7. Lord Chancellor
8. (Sir Thomas) Wyatt (the Younger)
9. Tobacco – accept Smoking
10. (Mrs Maria) Fitzherbert – accept Maria Smythe
11. A white hart – accept White male deer or stag
12. Crecy
13. Lord Melbourne – in full, William Lamb, 2nd Viscount Melbourne
14. A warming pan – hence the child was nicknamed 'the Warming Pan Baby'
15. Empress of India
16. Christopher Wren
17. 'Asleep'
18. John Morton – hence 'Morton's Fork'
19. He starved to death
20. (Bishop) Odo (of Bayeux and of Kent)
21. Kenya
22. Perkin Warbeck – also known as Peter Osbeck
23. (The Order of) The Garter
24. Tewkesbury
25. Catholic emancipation – in full, Roman Catholic Relief Bill or Act

26. (William Maxwell Aitken, Lord) Beaverbrook
27. 'The Cabal'
28. Katherine Swynford
29. Tranby Croft
30. 'No, I shall have mistresses'

General Knowledge 28.1
1. Buck's Fizz
2. Thermometer
3. *Jude the Obscure*
4. Fosse Way
5. A house
6. Maidstone
7. *Apocalypse Now*
8. Sea Horse or Pipefish
9. Cottage loaf
10. Banshee (or Bean Chaointe)
11. (Benjamin) Britten
12. Hyacinth
13. Carpetbagger
14. The *Golden Hind*
15. Patience
16. Tanzania
17. 1973
18. Helium
19. *Evita*
20. Menachem Begin
21. Medley
22. (Holy or Sacred) Basil – accept Tulsa
23. Pentagon
24. Elephant
25. (Piet) Mondrian
26. Staffa

27. *A Short History of Tractors in Ukrainian*
28. Kenneth MacAlpin or Kenneth I
29. Radiohead
30. Bette Davis

Specialist Subject 28.2 – Cinema 1910–2010
1. *Jaws*
2. (Ennio) Morricone
3. (Disney-)Pixar
4. (Federico) Fellini
5. (The Cowardly) Lion
6. *The Social Network*
7. (Luis) Buñuel
8. *Heat*
9. Harpo
10. *Donnie Darko*
11. Ian Dury
12. *The Matrix*
13. Billy Liar
14. *The Blob*
15. Simon Callow
16. *Get Carter*
17. Tony Blair
18. *Bugsy Malone*
19. Greta Garbo (Greta Lovisa Gustafsson)
20. *Bowling for Columbine*
21. Dirty Harry (Callahan)
22. *The Wicker Man*
23. Ayrton Senna
24. *High Society*
25. Kevin Spacey
26. *Women in Love*
27. Fred Astaire (or Frederick Austerlitz)

28. *Shaft*
29. Marcel Marceau (the famous mime artist!)
30. Venice (Film Festival)

General Knowledge 28.2
1. Glasnost (not Perestroika, which means 'Restructuring')
2. Moses
3. *The Rocky Horror Show*
4. Steppe
5. Del Boy or Derek Trotter (from *Only Fools and Horses*)
6. Hyena
7. Jamb (also known as a Reveal or Splay)
8. Canada
9. (Roederer) Cristal
10. Epidermis
11. *The Day of the Jackal*
12. Park Lane
13. Eminem
14. Egypt
15. (Martina) Navratilova
16. Alder
17. The Gods
18. Neptune
19. Pink Floyd
20. Eight
21. St Ives
22. Density
23. Haddock
24. Hudson Bay
25. Radar
26. Mexico
27. (Richard Brinsley) Sheridan
28. Snake

29. (Bela) Bartok
30. 'Work'

SHOW 29

Specialist Subject 29.1 – Three Great Composers: Mozart, Beethoven and Tchaikovsky

1. Beethoven's Fifth (Symphony)
2. Leopold
3. Ministry of Justice
4. Bonn
5. Marie Antoinette
6. 1812 Overture (it commemorated the 70th anniversary of Napoleon's retreat from the city)
7. (Joseph) Haydn
8. *The Marriage of Figaro* (or *Le Nozze di Figaro*)
9. Switzerland
10. 'Immortal Beloved'
11. A thousand and three
12. *Eugene Onegin* (or *Yevgeny Onegin*)
13. Heiligenstadt
14. *Cosi Fan Tutte*
15. Celesta or Celeste
16. The Congress of Vienna
17. *The Abduction from the Seraglio*
18. Fourth (Symphony in F Minor)
19. (Johann Wolfgang von) Goethe
20. *The Magic Flute* or *Die Zauberflöte*
21. (Gustav) Mahler
22. (Ludwig von) Köchel
23. 'Pathétique'
24. (Franz Xaver) Süssmayr
25. *The Nutcracker* (or *Shchelkunchik*)

26. (Friedrich von) Schiller
27. Oboe
28. Cholera
29. (Count Andreas von) Razumovsky
30. (Sir Peter) Shaffer – not Anthony Shaffer (his brother)

General Knowledge 29.1
1. Forty
2. Ornithology
3. (L.S.) Lowry
4. Vietnam
5. 'Waterloo Sunset'
6. Angevins (he was Count of Anjou)
7. Quentin Tarantino (who also wrote and directed the film)
8. Condor
9. Tzatziki
10. Jotunheim
11. (Edward) Gibbon
12. (Igor) Sikorsky
13. (Colin) Montgomerie – known as Monty
14. Kangaroos – accept Wallabies
15. Voltaire
16. River Tay
17. *The Man From U.N.C.L.E.*
18. (Aneurin) 'Nye' Bevan
19. Pas de Deux
20. Argus (Panoptes)
21. Amplitude Modulation
22. Gibson Desert
23. Sir John Mortimer
24. Seychelles
25. Woody Guthrie
26. Viagra

27. Stella McCartney
28. Apple
29. Iran
30. The Penguin

Specialist Subject 29.2 – Rivers, Mountains and Volcanoes of the World
1. Danube
2. Urals
3. Basel
4. Tanzania
5. (Black) Swan River
6. Argentina
7. Missouri
8. Hekla
9. Po
10. Mount Cook
11. Indus
12. Mount Logan
13. Montevideo
14. Mount Kosciusko
15. Khartoum
16. Portugal
17. Irrawaddy (or Ayayarwady)
18. Drakensberg Mountains or Quathlamba
19. Dawson City
20. Corsica
21. Volga
22. Kenya
23. Weser
24. Mount Etna
25. Turkey
26. Washington
27. Tagus

28. Ethiopia
29. Yangtze (known in Chinese as Chang Jiang)
30. Popocatepetl

General Knowledge 29.2

1. Central
2. Manchester (as it was the centre of the cotton industry)
3. Hooke or Hooke's Law
4. Woad
5. *The Inbetweeners*
6. Muezzin
7. Uffizi (Gallery)
8. Barnet
9. Samovar
10. Lungs
11. Emilia
12. (Valéry) Giscard d'Estaing
13. Arpeggio
14. Lake Michigan
15. (Charlie) Chaplin
16. Leveret
17. Basketball (not Football – neither Panathinaikos nor Maccabi Tel Aviv have ever won the European Cup or Champions' League)
18. (Operation) Torch
19. Morrissey
20. Pyrometer
21. Mary Quant
22. Holyhead or Caereybi
23. Hoisin
24. Saladin
25. Alexei Sayle
26. Erato
27. Stan Freberg

28. Beetles
29. Crosswords
30. *The Flintstones*

SHOW 30

Specialist Subject 30.1 – Flowers, Trees and Plants
1. Venus Fly-Trap
2. Purple
3. Poppy
4. Lime
5. Morning Glory
6. Coco De Mer (not The Coconut)
7. Daffodil
8. Patchouli
9. Fuchsia
10. Onion
11. (Native) Primrose
12. Dutch Elm disease
13. Rose
14. Joshua tree
15. White
16. Teak
17. Hyacinth
18. Elder
19. Edelweiss
20. Sunflower
21. Ebony
22. Azalea
23. Virginia creeper
24. Bracts
25. Beech tree
26. Ferns – accept Bracken

THE MASTERMIND QUIZ BOOK

27. Sisal
28. Monkey Puzzle tree
29. Keys
30. Walnut

General Knowledge 30.1
1. Mayday
2. Darjeeling
3. Bobby Moore (in full, Robert Frederick Chelsea Moore)
4. Florin
5. Crêpe Suzette
6. Fluorine
7. Descant
8. Parsis (or Parsees) – accept Zoroastrianism
9. Giotto (di Bondone)
10. Gorilla
11. *Tom Brown's Schooldays*
12. Justify or Justification
13. Two hours
14. (James) Keir Hardie
15. *Il Trovatore* or *The Troubadour*
16. Clytemnestra
17. Philip Pullman
18. Adenoids
19. *Extras*
20. Pillars of Hercules
21. *The English Patient*
22. Cambria
23. Pageboy
24. John Hancock
25. Mare or Horse
26. The Plough
27. Dusty Springfield

28. Venus
29. Sapling
30. Seven miniature Oscars

Specialist Subject 30.2 – The Novels of Evelyn Waugh
1. The General Strike
2. Uncle
3. (The Right Honourable) Walter Outrage
4. Italian Somaliland – accept Somalia
5. Mr Salter
6. The influence of Wales or the Welsh
7. Tony Last
8. Battle or Evacuation of Crete
9. Dante (Alighieri)
10. Harold Acton
11. 'Unreadable'
12. Prudence Courtney
13. *Little Dorrit*
14. Brendan Bracken
15. Charm
16. Nancy Mitford
17. (A bottle of) Whisky
18. Air Marshal Beech
19. *Put out More Flags*
20. Lady Diana Cooper
21. He hires a bus
22. Mr Prendergast
23. Bachelor of the Arts of Oxford University
24. A radio or wireless interview (with the BBC)
25. Villa Hermione
26. He enters a monastery or He becomes a monk
27. *Through the Looking-Glass*
28. The Guru Brahmin

29. 'Guernica Revisited'
30. Modern Art

General Knowledge 30.2
1. All Souls (of the Faithful Departed)
2. Land's End
3. Sun Records
4. Mary Seacole
5. Harold Lloyd
6. Carthusians
7. (Pizza) Calzone
8. Flags
9. *The Mousetrap*
10. Carborundum (also known as Crystolon or Carbolon)
11. Burgundy
12. Giant Squid
13. *The Ragged Trousered Philanthropists*
14. Albania
15. James Gandolfini
16. Cornelia
17. (Robert) Schumann
18. Nine degrees
19. John Donne
20. Nike
21. Surrealism
22. Swallowtail
23. Grand Slam
24. Lesotho
25. *The Italian Job*
26. Tuberculosis or Consumption
27. *Hair*
28. Purbeck
29. Mezzotint

30. Barry Goldwater

SHOW 31

Specialist Subject 31.1 – UK History since 1700

1. George II
2. Trieste
3. Income tax
4. Congress of Berlin
5. (James) Watt
6. Isandlwana
7. Death penalty – accept Executions
8. 'The unemployed'
9. Porphyria
10. (Richard Austen or 'Rab') Butler
11. Spion Kop (it inspired the use of the term 'Kop' at football grounds)
12. (Asiatic) Cholera
13. Orgreave
14. Alexander Graham Bell
15. Dreadnought (class)
16. The New Party
17. Twopenny Blue
18. (John) Maynard Keynes – later Lord Keynes
19. (Lines of the) Torres Vedras
20. Cern
21. 1952
22. (Henry) Bessemer
23. Lonrho – in full, London & Rhodesian Mining Company
24. (Sir Giles) Gilbert Scott
25. Kimberley
26. (General Henry) Shrapnel
27. ('Red' Ellen) Wilkinson

28. King of France
29. (Augustus) Pugin
30. Umbrella (tip)

General Knowledge 31.1
1. (Humphrey) Bogart
2. (Between adjacent) Ribs
3. Greece
4. Irwell
5. 'Amazing Grace'
6. Sub judice
7. Robin Redbreast
8. Faux pas
9. Sam Taylor-Wood
10. Giraffe
11. Taoism
12. Osborne (House)
13. (Robert) Kilroy-Silk
14. Pico
15. Teriyaki
16. (Papua) New Guinea
17. Baritone
18. Bicycle
19. Borat (Sadgiyev)
20. (Scottish) Crossbill
21. Snakes and Ladders
22. Ragnarök (not Götterdämmerung)
23. Cointreau (or any orange-based liqueur)
24. Jacaranda
25. Rosinante or Rocinante
26. Ammonia
27. UB40 (who took their name from an Unemployment Benefit form)
28. Apennines

29. Lucian Freud
30. '(I think it would be) A good idea'

Specialist Subject 31.2 – The 'Carry On' Films
1. *Carry On Sergeant*
2. Sid James
3. *Carry On At Your Convenience*
4. Third Foot and Mouth
5. Bicycle
6. *Carry On Camping*
7. Charles Hawtrey
8. *Carry On, Follow That Camel*
9. Elke Sommer
10. Oozalum Bird
11. *Carry On Matron*
12. Bernard Bresslaw
13. (Indian) Silk
14. *Carry On Henry*
15. Julius Caesar
16. Hattie Jacques
17. Death of Nelson
18. Jim Dale
19. Brighton
20. Phil Silvers
21. *Carry On Cowboy*
22. 'Frying Tonight'
23. Leslie Phillips
24. A daffodil
25. Kenny Lynch
26. Marcus Et Spencius
27. *Carry On Abroad*
28. Guy Fawkes
29. Senna Pod

30. (It flies off and) He swallows it

General Knowledge 31.2
1. *Friends*
2. C
3. Orson Welles
4. (The Battle of the) White Mountain or Hill
5. *Tosca*
6. (River) Dee
7. Primary colour
8. Orang-utan
9. (Bertolt) Brecht
10. (T.E.) Lawrence (of Arabia)
11. Bombe Glacée
12. Lima
13. Bougainvillea
14. Potassium (or Kalium)
15. Catalan Dragons – accept either
16. John Ball
17. 'Memory'
18. Bering Sea
19. Yerba Maté
20. Jefferson
21. *Rain Man*
22. Passeriformes
23. (Alfred) Sisley
24. Pleurisy
25. Horace (in full, Quintus Horatius Flaccus)
26. (Woollen) Cloth
27. Kinder Scout
28. Iron Maiden
29. Ithaca
30. 'Upper Class Twit of the Year'